Richard William Coppinger

Cruise of the Alert

Richard William Coppinger
Cruise of the Alert
ISBN/EAN: 9783742892263
Manufactured in Europe, USA, Canada, Australia, Japa
Cover: Foto ©ninafisch / pixelio.de

Manufactured and distributed by brebook publishing software (www.brebook.com)

Richard William Coppinger

Cruise of the Alert

CRUISE OF THE "ALERT."

FOUR YEARS IN

PATAGONIAN, POLYNESIAN, AND MASCARENE WATERS.

(1878—82.)

BY

R. W. COPPINGER, M.D.
(Staff-Surgeon Royal Navy, C.M.Z.S.)

With Sixteen full-page Woodcut Illustrations from Photographs by F. North, R.N., and from Sketches by the Author.

SECOND EDITION.

LONDON:
W. SWAN SONNENSCHEIN AND CO.,
PATERNOSTER SQUARE.
1884.

PREFACE.

IN preparing the following pages for the press, I have endeavoured to give a brief account, divested as much as possible of technicalities, of the principal points of interest in Natural History which came under observation during the wanderings of a surveying ship; while at the same time I have done my utmost, at the risk of rendering the narrative disconnected, to avoid trenching on ground which has been rendered familiar by the writings of travellers who have visited the same or similar places. And if in a few instances I have given some rather dry details regarding the appearance and surroundings of certain zoological specimens, it has been my intention, by an occasional reference to the more striking forms of life met with in each locality, to afford some assistance to those amateurs who, like myself, may desire to avail themselves of the opportunities afforded by the surveying ships of the British Navy for performing, although with rude appliances and very few books of reference, some useful and interesting work.

Large collections of zoological specimens were made, and as

ome to the Admiralty, whence they were transmitted to th[e] [B]ritish Museum, the authorities of that institution then submittir[g] [th]em to specialists for systematic description. For much kind[ly] [a]id in making these arrangements, as well as for advice an[d] [e]ncouragement received during the progress of the cruise, I a[m] [in]debted to Dr. Albert Günther, F.R.S., Keeper of Zoology in th[e] [B]ritish Museum.

I take this opportunity to thank Mr. Frederick North, R.N[.] [fo]r the use of a collection of photographs which were taken b[y] [h]im during the cruise under circumstances of peculiar difficult[y] [an]d of which most of the engravings in this work are repr[od]uctions.

I am also under obligations to all the other officers for assis[ta]nce rendered to me in various ways; and especially to tho[se] [o]fficers who acted successively as Senior Lieutenants, for th[e] [c]onsideration with which they tolerated those parts of m[y] [d]redging operations that necessarily interfered with the mai[nte]nance of good order and cleanliness on the ship's decks.

Finally, I have to thank my friend, Mr. R. Bowdler Sharp[e,] [th]e distinguished ornithologist of the British Museum, by who[se] [a]dvice and encouragement I was induced to submit these pag[es] [to] the public, for his assistance in perusing my MS., and offerir[g] [s]ome useful suggestions.

R. W. C.

TABLE OF CONTENTS.

INTRODUCTION.

PAGE

Object of the Voyage—Former Surveys of Straits of Magellan—Change of Programme—Selection of Ship—Equipment—Arrangements for Natural History Work—Change of Captain—List of Officers . . 1—4

CHAPTER I.

Departure from England—Storm Petrels—A Sparrow-hawk at Sea—Collecting Surface Organisms with Tow-net—Water-kite—Wire Sounding Apparatus—Land-swallow at Sea—Gulfweed—Phosphorescence of Seawater—Arrive at Madeira—Curious Town—Dredging Work—A Pinery—Discoloured Seawater—Petrels again—St. Vincent—Cape de Verdes—Pelagic Animals—Sounding near Abrolhos Bank—Dredging over Hotspur Bank—Dredging over Victoria Bank—Moths and Butterflies on the Ocean—Extraordinary Vitality of Sphynx Moths—Arrive at Monte Video—Gauchos—Trip into Interior of Uruguay—Buenos Ayres—Dr. Burmeister's Museum—Arrive at the Falklands—"Stone Runs." . . . . 5—33

CHAPTER II.

We enter Straits of Magellan—Reach Sandy Point—Gold and Coal—Surrounding Country—Elizabeth Island—Dredging—Fuegians at Port Famine—We enter Smyth's Channel—Canoe "Portage" at Isthmus Bay—Arrive at Tom Bay—A Fuegian Family—Trinidad Channel—Climate of Western Patagonia—Flora—Rock Formation—Soilcap—Natives—The Channel Tribe of Fuegians—Scarcity of Old People—Water-birds of Tom Bay—Sea Otters—A Concealed "Portage"—Habits of Gulls and Shags—Steamer Ducks—Landshells—Freshwater Fish—Deer . . . . 34—65

CHAPTER VI.

We proceed towards Skyring Water—Otway Water—Canal of Fitzroy Terrace-levels—Plants and Animals—Bay of the Mines—Previous Explorers—The Coal Mines—Altamirano Bay—Prospects of the Settlement—A Seal "Rookery"—Puerto Bueno—We proceed Northwards—Port Riofrio—Gray Harbour—Sailing for Coast of Chili—Small Pox amongst the Chilians—Discoloured Sea-water—Habits of Ant Thrush . . . . 127—143

CHAPTER VII.

Early History of Tahiti—Otaheite and Tahiti—Its appearance from Seaward—Harbour of Papiété—Produce—Matavai Bay—Tahiti annexed to France—Prince Tamitao—Annexation Festivities—King Pomare V.—Coral growing on Ship's Bottom—Nassau Island—Danger Islands—Tema Reef—Union Group—Nukunono—Oatáfu—Natives afflicted with a Skin Disease—Stone Implements—Religious Scruples—Metal Fish-hooks not appreciated—Capriciousness of Sharks—Lalla Rookh Bank . . . . 144—158

CHAPTER VIII.

Arrival at Fiji—Levuka—Ratu Joe comes on Board—Excursion to Bau in Viti Levu—We visit King Cacobau—A Native Feast—Lalis—Tapa—The Bure Kalou—Bakola—Old Fijian Atrocities—Double Canoe—Stone Adzes now becoming rare—Angona Drinking—Sir Arthur Gordon—Walk across Ovalau—The Kaicolos—An Imprudent Settler—Pine-apple Cultivation—*Periophthalmus*—Suva—Site of Future Capital—Sail towards Tonga Islands—Pelagic Animals—Early History of Tonga—Missionaries—Nukualofa—A Costly Pair of Gates—Visit to Bea—Davita—Evidence of Elevation of Island—King George of Tonga—Wellington Gnu—Curious Stone Monument—Trip to Village of Hifo—We are entertained by the Natives—Famous Caves—Eyeless Fish—Swifts behaving like Bats—Searching for Reefs—Discolouration of Seawater—Return to Levuka—Voyage

CHAPTER IX.

Refitting Ship at Sydney—Mr. Haswell joins us—We proceed Northwards along East Coast of Australia—Port Curtis, Queensland—A "Labour Vessel"—Mr. Eastlake—Marine Fauna abundant—Festivities at Gladstone—Birds—Percy Islands—Survey of Port Molle—Queensland Aborigines—"Black Police"—"Dispersing" Black fellows—Dredging Operations—A Parasitic Shell-fish—Port Denison—Visit to a Native Camp—Throwing the Boomerang—A Beche-de-mer Establishment at Lizard Island—Hostility of the Natives—Drawings by Aborigines at Clack Island—Albany Island, North-Eastern Australia . . . . 180—193

CHAPTER X.

Settlement at Thursday Island—Torres Straits Islanders—Pearl-Shell Fisheries—Value of the Shell—Pearls not abundant—Neighbouring Islands—Lizards—Landcrab—Landshells — Ferns — Birds — Booby Island—Arrive at Port Darwin, North-Western Australia—Submarine Cables—Trans-continental Telegraph—Palmerston—Northern Territory Goldfields—Aborigines at Port Darwin—Marine Fauna —Birds—Geese perching on Trees . . . . 194—208

CHAPTER XI.

Voyage from Port Darwin to Singapore—Through the Eastern Archipelago—We arrive at Singapore—Oceanic "Tiderips"—Bird Island, Seychelles—Seabirds on Land—Port Mahé, Seychelles—The Coco-de-Mer—Gigantic Tortoise—Produce of the Islands—Vanilla — A Primitive Crushing-mill — Dredging Operations — *Periophthalmus*—The Seychelles, of Granitic Structure—We visit the Amirante Group—African Islands—Abundance of *Orbitolites*—Crabs pursued by Eels—Eagle Island—Partridge shooting—Young Lizards—Darros Island—*Casuarinas*—Dredging—Poivre Island—Trees and Shrubs—Isle des Roches—Flora scanty—Land-birds—General Remarks on the Amirantes as a Group—"Fringing Reefs," but no "Barrier Reefs"—Signs of Elevation—Weather and Lee

CHAPTER XII.

Alphonse Island—Pearl-shell—Providence Island—Method of planting Cocoa-nuts—Edible Turtle—Flora—Red Coral—Cerf Islets—St. Pierre—Du Lise Island—Flora and Fauna—Erratic Stones on Coral Reef—Glorioso Island—We sail for Mozambique Island—And sight East Coast of Africa—Trade at Mozambique—Inhabitants—Caju—Shells of Foreshore—The Survey concluded—Homeward Bound—Cape of Good Hope—Egg of the *Epiornis*—Arrival at Plymouth . . . . 230—245

GENERAL INDEX . 246

INDEX OF NATURAL HISTORY TERMS . . 253

LIST OF ILLUSTRATIONS.

H.M.S. "ALERT" AT ANCHOR IN TOM BAY, WEST COAST OF PATAGONIA	*Facing title*
FUEGIAN AND AUSTRALIAN IMPLEMENTS	34
CANOE OF CHANNEL FUEGIANS	50
FUEGIAN "PORTAGE" FOR TRANSPORT OF CANOES OVERLAND	60
FUEGIANS OFFERING THEIR CHILDREN FOR BARTER	65
OUR FUEGIAN FRIENDS AT TILLY BAY, STRAITS OF MAGELLAN	104
FUEGIAN HUT AT TILLY BAY	120
FOOT OF GLACIER, AT GLACIER BAY, STRAITS OF MAGELLAN	124
FISH-HOOKS OF UNION ISLANDERS	143
WOMAN OF TAHITI	144
FISHERMAN OF TAHITI	148
KING CACOBAU OF FIJI, WIFE, AND RATU JOE	160
TOTOONGA VALLEY, OVALAU, FIJI	166
ANCIENT STONE MONUMENT AT TONGATABU	174
FACSIMILES OF DRAWINGS BY AUSTRALIAN ABORIGINES	192
ABORIGINES OF NORTH-WEST AUSTRALIA	204
"TRAVELLERS' TREES" IN GARDENS AT SINGAPORE	210

CRUISE OF THE "ALERT."

INTRODUCTION.

IN the summer of 1878 it was decided by the Lords of the Admiralty to equip a vessel for the threefold purpose of continuing the survey of the Straits of Magellan, of investigating the nature and exact position of certain doubtful reefs and islands in the South Pacific Ocean, and of surveying a portion of the northern and western coasts of Australia. The special object of the Magellan portion of the work was to make such a detailed survey of the sheltered channels extending southward from the Gulf of Peñas to Port Tamar as would enable vessels to pass from the Straits to the Pacific, and *vice versâ*, without having to encounter the wild and inhospitable outer coasts presented by the chain of desolate islands here fringing the western coasts of South America. It was also desirable that additional anchorages should be found and surveyed, where vessels might lie in safety while waiting for the cessation of a gale, or for a favourable tide to help them through the straits. The surveys made by the *Adventure* and *Beagle* in 1826-36, and by the *Nassau* in 1866-9, were excellent so far as they went, and so far as the requirements of their times were concerned; but the great increase of ocean navigation within the last few years had rendered it necessary that the charts should contain more minute surveys of certain places which were not formerly of importance. The South Pacific portion of our survey was to be mainly in connection with the recently acquired colony of the Fiji Islands, and was to be devoted to an exploration of the eastern passages leading to this group, with an investigation of the doubtful dangers reported in the vicinity of the great shipping tracts. Finally, on completing the above, and arriving at Australia, we were to spend a year and a half, or thereabouts, in surveying the line of reefs which fringe its whole western seaboard, the ill-defined position of which is a serious obstacle to the now extensive trade between Western Australia and the Dutch islands of the Malay Archipelago.

The latter part of the orders was subsequently changed, inasmuch as we were directed to omit the survey of the western shores of Australia, and were ordered instead, on completing the North Australian work, to proceed to Singapore, in the Straits of Malacca, to refit. Thence we were to return home by the Cape of Good Hope, stopping on our way at the Seychelles, Amirante Islands, and Mozambique, in order to fix astronomically the position of the Amirante group, and, as opportunities occurred, to take a line of soundings off the east coast of Africa.

The vessel selected for this special service was the *Alert*, a man-of-war sloop of 751 tons measurement and 60 horse-power nominal; and the command of the expedition was given to Capt. Sir George Nares, K.C.B. By a happy coincidence the same stout craft which had already done such good service in the Arctic Expedition of 1875-6, and which bears the honour of having attained the highest *northern* latitude, was selected as the ship in which Sir George Nares was now about to proceed on a voyage of exploration in high *southern* latitudes. She was officially commissioned on the 20th of August, with a complement of 120 officers and men, her equipments including apparatus for conducting deep sea sounding and dredging operations, and a miscellaneous collection of instruments not usually supplied to H.M.'s ships.

Object of the Voyage.

It being the wish of the enterprising hydrographer of the navy —Captain, now Sir Frederick Evans, K.C.B.—that the opportunities which this expedition would afford of making a valuable natural history collection in regions little known to science should not be thrown away, and Sir George Nares warmly seconding him in this wish, the Admiralty determined on appointing as surgeon an officer who, in addition to his duties as medical officer of the ship, would be inclined to devote his spare time to the cause of natural science. Sir George Nares, knowing my fondness for natural history, with characteristic kindness gave my application his support, and I had therefore the good fortune to be appointed as medical officer of the *Alert*, on the understanding that (so far as my medical duties permitted) I would not lose sight of the advantages which would accrue to science from a collection of natural-history objects illustrative of the fauna and flora of the countries visited in the course of the voyage.

During the four years over which my narrative extends, many changes took place in the *personnel* of the expedition. Scarcely a year had elapsed from the date of our departure from England, when we had to regret the loss of Sir George Nares, who left us at Valparaiso, and returned to England by mail steamer, in order to enter upon his duties as Director of the Marine Department of the Board of Trade. We were fortunate, however, in having as his successor Captain John Maclear—formerly of the *Challenger* exploring expedition—to whom I take this opportunity of expressing my thanks for the unvarying kindness which I have always experienced at his hands, as well as for much assistance and encouragement in the prosecution of our zoological work.

The following is a list of the officers:—

Captain Sir George S. Nares, K.C.B., F.R.S.; succeeded by Captain John Maclear, F.R.M.S.

Lieut. George R. Bethell; succeeded by Lieut. James Deedes.

Lieut. the Hon. Foley C. P. Vereker; succeeded by Lieut. George Rooper.

Lieut. Gordon S. Gunn (subsequently became senior lieutenant).

Nav. Lieut. William H. Petley.

Sub-Lieut. James H. C. East (subsequently served as lieutenant).

Sub-Lieut. Charles W. de la P. Beresford (left the ship at Singapore).

Staff-Surgeon Richard W. Coppinger, M.D.

Paymaster Frederick North.

Engineer, John Dinwoodie.

Engineer, William Cook.

Boatswain, Alfred Payne.

(Lieut. Grenfell joined the ship at Singapore, and remained until the close of the commission.)

CHAPTER I.

FROM ENGLAND TO THE FALKLANDS

AFTER various delays, owing to defects in machinery, we finally bade adieu to the shores of England on the 25th of September, 1878, taking our departure from Plymouth.

On the second day at sea the little storm-petrels appeared over our wake, and accompanied us, off and on, for most of our way to Madeira. These seemed to be of two kinds, the *Thalassidroma pelagica* and *Thalassidroma Leachii*, the latter being sufficiently recognizable from their having *forked* tails, in which respect they differ from other species of the genus. Many attempts were made to catch them by means of hooks baited with fat, skeins of thread, etc., but all to no purpose; and I rather fancy that in this thoroughfare of the ocean the wily creatures have had too much experience of the arts of man, and are therefore not to be caught so easily as their more ignorant brethren of the southern hemisphere.

On the 28th of September, when 155 miles to the westward of Cape Finisterre, and during a fresh easterly breeze, a sparrow-hawk made his appearance, at first hovering round the ship, and ultimately settling on the rigging. It had probably strayed too far from the shore in the pursuit of some tempting prey, and had then lost its reckoning, being eventually blown to seaward. At all events, it had travelled some long distance, as it evinced its weariness by resting quietly and contentedly on the main-topgallant rigging, until one of the seamen, who had managed to climb up unobserved, suddenly laid hands on it. On placing it in a meat-safe, which we extemporised as a cage, it ate ravenously, as well it might after its long journey.

When in the latitude of Lisbon, and 180 miles to the westward of the Portuguese coast, a large "sea-flier" bird paid us a visit, soaring over the waves in our vicinity, and evidently on the lookout for garbage from the ship. The plumage of the upper surface of wings and body was of a dusky brown colour, the under surface of the body was whitish, and the wings were long and pointed; in mode of flight he resembled a large tern. He did not long remain with us, probably not finding it a sufficiently productive hunting-ground. I may here mention that on the 6th of October, when a hundred miles from Madeira, we sighted a bird answering the same description.

All opportunities of plying the tow-net were duly availed of, but owing to the unusually rapid speed of the ship, these were few. However, we succeeded in capturing many specimens of living Foraminifers (mostly of the genus *Orbitolites*), stalk-eyed Crustaceans, Radiolarians, an Ianthina, a few Salpæ, and the pretty little Pteropod Mollusc, the *Criseis Aciculata*, besides many other organisms which the rapid motion of the net through the water had rendered unrecognizable. As it is usually found that these minute pelagic organisms are to be obtained from the surface in most abundance at night-time, and during the day retreat for some fathoms from the glare of the sunlight, I constructed a wooden apparatus on the principle of a kite, which I attached to the towing line at some three or four yards from the net, and which had the effect of dragging down the net some yards below the surface, and then retaining it at a uniform depth. It of course required to be adjusted each time to suit the required depth and the rate of the vessel, but it had this great advantage over the usual system of employing heavy weights, that the strain not being nearly so great, a light and manageable rope could be used; and that, moreover, the adjustment for depth could be readily made by altering the trim of this *water-kite*. When I first tried this apparatus, and before I had succeeded in trimming it satisfactorily, it caused great amusement to the blue-jackets by the playful manner in which it manœuvred under our stern, now diving deeply towards our rudder post (the shimmer of the white wood in the deep blue water reminding one of a dolphin), and now whimsically rising rapidly to the surface with an impetus that shot it fully six feet out of the water.

On the 4th of October, the captain made some experiments with the " Lucas deep-sea sounder." It consists of a strong brass drum carrying 2,000 fathoms of fine steel wire, and fitted with a cyclometer which registers on a dial the number of fathoms of wire run out. The sinker, which weighs 20 lbs., is made of lead, and has at its lower extremity a bull-dog snapper, which, on striking the ground, shuts up suddenly, so as to enclose a sample of the sea bottom. The apparatus is supposed to be capable of sounding to a depth of 500 fathoms in a vessel going 5 knots, and to 50 fathoms when going 12 knots. It is said to be a modification of an invention of Sir W. Thompson's. We subsequently used this largely, and found it to be a most convenient and expeditious method of sounding to depths of 500 fathoms, with the ship almost stationary. The wire could be wound up again while the ship was under way.

During the forenoon of this same day we saw, to our astonishment, a land swallow, which flew about the ship for a few minutes, and then went on his way rejoicing. He would have had to travel 254 miles to make the nearest land, which was the island of Porto Santo.

An erratic fragment of gulfweed (*Sargassum Bacciferum*) was entangled in the tow-net on the 5th of October, when we were 105 miles north-east of Madeira, a circumstance which is of interest as regards the distribution of the plant, the locality cited being considerably beyond the northern limit of the great eddy between the Gulf Stream and the Atlantic equatorial current, commonly called the Sargasso Sea. It was encrusted with a delicate white Polyzoon (*Membranipora*), and among other organisms carried on its fronds a pretty little *Spirorbis* shell, and several entomostracous Crustaceans of a deep-blue colour.

The phosphorescence of the sea is a trite subject, and one about which a very great deal has been written; but nevertheless, of its actual cause, or of the purposes which it is intended to serve, really very little is positively known. The animals to which it would seem mainly due are the small stalk-eyed Crustacea, the *Pyrocystis noctiluca*, and the Tunicate Molluscs. I have sometimes observed, when occupied at night in sifting the contents of a tow-net, that these organisms, as they were being sucked through the nozzle of the dip-tube, emitted flashes of light, so brilliant, that they could be distinctly seen even in a well-lighted room. During the voyage from England to Madeira, the wake of the ship was every night, with one exception, phosphorescent. The exception alluded to was on the night previous to our arrival at Madeira, when probably the unusual brilliancy of the moonlight caused the light-emitting creatures to retreat a few yards from the surface, as happens in the day-time. I have often noticed that while the phosphorescence of the comparatively still water abeam of the ship and on her quarter usually seems to emanate from large spherical masses of about a foot in diameter (commonly called "globes of fire"), yet the luminosity of the broken water in the vessel's immediate wake comes apparently from innumerable minute points. I have rarely captured any of the larger jellyfishes in the tow-net; and on those nights when I have observed the water lighted up the most brilliantly, the prevailing organisms have proved to be the small entomostracous Crustaceans.

The morning of the 7th of October broke cool and hazy, as we steamed up and dropped anchor in Funchal Roads, on the south side of the island of Madeira. Crowds of native boats, with their half-naked occupants, quickly thronged around; remaining, however, at a respectful distance, until the boat containing the haughty pratique officer came alongside. On the present occasion this portentous individual was contented with a very superficial inquiry into our sanitary condition, and after a few formal questions as to our tonnage, complement of crew, number of guns, and general condition, shoved off with the laconic exclamation, "All right!" We soon availed ourselves of this permission to visit the shore.

The most conspicuous objects in Funchal, as seen from the anchorage, are the "Loo Rock" (used as a fort and lighthouse), on the west side of the town, and on the centre of the crescent-shaped beach which fronts the town a remarkable and lofty cylindrical tower of dark-brown stone. This tower, we were informed, was built about the year 1800, and was intended as a support for a huge crane, which was to facilitate the loading and disembarkation of the cargo of merchant ships. The tower as it stands is about eighty feet in height, and as its base is now about forty yards distant from high-water mark on the beach, as an article of utility it is quite effete. Our surveyors have ascertained that the land has not been elevated since the first admiralty surveys. This they arrive at by a comparison of old and recent charts with known marks on the shore, and we are therefore inclined to believe that the beach has been silted up by accumulations ot basaltic rubble brought down by the two adjoining rivers, and here washed inshore by the sea. The tower is now without any appearance of the crane, and raises its plain cylindrical body in gloomy grandeur, reminding one of the old round towers of Ireland ; and, as in their case, its origin will probably some years hence be veiled in obscurity.

Madeira was considered to be looking unusually dingy, on account of a long season of drought, rain not having fallen for nine months. But some two or three days after our arrival a great religious ceremony took place at the village of Machico, eight miles to the eastward of Funchal. The object was to offer up prayers for rain ; and, sure enough, two days afterwards, rain fell abundantly !

During our stay here the dredge was several times brought into requisition. On the 8th of October, a party, consisting of the captain, Lieut. Vereker, some seamen, and myself, started in the steam cutter on a dredging expedition to the bay of Santa Cruz, which is distant about eight miles from Funchal. As we steamed along the coast, we had excellent opportunities of observing the sections exhibited by the cliffs of the varieties of volcanic rock, of which the upper crust of the island is mainly formed. At Point Garajas (Brazen Head), of which Lieut. Vereker made a good sketch, the north-east face of the cliff presents a magnificent dyke —a nearly vertical seam of dark lava, about three feet in width and two hundred feet in height, extending from summit to water line, and sealing up this long fissure in the older trachytic rock of the head. Farther on, masses of basalt resting unconformably on variously arranged layers of laterite tuff and trachyte, the latter in many places honeycombed in weird fantastic caverns, afforded a fertile subject for geological reveries into the early history of this now beautiful island. On reaching the bay of Santa Cruz, we lowered the dredge in thirty-five fathoms, finding, as we had half anticipated, that it was altogether too heavy to ride on the mass of sand that here forms the sea bottom. It buried itself like an anchor, and it was not without great difficulty that we could succeed in dislodging it. On bringing it up, we found it to contain some shells of the genera *Cardium, Pecten, Cyprœa, Oliva*, and *Dentalium*, a few small *Echini*, a Sertularian Polyp, several Annelids—among others, a *Nereis*—and Alcyonarians. We returned on board soon after dusk, having spent a most enjoyable, if not materially profitable, day. On subsequently dredging in fifty fathoms in the same bay, our work was more satisfactory; but besides some Crustaceans, an Ophiocoma, and an Asterias of a brilliant orange colour, obtained few specimens of any interest. On another day we tried the coast to the westward of Funchal; and as we moved along in the steam cutter, obtained, by means of the tow-net, several specimens of gulfweed entangling small sponges. The dredge, being put over in seven fathoms, procured for us many specimens of a *Cidaris*, studded with black spines three to four inches long, and whose oblate spheroidal tests of about two inches diameter were of a beautiful smalt colour. Off the same coast, in forty fathoms, the bottom was found to consist of black basaltic sand crowded with tooth-shells. This fine black sand seemed to form the sea-bottom along the south coast of the island as far out as the fifty fathom line, and from our experience does not prove a favourable berth for our friends the Mollusca and Annulosa.

Among the Crustaceans obtained in the above dredgings was a species of *Glaucothöe* new to science, which has since been described by Mr. E. J. Miers, of the British Museum, under the title of " *Glaucothöe rostrata*."

On the afternoon of the 12th of October, in company with Sir George Nares, and under the guidance of Dr. Grabham, a British doctor for many years resident in Madeira, we had an opportunity of inspecting a "pinery," established within the last two years by a Mr. Holloway, and by which he expects to amass a considerable fortune. This establishment, which lies to the north-east of the town, at an altitude of about three hundred feet, consists of a series of long, low hothouses with sloping glass roofs, painted white, and facing to the southward, and is heated entirely by the sun's rays. The material in which the pines are planted consists of the branches of the blackberry plant chopped to fragments, and spread out in a thick layer, and in this substitute for mould the young pines are placed, at intervals of about eighteen inches apart. They grow to an enormous size, as we ourselves witnessed ; and being cut when they show the least sign of ripening, and packed carefully in well-ventilated boxes, are shipped to London, where they fetch prices varying from twenty-five to thirty shillings each.

Dr. Grabham was kind enough to give us much interesting information concerning the natural history of the island, which, from his long experience and constant observation, was most valuable. He pointed out to us a considerable tract of land in the vicinity of the town which used to be thickly planted with vines, but which is now only devoted to the cultivation of sweet potatoes. During the last seven years the vine crops have been steadily decreasing, owing to the ravages of the *Phylloxera vastatrix*, and wine-making is now at a low ebb. The number of trees in the island was also rapidly diminishing, owing to the demand for fuel; and although efforts are made, by the cultivation of pine forests, to supply that want, the demand yet exceeds the supply. In a few years Madeira will no longer be, as its name implies, a land of *wood*. Although so late in the season, numbers of flowers were still in full bloom; the *Bougainvillea* with its dark-red bracts, and the yellow jasmine adorning the trellis-work; further up the hill the belladonna lily attracted attention, and on the heights were the old familiar furze blossoms, reminding us of the land we had left behind us.

On October 12th we weighed anchor, and proceeded to the southward. All that night and the following day we steamed quietly along in smooth water, with a long, shallow ground swell (of which, however, the old craft took advantage to display her extraordinary rolling powers), and late in the afternoon, just before dark, caught sight of Palmas, one of the Canary Islands, whose peak, 7,000 feet high, loomed conspicuously through a light bank of clouds. It was distant seventy miles. On the morning of the 15th we experienced for the first time the influence of the north-east trade wind, which wafted us along pleasantly at the rate of about seven knots. Up to this the only sign of animal life had been a solitary storm petrel, but on the following day a shoal of flying fish (*Exocetus volitans*) appeared, to pay their respects and greet us on our approach to the tropical zone. During the night, the wind, which had hitherto only behaved tolerably, fell light; and as the morning of the 17th dawned, we found ourselves flapping about in almost a complete calm. There were several merchant vessels in sight, with one of which, a fine-looking full-rigged clipper ship, we communicated by signal, when the usual dumb interchange of civilities took place; she informing us that she was the *Baron Collinson*, seventeen days out from Liverpool, and we in return giving the latest news we were aware of, viz., the failure of the Glasgow Bank. During the afternoon, a shark, which seemed to be the *Squalus glaucus*, hovered about our stern. It was accompanied by at least four "pilots" (*Naucrates ductor*), whose conspicuous darkblue body stripes showed out in striking contrast to the sombre hues of the shark, whose body formed the background.

It is during those tropical calms, usually so wearisome to the seaman, that the lover of natural history reaps his richest harvest. On the present occasion the tow-net brought up quantities of a minute *conferva* consisting of little bundles of delicate straw-coloured fibres, about one-eighth of an inch in length, and resembling, on a small scale, the familiar bundles of "faggots" as one sees them hawked in the streets. Under a high magnifying power the individual fibres composing these bundles were seen to consist of jointed segments marked with dots and transverse striæ as a diatom. When placed in spirit, they at once broke up into a shapeless fluffy mass. The surface water was thickly impregnated with them, yet not so as to impart any obvious discolouration. About dusk the trade wind suddenly returned, and a heavy shower of rain brought to a close a day of great interest.

On the 18th of October, many of us fore and aft were diligently expending our ingenuity in fishing for bonitoes, of which several (apparently the *Thinnus pelamis*) were to be seen about the ship; but, to our great chagrin, only one, a small specimen, was captured. The tow-net still brought up quantities of the *conferva* before mentioned, and multitudes of minute unattached specimens of the *Spirorbis nummulites*.

On the following day, as we lay all but becalmed, the storm-petrels (*Thalassidroma pelagica*) appeared in great numbers, settling on the water close to our stern, in flocks of twelve or fourteen, and feeding greedily on the rubbish thrown overboard. It seems that the natural food of these birds (which probably consists of the minute surface organisms) is not within their reach when the surface of the water is unbroken, and hence during calms they are more than commonly anxious to avail themselves of any offal thrown overboard. It was most interesting to observe the neat and graceful way in which they plant their webbed feet on the water, as with outstretched wings and legs erect they maintain a stationary attitude while pecking at the object of their fancy. They appeared to scrupulously avoid wetting the tarsi, and still to use the feet as a means of maintaining a fixed position on the surface of the water. I had never previously observed those untiring little navigators at rest in mid-ocean, but on this occasion we all saw them, with wings closed, floating as placidly on the water as ducks in a millpond. The old idea of their following ships only before and during stormy weather is, I believe, now quite exploded. I think that within the tropics, at all events, they are most numerous in the vicinity of ships during calm weather. Finding animal life scarce at the surface, I tried the tow-net sunk to a depth of about three fathoms, and having previously raked the surface, was enabled to institute a comparison; the result being that similar species were captured in both situations, but that a far greater number of individuals were present in the deeper water. During the daytime we obtained a number of Crustaceans, several *Atlanta* shells, *Globigerina bulloides*, and the same *conferva* as on the previous day. After dark I got a great quantity of highly phosphorescent Crustaceans, and one small cuttle-fish.

On the 20th the trade wind returned in full force, and the monotony of an otherwise uneventful day was varied by the appearance of a shoal of porpoises, which accompanied us for some time, moving along abreast of us and about two hundred yards off on our starboard beam, and making themselves conspicuous by their usual frisky behaviour.

On the afternoon of the 22nd the high land of San Antonio, the most northerly of the Cape de Verde Islands, hove in sight, far away on our starboard bow; but the evening closing in thick and dark, and this group being almost without lighthouses, the captain decided on laying-to until next morning. When about twenty miles off, we received a visit from a good-sized hawk, evidently out on a foraging tour; he hovered for awhile about our mastheads, reconnoitring our decks, and then soared away.

As we sailed along the east coast of San Antonio (the largest island of the Cape de Verde group), we observed a small outlying island rock, composed of closely packed vertical columnar masses of rock (probably basaltic), which, from their artificial appearance, reminded one forcibly of the Giant's Causeway, or of the Staffa Columns. The hills of the main island, which sloped up majestically from a low rocky beach to peaks five or six thousand feet high, were clothed with herbage, whose varying tints of green, to which the shadows of the secondary peaks added dusky patches of brown, created a most pleasing landscape.

We reached the harbour of Porto Santo, St. Vincent, on the afternoon of the 23rd of October, and soon after the anchor was dropped, those of us who could leave the ship proceeded to land. As we approached the beach, we were greatly struck by a contrivance, new to most of us, for carrying coals from the yard where it is stowed to the shipping wharves, a distance of nearly a quarter of a mile,—a row of posts, like those used for telegraph wires, placed about four yards apart, and supporting on iron rollers a long endless wire, to which are hung at intervals large metal buckets containing the coal. There is an incline from the depôt to the wharf, and consequently, as the full buckets travel down to the lower end of the circuit, and are canted so as to discharge their contents, the empty buckets pass up the incline back to the coalyard, and so a circuit is completed. Most of the large passenger steamers traversing the South Atlantic find St. Vincent a convenient place to stop at to replenish their bunkers, and it is to this coal trade that the island owes its importance.

After a cursory inspection of the little town, which presented a very neat and orderly appearance, we strolled out into the country, following the direction of the western shore of the bay. The country exhibited a tolerably green appearance, and we were informed that vegetation had been exceptionally good during the previous two years, owing to the rainfall having been much above the average. Of trees of course there were none to be seen, and of shrubs only a few stunted representatives, scattered singly or in patches. A species of rank grass, however, flourished, and here and there a rather stately fungus raised its head as if in defiance of its otherwise sterile surroundings, the blown sand of the foreshore supplying sufficient nutriment for its humble wants. Of dead shells a great variety were picked up on the beach between tide marks, including representatives of the genera *Arca, Patella, Cardium, Harpa, Littorina,* and *Strombus;* a very perfect *Spirula* shell was also noticed. The blown-sand ridges above high-water mark were everywhere perforated by the burrows of a very active grey-coloured crab (*Remites scutellatus*), whose feet terminated in sharp incurved claws admirably adapted for the creature's mining operations. Its burrows extended obliquely downwards, and to a depth of two feet from the surface of the blown-sand ridges. A couple of grasshoppers were the only other additions made on this occasion to our zoological collection.

The afternoon of the next day (24th October) I was enabled to devote to dredging operations, working over the bay at depths varying from two to twelve fathoms. From these I obtained some large and active specimens of a large wing-shell, the *Strombus pugilis*, whose gymnastic performances, when subsequently placed in a vessel of sea water, excited general interest. Armed with his long powerful foot, he struck out boldly in all directions, the operculated extremity acting like a sword blade, and alarming me for the safety of the seaweeds and other more delicate organisms which occupied the same vessel. When disposed to turn about, it protruded the foot so as to half encircle the shell, and by then rapidly straightening the organ the desired change of position was effected. It was very interesting to see the complete control which the animal thus exercised over its heavy and apparently unwieldy shell. In twelve fathoms of water we came upon a great quantity of blue-spined *Echini*, the tangles of the dredge in one short haul bringing up about two dozen. Fishing-lines were also brought into requisition, resulting in the capture of some fishes of a pale crimson colour, belonging to the blenny family.

In the evening of this day (24th October) we sailed from St. Vincent. Up to the 29th instant the north-east trade wind proved fairly propitious, but it now failed us completely; and as we were at this time in latitude 8° N., and there were otherwise unmistakable indications of our having arrived at the "Doldrums" (the region of equatorial calms), steam was had recourse to. Under this artificial stimulus we proceeded at a rate of from five to six knots, a speed unfortunately too great for the use of the tow-net; and on this occasion the circumstance was all the more vexatious, as the surface water seemed peculiarly rich in animal life. Ultimately, however, determining on sacrificing some bunting in the cause of science, I put a tow-net over the stern, and the captain aided me materially by towing from the end of the lower studding-sail boom a ten-foot trawl-net. Between the two we succeeded in capturing some water insects of the genus *Halobates*, several beautiful large *Ianthinæ*, but unfortunately with their fragile shells partly broken and severed from their rafts; also a *Physalia*, a small free-swimming *Actinia*, some discophorous Medusæ, and several Pteropod Molluscs of the genus *Hyalea*. For several consecutive days the surface water after dusk was thronged with the above-mentioned Medusæ, whose tough gelatinous discs, of three inches diameter, continually clogged up the meshes of the tow-net. On the 2nd of November we obtained some Globigerina forms, several Crustaceans, some minute Pteropods of the genus Cuvieria, and a host of minute Confervæ, of the kind met with previously to the northward of Madeira. On the afternoon of the 5th of November, when we were about a hundred miles from St. Paul's Rocks, we noticed that the little petrels, which for weeks had accompanied us in great numbers, were now feebly represented, and in the evening were completely gone. Perhaps they had found out their proximity to *terra firma*, and were gone for a run on shore. It is very strange how these birds, which follow ships over the ocean for thousands of miles, can manage to time their journeys so as to reach land for their breeding season. That the same individuals do follow ships for such great distances we have good evidence; for Captain King, in his voyage of the *Adventure* and *Beagle*, mentions a case in which the surgeon of a ship, coming home from Australia, having caught a Cape pigeon (*Dapteon capensis*), which had been following the ship, tied a piece of ribbon to it as a mark, and then set it free. The bird, recognized in this way, was observed to follow them for a distance of no less than 5,000 miles.

From the last date to the 9th of November, but little of interest occurred. One day a petrel (*Thalassidroma pelagica*) had been caught with a skein of thread; and on opening the body the crop was found to contain a number of stony particles, bits of cinders, minute shells, and otolites of fishes. In the tow-net we caught a number of Rhizopods, of $\frac{1}{20}$ inch diameter, which kept continually unfolding and shutting up their bodies in telescopic fashion. When quiescent, the animal is egg-shaped, and about the size of a mustard seed; but when elongated, it is twice that length, and exhibits a tubular sort of proboscis armed with an irregular circle of vibrating cilia. We also obtained a Pteropod resembling the Criseis aciculata, an Ianthina, and some hyaline amœbiform bodies, which were entirely beyond my powers of recognition. On the following day we got more of the pretty violet shells (*Ianthina fragilis*), several Crustaceans, including a large and perfect Glass-crab (*Phyllosoma*), and several large Salpæ and Medusæ.

On the 12th of November we entered the north limit of our surveying ground, being in latitude 17° S., and in the vicinity of the Abrolhos Bank. Here, in latitude 17° 18′ S., longitude 35° 34′ W., we made a cast with Bailie's deep-sea sounding apparatus; reaching bottom in 1,975 fathoms, and finding it to consist of "Globigerina mud," of a pasty tenacity, tinged with red, and containing a great mass of Globigerina tests, whole and fragmentary. Later in the day, when in latitude 17° 32′ S., longitude 35° 46′ W., we again sounded, getting bottom in 700 fathoms, and bringing up a sort of light-grey ooze. Towards evening we struck soundings in thirty-five fathoms, over the Hotspur Bank. There we made a successful haul of the dredge, finding the bottom composed of dead coral encrusted with Nullipores, Polyzoa, and slimy Algæ, and containing in its crevices some Crustaceans of the genera Actæa and Corallana, and a few Annelids. The stony masses of coral which we brought up were pierced in all directions by boring molluscs; and one specimen of a long elaborately woven sponge (which has since been described by Mr. S. O. Ridley, of the British Museum, as a new variety of *Cladochalina armigera*) was found attached to a lump of coral.

The next day we sounded in latitude 18° 4′ S., longitude 36° 1′ W., using the Lucas wire sounder. We reached bottom in 300 fathoms, the bulldog apparatus bringing up fragments of coral rock encrusted with calcareous Algæ. In the afternoon we passed into deeper water, sounding over the Globigerina ooze area, in 1,395 and 2,025 fathoms. The surface water again exhibited the same conferva-like bodies which were so abundantly obtained near Madeira. The Pyrocystis noctiluca was also largely represented; and in the evening the tow-net was found to contain small cuttle fish, some dead spirorbis shells, specimens of the Criscis ariculata, Cleodora pyramidata, and of a species of Hylea, and a thick fleshy Pteropod, a species of Pneumodermon, small globe fishes, many long, transparent, stalk-eyed Crustaceans, and other minute members of the same class of Arthropoda.

On the 14th of November we sounded in latitude $19°43'$ S., longitude $36°5'$ W., the bottom consisting of a pale chocolate-coloured tenacious mud. Towards evening we reached the position of the Montague Bank, which is indicated on the chart as a bank about three miles long, and in one part covered by only thirty-six fathoms of water. We sounded for this bank repeatedly, but in vain, nowhere getting bottom with 470 fathoms of line. The ship was now allowed to drift during the night-time, soundings being made from time to time; and towards morning we filled our sails to a northerly breeze, and stood on for the Victoria Bank. In the afternoon we met with a large school of sperm whales (*Physeter macrocephalus*), displaying to advantage, as usual, their huge cylindrical snouts, and alternately their great spreading tails; this circling exercise appearing to be a favourite amusement of theirs.

On reaching the Victoria Bank, we hauled the dredge in thirty-nine fathoms, but dropping on a rugged coral bottom, the bag was torn to pieces; however, the tangles contained numbers of an oval-shaped sponge, varying in length from a quarter of an inch to an inch, and studded with beautiful glassy spicules (determined by Mr. Ridley to be a new species of Chalina), and also numbers of the genera Vioa, Nardoa, Aphocera, and Grantia. Among Polyzoa, the genera Cañda, Membranipora, Cribrillina, Gigantopora, Rhyncopora, Smittia, and Cellepora were represented. Our operations in the Abrolhos region being now at an end, we shaped a course for Monte Video.

On the 22nd of November, when we were a hundred miles from the Brazilian coast, and in about the latitude of Rio, great numbers of moths appeared, hovering about the ship, and settling on the rigging. The wind was at the time blowing freshly from the westward; but the moths appeared, strange to say, as if coming up from the south-eastward. Conspicuous among them by their great numbers as well as by their formidable appearance, were the Sphinx moths. These large insects seemed gifted with marvellous powers of flight; for although the wind amounted to a fresh breeze, I noticed that they were not only able to hold their own, but even to make headway against it. We concluded, however, that nearer in shore the wind was much stronger, perhaps reaching us so as an upper current, and that it had consequently blown them off the land. Later in the day the Lepidoptera were represented in still greater variety, so that altogether the ship exhibited an unusually sportive appearance; men and officers alike striking out with their caps here and there, as they pursued the objects of their fancy. In the course of the day I collected no less than seventeen species, of which fourteen were moths, and the remainder butterflies. As illustrating the great tenacity of life of the Sphinx moths, I may mention that, in the case of one refractory individual, it was only after employing all the deadly resources at the time at my command, viz., prussic acid, ammonia, oxalic acid, chloroform, crushing the thorax, etc., that I could succeed in removing all the ordinary manifestations of life. However, as, after long incarceration in a bottle filled with the fumes of chloroform, he at length appeared to have succumbed, I proceeded to remove the contents of his large fleshy body. This done, I filled in the body with cotton wadding, and placing the specimen on one side, proceeded to operate on another. But no sooner had I put down the specimen thus prepared, than it proceeded to kick about in a most vigorous way, and otherwise gave unmistakable signs of vitality. On turning it on its legs, it crawled about, clung to my finger, and seemed to imply that it could get on just as well with a cotton interior as with the whole complicated apparatus of intestine and so forth, which it had given me so much trouble to remove.

It was a strange coincidence, that among the contents of the tow-net on this occasion was a large black Chrysalis. It also contained a great number of little phosphorescent spheres, which, under a high magnifying power, proved to be similar to the bodies described by Sir Wyville Thompson, under the term *Pyrocystis noctiluca*. On the same day we entered the Albatross region, one large white bird (*Diomedea exulans*) and several sooties (*Diomedea fuliginosa*) soaring around our ship. Some land birds were also seen, one of which, a species of finch (?) was captured and preserved.

On the 24th of November we approached within eighty miles of the Brazilian coast, and on getting soundings in forty-eight fathoms, immediately put the dredge overboard. The hempen tangles contained starfishes of three or four species, and the bag brought up a mass of bluish tenacious mud, which, on sifting, was found to contain some Crustaceans and tube-building Annelids, and many small shells, living and dead, of the genera *Dentalium*, *Hyalea*, *Arca*, and others. About the same time a turtle was observed floating on the water.

On the forenoon of the 26th, land—the coast of Uruguay—was in view on our starboard beam, a long low line of beach, whose uniform outline was broken by a conspicuous tall lighthouse, which stamped the locality as Cape Santa Maria. A few hours later we obtained a view of Lobos Islands, a bare-looking uninviting mass of rock, situated just off Maldonado Point; and as we now fairly entered the estuary of the Plate, a number of large gulls (apparently of the genus Dominicanus) joined us, eagerly picking up any offal cast overboard.

We arrived at Monte Video on the 27th of November, and stayed until the 14th of December, during this time making several trips into the country.

On one occasion I went by train to a place called Colon, about ten miles to the N.W. of Monte Video. Starting from the central station of the Northern Railway, I took my seat in a clean well-fitted carriage, with two other passengers, one of whom, my *vis-à-vis*, might have realized one's ideas of a Guy Fawkes. In the course of the journey, this individual somewhat surprised me by diving his hand into a back coat pocket, and producing therefrom a formidable-looking silver-sheathed dagger, which, however, to my relief, he quietly laid down beside him on the seat, perhaps that he might the more conveniently stretch himself out ; possibly because he thought me a suspicious companion, and wished to show in time that he was not unprepared in case of an attack.

About Colon the country was open enough, presenting to the eye a great bare tract of weedy-looking land varied by gently undulating hills, and studded with oxen innumerable; the farm-houses, low structures disposed about half a mile apart, hardly breaking the monotony of the landscape. Here and there a gaily caparisoned Gaucho cantered about, apparently without any fixed object, except to enjoy his liberty, and gave a picturesque character to the scene. These Gauchos are really fine-looking fellows, well mounted, and most excellent horsemen. They have about them a certain air of well-fed contentment, which, in spite of their known ferocity, almost elicits admiration. It is a popular error to apply the term "Gaucho" indiscriminately to all the horse-riding community of the lower classes, for the term is properly only applicable to those homeless wandering horse-riders whose sole worldly possession consists of a horse and its trappings, who roam about from place to place, picking up whatever they can appropriate by fair means or foul, and who, consequently, do not enjoy a very high reputation among the settled inhabitants. The word "Gaucho" is looked upon as a term of reproach, and an honest, self-respecting peasant so addressed would reply, "No, Señor, no soy Gaucho, soy Paysano." By a clever stroke of policy the present dictator of Uruguay, Señor Letore, has almost succeeded in putting a stop to the infamous practice of "cattle lifting," formerly so common among the "Gauchos." Their equipment usually includes a long strip of hide, ostensibly carried as a tether for the horse, but frequently turned to account as a lasso. A law has now been enacted, and is rigidly enforced, restricting the length of this rope to five "brazeros," *i.e.*, five arm spans; and as it is in consequence much too short to answer the purpose of a lasso, these mounted tramps are no longer able to capture stray bullocks for the sole pleasure of gouging out the tongue as a dainty dish. Indeed, a gentleman of Durazno, for many years resident in the country, informed me that it was now no uncommon thing to see a Gaucho carrying a hempen rope instead of a thong, the want of a lasso leaving him without the means of helping himself to a cowhide.

About Colon the prevailing plants were a large thistle and a purple-flowered *Echium*, and these so predominated as at a distance to seem to cover the entire surface of the ground. A light fall of rain, and a puffy breeze, combined to make it a bad day for insect hunting, and accordingly very few of these creatures were seen or captured. Of birds, the cardinal grosbeak, partridges, and pigeons, were abundant.

Some days subsequently we received, through the courtesy of the directors of the railway company, permission to travel free to the extremity of their line, and of this indulgence we availed ourselves so far as to make a trip to Durazno, the northern terminus of the railway. Accordingly, a party consisting of the captain and four of us ward-room officers started by a train leaving the central terminus at seven in the morning. This railway, which has been for eleven years in existence, and for a long time struggling against unfavourable circumstances (rebellion and so forth), is now gradually assuming a prosperous condition, and has been extended so far that it now pierces the republic of Uruguay in a northern direction, to a distance of 128 miles from Monte Video. As we emerged from the precincts of the town, and passed through a hamlet called "Bella-Vista," on the shores of the bay, we noticed here and there woods of the eucalyptus tree growing in great luxuriance to a height of eighty and even a hundred feet, the foliage of adjoining trees being so interlocked as to afford considerable patches of shelter from the sun's rays. Sir George Nares, who has had some experience of these trees in Australia, where they are indigenous, said that he had rarely seen them clad with so dense a foliage. We were told that these trees had been imported and planted only twelve years previously; yet such is their rapidity of growth, that they are now of the magnitude of forest trees. On reaching a distance of about twelve miles from Monte Video, the number of trees (none of which, except the willows, were indigenous) had so far decreased, that the few solitary representatives which dotted the landscape served only to render the paucity of the race the more remarkable. The surface configuration of the land was everywhere the same—a gently undulating grass-covered plain, where the depths from crest to hollow averaged about thirty feet, admitting a range of vision of about twelve miles from the summit of each rise. Of ravines, fissures, or gullies, there were none; and as the railway track had evaded the difficulties of levelling by pursuing a most meandering course, not even a cutting was to be seen to afford means for arriving at a geological examination of the district. About the station of Independencia, rock was to be seen for the first time, consisting of a coarse-grained (apparently felspathic) granite, showing itself through the alluvial soil in the shape of low rounded masses, or as boulders disseminated in streams directed radially from the outcropping source. At the next station, appropriately named "Las Piedras" (the stones), the rock was in greater proportion; and during the remainder of our journey north, perhaps once in every ten miles, the wide expanse of grass-land would be varied by an odd-looking outcrop of granite. Stone was evidently a rare commodity in these parts, most of the huts being built of sticks and mud.

As far as Santa Lucia, a station about forty miles from Monte Video, the land (divided into fields by hedgerows of aloes) was studded thickly enough with large prickly thistles of a very coarse description; but to the northward of this position the prominent features of the landscape underwent a change. Trees disappeared altogether, and except along the river banks, where some bushes resembling bog-myrtle eked out an existence, no shrubs were to be seen. Thistles were still present, but in very small numbers, and indeed there was little to meet the eye but a wide expanse of grass-land dotted here and there with herds of oxen, sheep, and horses (which seemed in very small proportion to the acreage), and exhibiting, at distances of about two miles apart, small one-storied huts. For ploughing and other agricultural work, oxen seemed to be used, to the exclusion of horses; which is all the more strange, as the latter here exist in great abundance, and are so cheap as to create that equestrian peasantry which to a European visitor is, I think, the most striking characteristic of the country.

As one of the up-trains passed by us at the station of Joashim Suarez, we noticed several trucks piled up with ox skulls and other bones, and on enquiry ascertained that they were for exportation to England, to be used in sugar-refining factories: the bones were piled up so high on the trucks as to tower above the engine, so that as the train approached us end-on, they formed a ghastly sort of figure-head.

At Santa Lucia the train stopped half an hour for refreshments, and all hands adjourned to an hotel close by the railway station, where a good breakfast, consisting of many courses (including beefsteak and potatoes), was satisfactorily disposed of. The charge for this repast was moderate, being only six reals= 3s. 6d. a head.

Of birds a great many were to be seen as we travelled along. Looking forward from the carriage windows, we could see ground doves of a dull slate colour, rising from the track, and sheering off to either side in great flocks, as the train advanced. A species of lapwing, with bluish-grey plumage barred with white across the wings, and displaying a pair of long red legs, kept us continually alive to its presence by its harsh double cry. Partridges were also abundant. These birds are strictly preserved all over Uruguay, and during the breeding season, from September to March, no shooting of any kind is allowed without special permission. We saw one flock of ostriches stalking about unconcernedly among the cattle. We were subsequently told that the ostriches in this district were all allowed to run wild, the value of the feathers not repaying the cost of farming. Of deer, the largest indigenous mammal, we saw only one individual, browsing quietly among a herd of cattle. They are allowed to come or go as they please, not being sought after or utilized by the inhabitants.

On arriving at Durazno we were most hospitably received and entertained by Mr. Ware, the engineer of the railway, under whose guidance we inspected the sights of this dilapidated country town, and then proceeded to explore the banks of the river Yi, a tributary of the Rio Negro, where a great variety of animal life was to be seen. There was here a large lagoon bordered with low bushes, a favourite haunt of the largest living rodent, the capybara or "carpincho," as the natives call it, and also largely stocked with birds. Snipe and dottrel were here so tame as to allow one to approach within a few yards of them. In the course of the day we had the good fortune to meet a Mr. Edye, an Englishman, who, during thirteen years' residence in the Plate, had acquired a considerable insight into the natural history of the country. He told us that a great variety of birds inhabit the low bushes of the "Monte" (as they call the shallow valley of the river), including three species of the cardinal, one humming bird, the calandria or South American nightingale, etc. With reference to the tucutuco (*Ctenomys*), he assured us, contrary to the opinion expressed by Dr. Darwin, in his "Journal of a Naturalist," as to the animals never coming to the surface, that the little rodents were commonly to be seen near their holes about the time of dusk, and that they invariably retreated to the burrows on the near approach of a human being. He considered it almost impossible to catch them, but had no doubt about their habit of coming to the surface. As we strolled along the river banks, we saw and captured a black snake about two and a half feet long, which was swimming gracefully from bank to bank, with its head elevated about two inches from the top of the water. We also got some living specimens of a river mussel, which is here used as fish bait.

Everywhere among the English-speaking community we heard the same gloomy accounts of the dulness of trade, arising from the yet unsettled state of the country. All agreed that the present Dictator was managing the country admirably, but expressed their fears that he would some day be "wiped out," as others had been before him, and that the country would again relapse into a state of anarchy and brigandage.

Some days later I had an opportunity of visiting Buenos Ayres, the capital of the Argentine Republic, situated on the opposite or south shore of the river Plate. Accompanied by Lieut. Gunn, I started from Monte Video on the evening of the 9th of December, taking passage on board one of the river steamers (*Villa de Salto*), then plying daily between the two cities. The distance, 120 miles, is usually traversed at night-time, and in this arrangement sight-seers lose nothing, as, owing to the lowness of the banks and the great width of the river, the opposite shores are barely visible from a position in mid-channel. Our fellow-passengers, about eighty in number, represented Spanish, Italian, and English nationalities, and among the latter we were fortunate enough to meet two gentlemen residing in the country, to whom, as well as to the captain, a jovial, hospitable American, we were indebted for much interesting information concerning the men and manners of the country. After dinner—a long, ponderous affair—had been disposed of, a general dispersion took place, the gentlemen to smoke, and the ladies to their cabins; but in an hour or so the latter again appeared in the saloon, arrayed in evening dress of a more gay and airy character than that worn at dinner, and they now applied themselves diligently to the luxury of maté drinking. The fluid known as maté is an infusion of the leaves of the *Ilex Paraguayensis*, commonly called Paraguay tea, and is usually sucked through metal tubes about ten inches long, from a gracefully carved globular wooden receptacle about the size of an orange. One stock of "yerba" seemed to stand a great many waterings and sugarings, the necessary manipulations for which furnished the ladies with a suitable occupation. It was amusing to watch the eagerness with which the latter sucked away at their maté tubes, the attitude reminding one of a boy using a decoy whistle.

We anchored off the town of Buenos Ayres at an early hour the next morning, and here the inefficiency of the landing arrangements were made unpleasantly manifest. Three different means of locomotion were resorted to, in order to convey us from the steamer to the shore. We were pulled in a small boat for a portion of the way; then, as the boat grounded, the rowers got out, and, wading alongside, dragged it on for a few hundred yards more. We were then transferred, with our baggage, to a high-wheeled cart, drawn by two horses, which brought us through the last quarter of a mile of shallow water fringing the shore. The cost of effecting a landing was no inconsiderable item in the expense of our trip, and was moreover one calculated to prejudice unfavourably one's first impression of Buenos Ayres.

After securing rooms at the Hotel Universal, and breakfasting at the Strangers' Club, where we were most kindly received by the secretary, Mr. Wilson, we proceeded in search of the muŝeum, so celebrated for its collection of fossil remains of the extinct South American mammals, arranged under the direction of Dr. Burmeister. We found the learned Professor enveloped in white dust, and busily engaged in restoring with plaster of Paris the spinous process of the vertebra of one of his specimens; and on explaining the object of our visit, he kindly drew our attention to the principal objects of interest in his collection. This museum has already been fully described, and I need hardly allude to the splendid specimens which it possesses of the Glyptodon, Machairodon, Toxodon, Mylodon, and other fossils; its beautiful specimens of the *Chlamydophorus retusus* (a mole-like armadillo), the leathery turtle (*Sphargis coriacea*), the epiodon, etc. The Professor pointed with great pride to a recent specimen of armadillo, with the young one attached to its hind-quarters in a peculiar manner.

On the same day we inspected the Anthropological Museum, which is in a large building in the Plaza Victoria, opposite the old market, where we saw a fine collection of Tehuelche and Araucanian skulls, recently made by Señor Moreno in his travels through Patagonia. Among others was the skull of "Sam Slick," a son of the celebrated Casimiro, the Patagonian cacique, so well known for many years in the vicinity of Magellan Straits. We also saw a mummified specimen of a Patagonian, recently found in a cave at Punta Walichii, near the head waters of the Santa Cruz river.

In the course of the day we called upon Mr. Mulhall, the enterprising and courteous editor of the *Buenos Ayrean Standard*, and from him we acquired much valuable information as to the condition of the country. On taking up the *Standard* next morning, we found ourselves treated to an editorial notice chronicling our visit to the Argentine capital, and referring to the past and present services of H.M.S. *Alert*.

Coming fresh from so neat and trim a town as Monte Video, Buenos Ayres was not to be expected to impress one very favourably. It seemed, indeed, to be a great straggling town that, having arrived at a certain degree of civilization, had now for some years back considered itself entitled to rest on its laurels, and gradually fall into decay. Streets, plazas, and tramways were in a wretched state of neglect; and such were the great ruts which time and traffic had made in the streets, that baggage-carts might be seen brought to a dead lock, even in the principal thoroughfares. Buenos Ayres can boast of several fine old public buildings, among which the cathedral, with its classic front, stands pre-eminent; and although there are some fine pieces of modern architecture, such as the Bolsa, or Exchange, the latter are so stowed away among lofty houses in narrow streets, that they require to be specially looked for to be noticed at all. I must qualify the above observations by mentioning that these are the impressions of only two days' sojourn in Buenos Ayres.

Some days later, His Excellency the Governor of the Falkland Islands (Mr. Callaghan) and his wife arrived at Monte Video, *en route* for his seat of government; and as the sailing schooner, which was the only regular means of communication between Monte Video and the Falklands, was then crowded with passengers, the Governor gladly accepted Sir George Nares's kind invitation to take him as his guest on board the *Alert*.

We left Monte Video on the 14th of December, and on the 26th, amid a furious storm of wind and hail, anchored in Stanley Harbour, Falkland Islands. Here we found that the great topic of conversation was a landslip of peat, which had occurred about a month previous to our arrival, laying waste a portion of the little settlement. On the summit of a hill above the east end of the town, a circular patch of turf, about two hundred yards in diameter, had collapsed; and at the same time a broad stream, four feet high, of semi-fluid peat, flowed down the hillside to the sea, in its course sweeping away walls and gardens, and partly burying the houses. This phenomenon, occurring at night, caused great consternation among the inhabitants of such an uneventful little place; but after the people had shaken themselves together somewhat, and recovered from their surprise, they found that after all no great damage had been done. The appearance of the peat avalanche, as seen from the ship, was very peculiar, and in many respects the whole occurrence resembled a lava flow.

On the evening of our arrival, we were most hospitably entertained at Government House, where we had also the pleasure of meeting all the rank and fashion of this part of the colony.

The next day, being fine, I determined to devote to an inspection of the "stone runs," which have been rendered so famous in the geology of the Falklands by the writings of Darwin, Wyville Thompson, and others. In this excursion I was fortunate in having the assistance of Dr. Watts, the colonial surgeon, a gentleman who, from his long experience of the group, was well acquainted with all the salient points in its natural history. The "run" which we visited lay in the hollow of a winding valley, situated about two miles to the westward of the settlement of Stanley. The rocks, heaped together confusedly, formed a so-called "stone river," varying in width from fifty to two hundred yards, and extending up the valley as a single "stream" for about one mile and a half, to a point where it seemed as if originated by a confluence of tributary streams flowing from the surrounding hills. The stones, composed of quartzite, presented a roughly rounded appearance, which was seemingly due to excessive weathering; and they were so covered with lichens, as to appear of a uniform grey colour. Those which lay below the surface were of a rust colour, and, by all accounts, the upturned stones required an exposure of many years to assume the uniform grey tint of the surface layer. The margin of the "run" was distinctly defined by an abrupt edge of swampy soil, with its tangled vegetation of diddle-dee, tea-plant, and balsam bog. Now, why are the stones of the "run" so entirely destitute of soil? and why do they exhibit a margin so sharp and well defined, yet without the elevated, rounded appearance of a river bank? Sir Wyville Thompson's theory, it seems to me, falls short of explaining this. I have as yet seen too little of the country to justify me in forming a fixed opinion; but I am, so far, inclined to think that these "streams of stones" are of a date *anterior* to the existence of peat on the island, and that the peat has been approaching the valleys from the elevated land by growth and slippage, and in its descent has encountered difficulty in obtaining a footing in those places where the stones are large, and being heaped to a great depth, act like a gigantic drain, and so prevent any soil from forming. As far as I can ascertain, no attempt has ever been made to estimate the rate of movement (if any) of these "runs," and there is no evidence whatever of their motion during the present century. There is not sufficient land comprised by the watershed to form torrents capable of removing the dense mass of peaty soil, which, according to Sir W. Thompson's theory, would have been necessary for the transportation of the large blocks of stone that are here accumulated. The inhabitants remark, and I think with truth, that the summits of the hills and the upper slopes are as a rule more wet and boggy than the hollows below. This supports my view of the *drainage* being greatest in the valleys where the big stones were originally packed to a greater depth, and towards which the peat is now encroaching. It is worthy of remark that the surface of the stream is tolerably flat, and does not indicate a process of accumulation by flow from either side.

To Dr. Watts, my guide on this occasion, I was also indebted for a skin of the Falkland Island fox, an animal now almost extinct, a skull of the sea elephant, and a dried specimen of the petrel, which is known here as the "fire bird," from its habit of dashing itself against the lantern of the lighthouse, at whose base dead specimens are occasionally found.

CHAPTER II.

EXPERIENCES IN PATAGONIA.

WE left the Falkland Islands on the evening of the 27th, and sailed to the westward. On the morning of the 1st of January, 1879, we entered the eastern entrance of the Straits of Magellan, passing within easy sight of Cape Virgins and Dungeness Point. As we approached the latter, we noticed a herd of guanacoes browsing quietly near the beach, as if a passing ship were an object familiar to their eyes. This, our first impression of the famous Straits, was certainly favourable. A winding channel, the glassy smoothness of whose surface was only broken by the splashing of cormorants, steamer ducks, and other sea-birds, stretched away to the westward. On the north side were the low undulating plains of Patagonia, covered with their summer mantle of greenish-yellow vegetation; while to the southward a few widely separated wreaths of blue smoke, ascending from the gloomy shores of Tierra del Fuego, marked out the dwelling-place of one of the most remarkable varieties of the human species. Favoured by the tide, we passed rapidly through the first Narrows, and at 6.30 in the evening had got as far as Cape Gregory. Here the flood-tide setting strongly to the westward, fairly brought us to a standstill, so we steamed in towards the north shore, and anchored close under Cape Gregory. A party of us who were bent on exploring soon landed, and proceeded in various directions in quest of game, and in the few remaining hours of daylight we succeeded in getting several

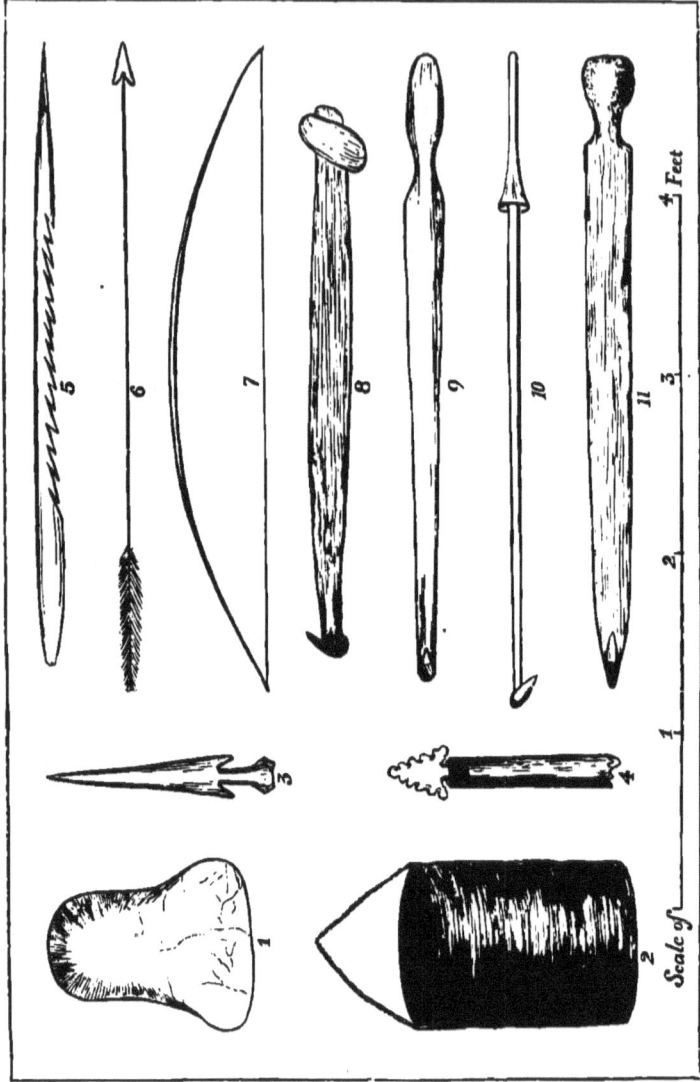

FUEGIAN IMPLEMENTS 1 TO 7.—AUSTRALIAN "WOOMERAHS" 8 TO 11.

1. Stone Axe-head. 2. Bark Bucket. 3. Bone Harpoon-head. 4. Glass Spear-head. 5. Bone-Spear-head, used in fishing. 6. Glass-tipped Arrow. 7. Bow. 8. "Woomerah," or Throwing-stick used by natives of Torres Straits. 9, 10, 11. "Woomerahs" used by Aborigines of North-West Australia.

[To face p. 34.

ducks, some small birds, and a young fox. The ground was for the most part covered with a sort of rank grass, through which bushes of the Berberry, *Empetrum rubrum*, and *Myrtus nummularia*, grew luxuriantly. A very pretty dwarf calceolaria was also abundant. The only quadruped seen was a fox, but the tucutucos (*Ctenomys*) must have been very numerous, for the ground was riddled in all directions by their burrows. Some of our party, who strolled along the beach towards Gregory Bay, found a small settlement of Frenchmen, who, it seemed, had recently come out here to try their hands at farming. After our arrival on board, one of the men brought me a specimen of a *Myxine*, which had come up on his fishing line, not attached to the hook, but adhering by its viscid secretion to the line at some distance above the hook. Of this curious fish I subsequently obtained many specimens in the western Patagonian channels.

We got under way again before daylight, and about eight in the morning we arrived at Sandy Point. This interesting little Chilian settlement was established in the year 1843, and although a great portion of it was burnt to the ground during the mutiny of 1877, it yet shows signs of ultimately becoming a place of considerable importance. Great credit is due to the Chilian Government for their perseverance in maintaining a settlement in this wild region, notwithstanding the sad fate of the colony which was established by Sarmiento in 1580, at a bay to the westward of Sandy Point, which he named "Bahia de la Gente." On Sarmiento's return, eight years subsequently, it was discovered that nearly all the colonists had perished of starvation. That bay has since been called Port Famine. Of late years the Straits of Magellan have been largely availed of by men-of-war and merchant steamers. Two lines of mail steamers, viz., the P. S. N. C. and the Kosmos line, now run bi-monthly through the Straits; and as all these vessels touch regularly at Sandy Point, the colonists are kept in frequent communication with the rest of the civilized world. For some years after its foundation the population consisted mainly of convicts, undergoing penal servitude, who were kept in control by a small garrison ; but since the mutiny of November 1877, the importation of convicts has ceased, and as a consequence labour has become scarce. At the time of our visit there were 1,100 inhabitants, including the garrison, which now consists of 120 men, rank and file, all of whom are armed with the Winchester repeating rifle.

The country possesses at least two great sources of mineral wealth, viz., gold and coal. When the coal mines were first established, sanguine ideas were entertained of their successful working. But commercial difficulties arose. The company who were working the mines became involved in a lawsuit, which, whatever may have been the rights of the case, has at all events put a stop to mining operations ; and at the time of our visit the railway leading to the mine seemed to be going to decay ; and the rolling stock, in a disjointed state, scattered about the wharf and line, testified to the stagnant condition of affairs.

I was here fortunate in finding a friend in the Government (Chilian) surgeon of the settlement—Dr. Fenton—with whose assistance and guidance I made some pleasant trips into the country adjoining Sandy Point. On our first day there he kindly provided horses, and took me for a ride into the forest, to the end of the settlement. There I saw for the first time the evergreen and deciduous beeches, the winter's bark as well as the berberry, diddle-dee, and other plants, of which we saw a great deal subsequently, during our Patagonian surveys. As we crossed a flat dreary plain which lay between the margin of the forest and the sea coast, we encountered a great number of very bold hawks, which alighted on the big thistles near our bridle path, and coolly stared at us as we went by. We also saw flocks of Bandurria, a species of black and white ibis, which is common in these parts, but being sought after by the

Chilians as an article of food, has naturally become distrustful of the ways of man, and is difficult to approach. On returning to the settlement, we found some excitement prevailing, for two of the inhabitants had just been drowned by the capsizing of a boat near the landing-place. With southerly winds, heavy rollers break along the beach; and as there is no protection in the shape of a breakwater (for boats), communication with the shore is dangerous while these winds continue. It appeared that a party of five were returning from a hulk in the roadstead, where an auction was being held, and on nearing the shore the boat got broadside on to the rollers, and capsized. Two were drowned. The other three narrowly escaped a similar fate, and owed their preservation to the gallant conduct of two of our bluejackets, who, happening to be on shore near the scene of the disaster, plunged boldly in at the risk of their lives, and brought the survivors to land.

On the following day two of us rode along the shore to the southward of the town for a distance of about six miles, when we struck into the woods, following a cart track which led us to a sawmill in the heart of the forest, belonging to Mr. Dunsmuir, the British Vice-consul. Here we shot a small owl, specimens of the Magellan thrush, and a diminutive bird of a general black colour, with a rusty-red collar, the *Centrites niger*. The beach was in places covered with dense clusters of mussels, and strewn with the dead shells of Volutes, Arcas, and Patellas, the tests of crabs, and the calcareous remains of a small Cidaris. We were greatly struck with the sagacity of our little horses—requiring little or no management, going for the most part at an easy canter, and climbing over logs, trunks of fallen trees, and banks, with the agility of goats. On our dismounting, and leaving the bridles trailing on the ground, they remained quite patiently, without showing the least inclination to make off, although we several times discharged our guns close to their heads.

We left Sandy Point on the afternoon of the 4th, and proceeded under steam to Peckett Harbour, an anchorage about twenty-five miles to the north-east of the colony. Arriving about four p.m., all of us who could, landed, and set off in pursuit of game. Even here, so little to the eastward of Sandy Point, the aspect of the country was completely different. The land was entirely devoid of trees, and the only plants of any size were the barberry and balsam bog, the latter growing as luxuriantly as at the Falklands. Walking was laborious, for the ground was everywhere riddled with the burrows of the tucutuco, a curious rodent (*Ctenomys*), which the Chilians call *carouru*. There was a fresh breeze blowing, and the birds were consequently very wild, and by no means numerous. We obtained specimens of the crested duck (*Anas cristata*), upland goose (*Chloephaga magellanica*), grebe, plover, soldier starling, snipe, sandpiper, and *Centrites niger*. The tucutucos here evidently differ in their habits from those described by Mr. Darwin, for they come out of their burrows occasionally (I believe at dusk), and one was caught by Lieut. Vereker, and given to me.

The next day we were again under way, and having taken on board some horses belonging to Mr. Dunsmuir, the British Vice-consul of Sandy Point, proceeded towards Elizabeth Island, a few miles off. This island has recently been rented from the Chilian Government by Mr. Dunsmuir, and proves of value for stock farming. Tucutucos have not yet succeeded in reaching it, a matter of no small importance as regards the value of the land, for their mining operations are almost ruinous to the pasturage. The island is about six miles long and four miles broad, and consists of an elevated plateau of undulating grass land, terminating at its margin in cliffs three hundred feet high, which front the sea. Mr. Dunsmuir has stocked it with four hundred sheep, who are left usually in charge of a shepherd and his family; and he has also, for commercial purposes, adopted measures for the protection of the upland geese, which breed in large numbers on the island. The object of our visit was to bring over for him some horses, which were required for the working of the island. As we steamed round its eastern end, myriads of terns rose in a cloud from the low sandy pits, where they had their breeding place.

After getting out the horses, and letting them swim on shore, we dropped our anchor, and soon afterwards many of us landed to explore. It was the breeding time of the upland geese, and the birds were consequently very tame, and afforded little sport in shooting. Along the beach below the cliffs a variety of birds were to be seen, including oyster-catchers, steamer-ducks, and a species of Cinclodes. As I walked by the foot of the cliffs, a steamer-duck would occasionally rush out from its retreat, and make for the water, cackling vigorously as it waddled over the shingle. As these birds steamed out seaward, they seemed undoubtedly to flap their wings in unison; but there was a sort of wabble in their swimming motion, arising probably from the alternate paddling of the feet. On the heights above, I shot several military starlings, and others of our party obtained some brown ducks (*Anas cristata*) and snipe.

The cliff was apparently breaking away in many places, exposing fresh sections of its face, and exhibiting pebbles, rounded stones, and rocks imbedded in the clayey mass, a feature which is characteristic of this part of the coast. Lines of stratification, of varying degrees of fineness, were to be seen; and in several places, at about fifty feet from the summit of the cliff, streams of water oozed out from the seams. I could detect no trace of a fossil. Along the beach lay many dead shells of the genera Voluta, Arca, Patella, Mytilus, and Trophon. During this walk I noticed about six different species of butterflies and a few beetles.

The dredge had been laid out from the ship on anchoring, so that it might profit by the swinging of the ship; and when we hauled it up in the evening, it contained a quantity of dead barnacles covered with ophiurids, and also shells of the genera Trochus and Trophon, Amphipod Crustaceans, Annelids, and some red, jelly-like Gephyreans. These were all entangled in a mass of red seaweed, interlaced with stalks of the Macrocystis.

Early next morning (January 7th) we steamed back to Sandy Point. As we approached the anchorage, we noticed dense clouds of smoke rising from the woods some distance inland, and it soon transpired that the forest in the vicinity of the Consul's sawmills was on fire. In the afternoon I rode out with Dr. Fenton to the scene, and we found the troops of the garrison employed in felling trees, so as to make a sort of lane through the woods to leeward of the fire, in order, if possible, to limit its ravages. Dr. Fenton afterwards came on board, and gave us an interesting account of the mutiny of 1877, in which he and his wife narrowly escaped being shot. His house, like most others, was burnt down on that occasion. Sixty of the peaceable inhabitants were shot by the mutineers, and nine of the latter were subsequently executed. Those of the population who escaped had fled to the woods, and there fortified themselves against an attack. Eventually the mutiny was quelled by the arrival of the Chilian gunboat *Magellanes*, at whose approach the mutineers fled away into the pampas.

At two o'clock in the afternoon of the following day we weighed anchor and proceeded to the westward. We had scarcely left Sandy Point a few miles behind us, when the character of the scenery underwent a marked change. The straits narrowed, its shores rose in lofty hills, whose lightly inclined slopes were clothed with forest from the summits to the water's edge, and we exchanged the clear blue sky of Patagonia for an atmosphere of mists and rain squalls. As we passed by Port Famine, two Fuegian canoes pulled off to us from the southern shores, the natives hailing us vociferously for "*galleta tabac*" (biscuit and tobacco). However, we could not spare time to interview them, and they turned back disappointed, and moreover evidencing signs of indignation. When abreast of Borja Bay, we experienced such a succession of heavy squalls from the westward, that we were compelled to put in for shelter, and accordingly anchored. On landing, we found the trees placarded in various places with wooden records of ships that had called there; and on pushing our way through the bushes adjoining the beach, we were not a little surprised at stumbling across a coffin, which from its position seemed to have been hurriedly deposited there by a passing ship. It bore an inscription stating that it contained the remains of some person who had belonged to the Chilian man-of-war *Almirante Cochrane.* Animal life was at a discount; only a few moths, a Cinclodes, a brace of duck, and a few gulls being seen. The vegetation was luxuriant, and the Philesia, berberry, and diddle-dee plants were in full bloom. We stopped for only a few hours; for on the wind lulling we again proceeded on our course. Passing through the "Long Reach," the scenery became of a most imposing character; several straggling, highly inclined glaciers creeping down on either side through the deep mountain gorges, their dazzling whiteness contrasting strikingly with the richly verdured hillsides, and the lofty snow-covered mountain summits beyond fading away imperceptibly into a hazy sky. Later in the evening we anchored in Playa Parda Cove, a beautiful little land-locked basin, and most of us landed at once, to spend the last few remaining hours of daylight. A solitary steamer-duck was seen, but for the rest animal life was unrepresented. As at Borja Bay, several little billets of wood, attached conspicuously to trees bordering the shore, recorded the visits of previous explorers to these outlandish regions.

On the morning of the 10th we left Playa Parda, and steamed northward through the Sarmiento Channels. In the afternoon, as we were passing by Fortune Bay, we sighted and exchanged signals with the Chilian man-of-war *Chacabuco*, a vessel which was now employed in surveying certain portions of the Straits. Our halting-place for this evening was at Isthmus Bay, where we anchored about six p.m. At the head of this bay, where a narrow neck of lowland separated us from the waters of Oracion Sound, was the remains of a Fuegian encampment, which, to judge from the appearance of the shell heaps, could not have been left for more than a year uninhabited. Across the isthmus was a "portage" for boats, consisting of rudely-cut stakes laid on the ground parallel to each other, and a few yards apart, like railway sleepers. The aspect of the green forest encircling this charming little bay was variegated with a luxuriant display of really beautiful flowers, among which were conspicuous the *Philesia buxifolia*, *Fuchsia magellanica*, *Gaultheria antarctica*, *Berberis ilicifolia*, and a number of composites of different species. A kind of cedar, the *Libocedrus tetragonus* ("cipres" of the Chilotes), was here also very abundant, furnishing good straight poles suitable for various purposes. Its four-sided arrangement of leaves at once attracts attention.

We got under way early in the morning, and proceeded up the Sarmiento Channels, passing by the Chilian ship *Chacabuco* in the midst of a rain squall. No natives were to be seen. The channel here narrowed, and the scenery of the opposing shores became of a grand yet rather sombre character, the round-topped granite mountains which seemed to overhang us, with their streaky patches of forest creeping up the gullies, being enveloped in a hazy mist, and presenting a sort of draggled appearance, as if rain had been falling over their rocky faces for ages.

About five in the evening we entered Mayne Harbour, a few cormorants and steamer-ducks sheering off with much splashing, as we slipped between the islets that almost block up the entrance.

So we continued to wend our way through these desolate channels, looking into nearly every anchorage on the way, and usually anchoring for the night, until the 14th of January, when we reached "Tom Bay," which was to be our base of operations for the ensuing survey of the Trinidad Channel. Some hours after we had anchored, a native boat suddenly emerged from a narrow channel opening into the bay, and paddled towards the ship, displaying a green branch in the bows of the boat, while one individual standing up waved a small white cloth, no doubt intended as a flag of truce. Our people on board made amicable demonstrations in response, by waving handkerchiefs and so forth, and then slowly and warily the natives approached. This was our first experience of representatives of the Channel tribe of Fuegians. There were altogether eight of them. But I must not omit to mention the dogs, five in number, as the latter formed by far the most respectable portion of the community; for it would indeed be difficult to imagine a more diabolical cast of countenance than that presented by these savages. Their clothing consisted of a squarish scrap of sealskin looped round the neck, sometimes hanging over the back, sometimes resting on the shoulders, but apparently worn more by way of ornament than for any protection which it afforded; and a very narrow waist-cloth, which simple garment was sometimes deemed superfluous. An elderly lady of a saturnine cast of countenance sat on a wisp of grass in the stern of the canoe, and manœuvred the steering oar. They could not be induced to come on board the ship, and from their guarded demeanour would seem to have had rather unfavourable experiences of civilized man. After bartering their bits of seal and other skins, and getting some biscuit, tobacco, and knives, they paddled away, and established themselves on an islet about half a mile from the ship, where we saw that the skeleton frameworks of some old huts were standing.

On the following day a small party, consisting of North (the paymaster), three seamen, and myself, pulled over to the native camp. We were received on landing by four men with bludgeons in their hands, who did not seem at all glad to see us, and who seemed apprehensive of our approaching the hut, where the women had been jealously shut up. However, by a few presents of tobacco and biscuit, we established tolerably amicable relations, and were permitted to examine the canoe, which lay hauled half out of the water. It was composed of five planks, of which one, about twenty feet long and two and a half feet wide, formed the bottom, while the other four, each one and a half foot in width, formed the sides. The bottom plank was turned up at the ends, so as to form a flat bow and stern of nearly similar shape; and to this plank, as well as to each other, the side pieces were secured by a lacing passed through rude square-shaped holes about an inch in area, which were made in an even row close to the edges of the planks. The lacing used for this purpose is the tough stem of a bignoniaceous creeper (the *Campsidum chilense*), which is commonly seen twining round the tall forest trees, forming festoons from branch to branch, and again extending from the horizontal branches vertically downwards like the cordage of a ship. Caulking was effected by stuffing the seams with moss and strips of the winter's bark (bark of the *Drimys winteri*), over which the lacing was carried; and the square-shaped holes were plugged with some pulpy vegetable matter, of which moss seemed to be the chief constituent. The oars were made of young stems of the *Libocedrus tetragonus*, to one end of which elliptical pieces of wood were lashed by way of blades. These oars were used in the ordinary way, the loom resting on crescentic-shaped crutches, fashioned out of a single piece of wood, and lashed to the gunwale. The everlasting Fuegian fire, from which Tierra del Fuego derives its name, burned in the middle of the boat, resting on a bed of clay; and the half-decomposed head of a seal, which either the natives or the dogs had recently been gnawing, completed the furniture of this crazy vessel. The hut in which the women were shut up was a haycock-shaped arrangement, composed of a skeleton framework of boughs, over which were thrown several old skins of the sea-lion (*Otaria jubata*). The chief of this party, who was, by the way, the tallest Fuegian ever seen by us, we found by measurement to be five feet four inches in height. One hut accommodated the entire party, consisting, as I have said, of four men, four women, and five dogs.

The greater part of the subsequent four months was spent in the vicinity of the Trinidad Channel, which it was our special duty to survey; and as our movements during this period were most erratic, and we frequently paid five or six different visits to the same parts, I shall for a time abandon all chronological order, and speak of events according to the places in which they occurred.

But in the first place, in order to render my narrative more intelligible, I shall here give a brief general description of this region, referring to its climate, natural features, and inhabitants.

The weather is peculiar, for the rainfall is excessive, and as a rule there is not more than one moderately dry day out of the seven.

The peaks and ridges of the broken-up range of mountains, of which the islands and coast are formed, intercept the moisture-laden clouds which are being continually wafted from seaward by the prevailing westerly winds, frequent and long-continued downpours being the result. From observations taken with the rain gauge, we estimate the average daily rainfall to be 0·41 inch, and that of the wettest month of which we have had experience, viz., the month of April, 0·522 inch. The annual rainfall, estimated from the mean of eight months' observations, we find to be 149·65 inches. The mean annual temperature, estimated similarly from observations extending over the months of January, February, March, April, May, (nine days of) October, November, and December, we found to be 49·2, the extremes of temperature being 36° and 60°. When we reflect that the annual rainfall in London is about 23·5 inches, while the yearly average of temperature is 46·9 Fahr., we can realize the extent to which rainy weather prevails in this land, and the comparative coldness of its nevertheless equable climate. We were told by the master of a sealing schooner that the climate of Western Fuegia varied but little throughout the year, and that in his opinion the finest weather was to be found in mid-winter; and, indeed, on entering the channels in the month of October—that is, in the early spring—we ourselves found the appearance of the country but little different from our recollections of the previous midsummer. There was, perhaps, more snow on the hill-tops, but there was none at all on the lower slopes of the hills, and the evergreen vegetation seemed almost as luxuriant as during midsummer.

As might be expected from the large rainfall and comparatively equable temperature, this climate is very favourable to the growth of cryptogamous plants; ferns, mosses, and Hepaticæ abound, clothing the stems of dead and living trees, and occupying every shady nook and crevice. Among the ferns most commonly seen were several beautiful species of the genus Hymenophyllum. Of flowering plants there were also some of great beauty, the most attractive of which were the Philesia buixfolia, the Desfontainea Hookeri, the Berberis ilicifolia, the B. empetrifolia, and the Embothrium coccineum. The former is a sort of under-shrub, of creeping habit, and is most commonly seen twining round the stem of the evergreen and antarctic beeches, to a height of six or eight feet from the ground, its lovely, rose-coloured, bell-shaped flowers showing to great advantage against the delicate background of ferns and mosses, which, growing from the bark of the tree, display the flowers, but almost conceal the branches of the twining Philesia. There is another beautiful plant, of the same natural order, met with in Southern Chili, which the people take great pride in, showing to strangers as the glory of their gardens. It is called the "Copigue" (*Lapageria rosea*). The only trees which attain to any reasonable size as such are the evergreen and antarctic beeches (*Fagus antarctica* and *F. betuloides*), the winter's bark (*Drimys winteri*), and the cypres (*Libocedrus tetragonus*). The bark of the *Drimys winteri* was formerly employed in medicine, but has latterly fallen into disuse, partly from the difficulty of obtaining the genuine article in Europe. It has tonic and stimulant properties. The infusion of the dried bark is so hot and peppery as to burn the tongue and throat; but, strangely enough, the spirit tincture extracts the tonic bitter with but very little of the peppery principle.

The summits of the low hills, which are usually bare of trees or brushwood, are covered with a sort of swamp formed of astelias, gaimardeas, and calthas, whose interlacing roots form a more or less compact sod, which, as one walks on it, shakes from the fluctuation of the bog water beneath.

The rock of the district is a cross-grained syenite, intersected with dykes of greenstone, of very variable thickness. This is the prevalent rock; but about Port Rosario, on the north side of "Madre de Dios" island, there is an outcrop of limestone. The latter is of a pale-blue colour, in some cases assuming the character of marble; and when much exposed to the weather, presents a curious honey-combed appearance, due to the solvent action of the rain. This rock is unfossiliferous. The disintegration of the syenite from the usual atmospheric agencies is rapid enough; but the resulting detritus does not contribute to form a good clay.

If an artificial section be made of the soilcap, or if advantage be taken of a landslip to examine it carefully, it will be seen to be composed of a dense network of interlacing roots, containing in its interstices a small quantity of black mould, the latter increasing in proportion as the basement rock is reached. This spongy mass of tangled vegetation, ever saturated with moisture, is the soil on which the trees clothing the hillsides take root. On the little plateaus about the hill-tops, however, it only contains the roots of the marsh plants above mentioned, and those of an odd stunted bush. On first coming to this region, I was much struck on seeing that the forest approaches so close to the water's edge, and that the banks overhang so much that frequently the branches of the trees dip into the salt water; and in some places a black snag projecting above the surface of the inshore water tells the fate of a tree that had perished from immersion. These phenomena, among others to be hereafter alluded to, are, I think, to be attributed to a slow but steady sliding motion of the soilcap over its rocky foundation on the sloping hillsides, a motion which is in many respects analogous to the flow of a glacier.

Of the natives inhabiting the Patagonian channels between the Gulf of Penas and Smyth's channels, very little is known; and I am the more inclined to attempt a description of their physical characteristics and habits of life, because of all the savage tribes of whom I have had experience—including the Australian aborigines, who are generally credited with being of the lowest order—I believe that the people whom I am about to describe bear away the palm as the most primitive among all the varieties of the human species. They are certainly closely related to the Fuegians who live south of the main Straits of Magellan, from whom, however, they differ sufficiently to show a tribal distinction. Fitzroy, in enumerating six tribes of Fuegians, denominates those of whom I speak as "the Channel or Chonos tribe." They lead a wandering life, constantly shifting in their canoes from place to place, and travelling in families of about twelve individuals, all of whom stow in the same canoe, and sleep in the same hut. We have never been able to ascertain the precise relationship existing between the different members of these families; but a party of twelve would probably consist of three men, five women, and four children.

For the greater part of the year they live almost entirely on mussels and limpets, this simple fare being only varied occasionally by the capture of a seal, a small otter, or of an equally small coypu. That they get this kind of fresh meat but rarely is evident from our inspection of their midden heaps, hillocks of refuse in the vicinity of the huts, consisting mainly of shells. I must not omit to mention, however, that bones of the steamer-duck and cormorant are also found about the huts, but not in any quantity. During the months of December and January, the Magellan seals "haul up" to breed on the rocks of the outer coasts, and during this season there is a great gathering of natives about the "rookeries," as the sealers call them, so that for a short portion of the year these unfortunate wretches can luxuriate upon a diet of fresh meat.

They are of low stature, the men averaging 5 ft. 1 in. in height, while the women are still shorter. Of eight men whom I measured carefully, the extremes were 4 ft. 10 in. and 5 ft. 3 in.; so that there is a strong contrast between them and their neighbours in the same latitude, the Patagonians, whose average stature (I speak of the men only) is 5 ft. 10 in. Their complexion is of an ochrey copper colour; the eyes are dark, and placed close together; the upper eyelid curving downwards abruptly as it approaches the nasal side, or inner canthus, in such a way as to give an appearance of obliquity in the eye, which reminds one of that feature in the face of a Japanese. The sclerotics, or so-called "white" of the eye, have a yellow tinge, and in the adults the conjunctiva is injected or bloodshot, probably from their habit of sitting over a smoky wood fire. The upper lip is thin and curved; and when a grimace is made, it tightly embraces the teeth, so as to communicate a peculiarly wicked expression to the countenance. The maxillæ are broad, and the teeth are of glistening whiteness. In the female the front teeth present an even regular line; but in the male adult there is usually a front tooth missing, as if knocked out designedly. The hair is long, black, and coarse, and is peculiar in growing sometimes from the temples, as well as from the scalp, a circumstance from which the forehead acquires a narrow pyramidal appearance. There are no whiskers, but on the lips and chin a few scattered hairs are seen. The upper extremities and trunk are well formed, but the legs are very poorly developed, so much so as to seem out of proportion to the rest of the body. The skin overlying the kneecaps is particularly loose, baggy, and wrinkled when the native stands erect, a circumstance which, in the case of the southern Fuegian, is very justly attributed (*vide* Voyage of *Adventure* and *Beagle*,

p. 176) to the practice of frequently sitting on the heels, with the legs flexed to a maximum.

Some of the emotions are expressed by very decided contortions of the features and limbs. Delight, when intense, is shown by a display of the closed teeth, accompanied by a clucking sound, and a curious up and down bobbing motion of the body. Eagerness is expressed by a clucking sound and a frothing of the lips. Anger is characterised by a tightening of the upper lip, a protrusion of the lower jaw or mandible, and a slight display of the upper incisors.

The men are almost entirely naked, sometimes wearing a square piece of sealskin suspended from the neck, and hanging over either shoulder. This seems to be intended as a sort of weather screen; but, strangely enough, it is one of the first things parted with when a chance of bartering occurs. Although so careless about protecting their bodies against the rigour of the weather, it was nevertheless evident that they were keenly sensible to the cold; for they were frequently to be seen with their teeth chattering, and trembling from head to foot, as the rain, wind, and spray swept over their unprotected skins. The women generally have a large skin mantle, which they wear with the hair turned outwards. Those with infants carry the child in a pouch between the shoulders; but those not so burdened readily part with their only covering for a plug of tobacco. That these people should attach any value to tobacco is difficult to understand; for not only are they unprovided with native pipes in which to smoke it, but, as far as we could judge, they had never enjoyed sufficient opportunities of doing so to render the *process* anything but highly unpleasant, although its *anticipation* undoubtedly afforded them great pleasure. In fact, one or two whiffs of smoke were sufficient to put a man into the nauseated and giddy condition familiar to every schoolboy when he makes his first trial of tobacco.

Although the dress of the women is, as I have mentioned, far

CANOE OF "CHANNEL FUEGIANS" HAULED UP ON BEACH.

from elaborate, they otherwise evinced the usual love of their sex for articles intended to be ornamental. They commonly wore round their throats necklaces composed of margarita shells, porpoise teeth, or fragments of calcareous worm-tubes, strung together. Their faces, as well as those of the men, were sometimes daubed with black charcoal, and sometimes with a paste composed of white wood-ashes, but with what precise object we did not ascertain.

The affection of these savages for their children does not seem to be of a very stable character; for, by all accounts, they are willing to part with them for a trifling consideration. A Fuegian boy, christened Tom Picton, whom we took on board in the Trinidad Channel, quitted his relations without any manifestation of reluctance; and they, on their part, were readily conciliated by the gift of a few necklaces and some biscuit. In Byron's narrative of the loss of the *Wager*, there is a most interesting account of his wanderings among the natives of the Gulf of Peñas. He mentions that, on one occasion, a savage was so exasperated with his son, a child of three years, who had accidentally dropped into the water a basket containing some sea-eggs (*Echini*), that he "caught the boy up in his arms, and dashed him with the utmost violence against the stones," the child dying soon afterwards.

Their hunting appliances are few and simple; the canoe is a rude structure, but answers its purpose well enough. It is constructed of five planks, of which one, about 20 ft. by 2½ in width, forms the bottom, and the other four, each 1½ ft. wide, form the sides. The bottom plank is turned up at the ends, so as to form a flat bow and stern of nearly similar shape; and to this, as well as to each other, the side planks are laced by the long flexible stem of a creeping plant, which is passed through rude squarish holes, about one inch in area, which are made in an even row close to the edges of the planks. The material used for the lacing appeared to be the stem of the *Campsidium chilense*, a creeper which grows to a great length, is very abundant, and is remarkable for its exceeding toughness. Caulking is effected by stuffing the seams with bark, over which a lacing is carried, and the squarish holes are finally plugged with some vegetable pulpy matter, of which moss is the chief constituent. Two oars, with very large broad blades, are used for propelling the boat, and not paddles, as in the case of the southern Fuegians. A young woman, seated in the stern sheets, steers very dexterously with a short paddle. Such rude boats leak, of course, a good deal, and hence require constant baling out. This office is performed by the *old* woman of the party, who, crouching amidships, bales out the water with a bark bucket.

Spears of two kinds are used, one for fishing, the other for sealing. The one for sealing, which is rather a harpoon than a spear, has an arrow-shaped bone head, which is movable, and is attached by a slack line of hide to the spear shaft. The use of the loose line is probably to facilitate the capture of the seal, into which the movable arrow-head has been driven by the impetus conveyed through the detachable shaft. A harpoon similarly constructed is used by the Eskimo hunters for a like purpose. The fish spear is a formidable weapon, having a long bone head securely fixed to the shaft, and with many deep serrations along one side. The shafts of both are about eight feet long, and are made of the young stems of a coniferous tree, the *Libocedrus tetragonus*.

Every party that we met with was provided with an iron axe of some kind. The axes are usually made of bits of scrap iron which have been picked up from wrecks, or obtained by barter from passing vessels. Sometimes, though rarely, an axe of civilization pattern is seen. In other cases the piece of iron, having been ground into a rude triangular shape, is fitted into a wooden handle, as some of the old stone celts are supposed to have been ; that is to say, the small end of the axehead is jammed into a hole made near the end of a stout piece of stick. I may here mention that, in spite of a most diligent search, I have once, but only once, succeeded in finding a STONE axchead. It was of very primitive shape—being only in part ground—and was found lying among the shells of a very old abandoned kitchen-midden.

For holding drinking water they use large cylindrical buckets, which are made from the bark of the *Drimys winteri;* the single scroll-shaped piece which forms the cylinder and the disc-shaped bottom being sewn together with rushes. From this same kind of rush plant, which they use so frequently for making temporary hitches, they make three-plaited ropes for mooring the canoes, and also baskets to hold shell fish. The kind of plait used in fashioning their baskets is a simple network, which must, however, be tedious to construct, owing to the necessity for frequently splicing the rushes.

Their huts somewhat resemble small haycocks in general shape, but are rather oblong, the floor (which is never excavated, as in the case of some of the southern Fuegians) usually measuring ten by twelve feet; the height in the centre is six feet, so that one of us could always stand upright when in the middle of the hut. A skeleton framework is made of boughs, whose thicker ends are stuck in the ground, while the terminal twigs are made to interlace, and are moreover secured to each other by rush lashings. The required amount of shelter is obtained by placing leafy boughs and dried sealskins over the framework of the hut. A fire is kept burning in the centre; and when the boat is about to be used, a few burning sticks are transferred to it, and kept alight on a clay flooring amidships.

I have never seen their appliances for striking a light, but I have no doubt they use iron pyrites, with dried moss or down for tinder, as do the southern Fuegians, from whom I have obtained these appliances. These materials for obtaining fire are very judiciously guarded, and are the only articles among the properties of a canoe which are not submitted for barter. The "Pecheray" Fuegians keep their stock of tinder in water-tight pouches, made of the dried intestine of the seal. (?)

Neither stone slings, bows and arrows, nor bolas, are used by the Channel Fuegians, so that altogether, with respect to hunting appliances, they are in a more primitive state than any of the southern tribes.

The remains of the deceased, so far as we have known, are deposited in caves in out-of-the-way localities. During the voyage of Sarmiento, towards the latter end of the 16th century, a cave containing human remains was found in a small island called the " Roca Partida," or cleft rock ; and subsequently, when the shipwrecked crew of the *Wager*, one of Commodore Anson's ships, were wandering about the Gulf of Peñas, Mr. Wilson, the surgeon, discovered near the seashore a large cave which contained the skeletons of several human beings (*vide* Byron's narrative of the loss of the *Wager*, Burney's Voyages). During the surveying cruise of H.M.S. *Nassau*, in 1866-9, a diligent search was made for such burial places, but without success ; but, on the other hand, no signs were observed of any other method of disposing of the dead, either by fire, as in the case of some of the southern tribes, or by covering the bodies with branches of trees, as described by Fitzroy. However, during our late survey of the Trinidad Channel, we found a small cave containing portions of two skeletons in a limestone islet, near Port Rosario, on the north side of Madre de Dios Island ; and this would seem to have been used as a burial-place, at some very remote period. The remains have been deposited in the British Museum.

It has been stated by the late Admiral Fitzroy, on the authority of Mr. Low, a sealing captain, that during times of great scarcity of food, these savages do not scruple to resort to cannibalism, and that for this purpose they select as victims the old women of the party, killing them by squeezing their throats, while holding their heads over the smoke of a green wood fire. Mr. Low's evidence on this point is so circumstantial, being derived from a native interpreter who served on board his ship for fourteen months, that it can hardly be doubted. On this subject I can only add that we noticed a singularly small proportion of old people, whether male or female, among the parties of natives with whom we met. This circumstance may support Mr. Low's opinion, or it may be the natural consequence of the short span of life which is allotted to these wretched people.

Regarding the treachery of these savages, there can be no doubt. Their faces alone indicate it, but unfortunately further evidence is not wanting. We recently met with a small sealing schooner, the *Annita*, of Sandy Point, the master of which—a Frenchman, named Lamire—gave us a detailed account of an attack made upon his vessel about two years ago, when he was "sealing" at the north end of Picton Channel. He lay at anchor one night in fancied security, when he was surprised by a large party of natives who came alongside in seven canoes. A dreadful struggle ensued, in which his crew defended themselves with their guns against the axes, spears, sticks, and stones, of their savage assailants. The natives were eventually driven off, but not before five of the sealers had lost their lives. The sealers are now well aware of the anxiety of the natives to gain possession of their vessels, and consequently put no trust in their overtures of friendship. A white man is feared only so long as his party is known to be the strongest.

Fitzroy has described six tribes of Fuegians who speak different dialects, and also differ somewhat in their habits. These are (1) the Yacanas, or inhabitants of the north portion of King Charles's South Land; (2) the Tekeenicas, who live in southeastern Fuegia; (3) the Alikhoolips, who inhabit the South-Western Islands; (4) the Pecherays, a small tribe of savages who hover about the middle and western part of the Straits of Magellan; (5) the Huemuls, so called from the Chilian name of a deer which has been found about Skyring Water and Obstruction Sound, the head-quarters of this tribe; and (6) the Fuegians who inhabit the shores and islands of western Patagonia, between the parallels of 47° and 52°, and whom Fitzroy denominates the Chonos or Channel Fuegians. In Fitzroy's account of the Fuegians, he naturally selected as his type the people with whom he was best acquainted, viz., the Tekeenicas, who inhabit the shores of the Beagle Channel. These people build conical wigwams, which are made of large poles leaning to from a circular base, with their upper ends meeting in a point. Their canoes are built of bark, and are small and skiff-shaped. They also use bows and arrows, and stone slings, and in this respect are considerably in advance of the Channel Fuegians.

In their methods of disposing of the dead, the Fuegian tribes differ somewhat strangely. Fitzroy tells us that among the Tekeenicas, Alikhoolips, and Pecherays, the bodies of the dead are carried a long way into the interior of the forest, where they are placed upon broken timber, and then covered up with branches. On this subject some information has recently been obtained from the missionaries, who have now for some years maintained a settlement at a place called Ushuwia, in the Beagle Channel. We heard, on the authority of these gentlemen, that a form of cremation is now commonly practised among the Tekeenicas, and that charred human bones may often be found among the embers of the funeral pyre. The Fuegians of the Western Channels, as I have mentioned already, deposit their dead in caves.

To continue with Tom Bay. The month of January is here the breeding season with most of the water birds. About the middle of the month the steamer-ducks (*Tachyeres cinereus*) and the kelp geese (*Bernicla antarctica*) were paddling about with their young ones; and the oyster-catchers (*Hæmatopus leucopus*, and *ater*), with their young broods, occupied the small low rocky islets, where they made themselves conspicuous by their shrill piping cry. We remarked that the kelp geese, which, as a rule, never wet their feet, except with the damp seaweed of the fore-shore,

Our Bird Visitors at Tom Bay. 57

take to the water as soon as the young are hatched, being probably induced to do so in order the better to protect their goslings from the hawks and rats. The male and female adult birds differ remarkably in plumage; that of the female being almost black, with a few white dots and dashes, whereas the feathers of the male are perfectly white. The sombre colour of the female is probably intended as a protection during the hatching time, when she remains almost continuously on the eggs, while the gander does sentry in some conspicuous position adjacent. Whenever at this time of the year a solitary gander is seen standing on a projecting point or headland, it may safely be inferred that his faithful consort is on her nest somewhere within sixty yards. Even under these circumstances it is by no means an easy matter to find the nest; for the black plumage of the female assimilates with the dark wind-blown seaweed and rank grass in which her nest is made, and she lies so close that she will not stir until almost walked on. While the birds are immature (*i.e.*, less than one year old) the sexes are scarcely distinguishable, the plumage of both male and female being an almost equal mixture of white and black colours.

The ashy-headed brent goose (*Chloephaga poliocephala*), remarkable for the splendid chestnut colour of its breast, is the only other goose met with in these western channels. The common Magellan and Falkland Islands goose (*C. Magellanica*) does not, as a rule, extend its range to the damp western regions.

About the islets adjacent to the Tom Bay anchorage were great numbers of abandoned huts, and at some the size of the shell mounds and the compactness of the bottom layers indicated considerable antiquity. These mounds are principally composed of mussel and limpet shells, the latter predominating; and among the interstices were great numbers of insects and worms. There was one very old grass-covered mound near our anchorage, of which we made a thorough examination by digging cross-section trenches. Besides the usual shells, there were a few seal bones and sterna of birds, and at a depth of four feet from the surface we found a partly disintegrated bone spear-head, which was different in shape from any which we saw among the natives either before or subsequently. Instead of being rounded, it was flattened from side to side, like a very large arrow-head. In most of the other shell heaps which we examined, bones of the nutria (*Myopotamus coypu*) and of the otter (*Lutra felina*) were observed.

To the westward of our anchorage (*i.e.*, in the large island of Madre de Dios) was a long narrow inlet, partly overhung with trees, which communicated by a shallow bar with a brackish lagoon of about thirty acres in extent. At low water there was only about three feet of water on the bar, and we could then see that the bottom was covered with huge white sessile barnacles (the "picos" of the Chilians), growing closely together. During the ebb and flood tides the current ran fiercely over this bar, so as to render it an exceedingly difficult matter to pull through the channel when the tide was adverse. This lagoon was a favourite haunt of the Magellan sea otter (*Lutra felina*), which is abundant in all these waters, but is very difficult to kill without the aid of dogs. Its "runs" are generally strewn with the shells of a large spiny crab (the *Lithodes antarctica*), which appears to form its principal food. I have seen an otter rise to the surface with one of these hideous crabs in its mouth, as unpalatable a morsel, one would think—for it is armed all over with strong spines—as a "knuckleduster." In the *Alert*, the great feat of sportsmanship was to shoot and bag an otter; for if the animal be not struck in the head, and killed outright at the first shot, it is almost certain to make a long dive, crawl up the beach in the shade of the overhanging bushes, and escape.

When exploring in a small boat the winding shores of this lagoon, we one day came upon a little sequestered cove, where there was a luxuriant growth of *Desfontainea* bushes, and on landing on the shingly beach we saw, by the way in which the larger stones had been moved aside, that the place had been used by the natives

A Native "Portage." 59

for hauling up their canoes. On walking through the long rank grass, which encroached on the beach, we tripped over some logs which seemed to have been arranged artificially, and we then discovered that we were at the extremity of a "portage," intended for conveying boats overland. On tracing it up, we found a sort of causeway leading into the forest; and after following it for about three hundred yards, we ascertained that we had crossed a narrow isthmus, of whose existence we were previously unaware, and had reached the shore of an arm of the sea (probably Delgado Bay), which communicates with the Trinidad Channel not many miles to the eastward of Port Henry. It was evident that by means of this "portage" the natives were able to proceed from Concepcion Channel, viâ Tom Bay, towards the outer coasts, without undertaking the much longer and more hazardous journey through the main channels round Point Brazo. The logs forming the "portage" were partly imbedded in the ground, and were arranged parallel to each other, like the sleepers of a railway, and at a distance of about two feet apart. There was, however, no appearance of the natives having recently visited the place. We had reason to believe that these "portages" were of frequent occurrence, and were largely used by the natives, and that it was owing to the facilities thus afforded them for crossing isthmuses and the necks of promontories that they were enabled to surprise sailing vessels at anchor, approaching them unobserved from the landlocked side of bays and inlets at a time when the attention of the sailors on "look-out" was naturally only directed towards the entrance of the harbour which had previously seemed to them to be untenanted. The "portages" are so concealed by a luxuriant growth of grass and brushwood that they readily escape observation.

The brackish lagoons, which are fed continuously by freshwater streams, and receive an influx of sea water while the flood tide is making, are a peculiar feature of this Patagonian archipelago, and we usually found that the outlets were excellent places for catching fish. Our fishing parties were in the habit of placing a "trammel" net across the outlet while the tide was ebbing, and in this way entrapped great quantities of mullet and mackerel; sometimes upwards of eighty, ranging in weight from two to eleven pounds per fish, being taken at one haul.

I collected some green flocculent matter from the surface of one of these lagoons, and found it to consist almost entirely of diatoms.

One fine day in April we noticed a great concourse of gulls and shags, attracted by a shoal of fish, in the pursuit of which they ventured unusually close to the ship. This gave us an opportunity of observing that the common brown gull of the channels, the female of *L. Dominicanus*, behaves towards the male bird in many respects like a skua. No sooner would one of the "black-backed" (male) birds capture a fish, and rise from the surface, than he would be attacked by one of the brown birds, and chased vigorously about the harbour; the predatory bird not desisting from the pursuit until the coveted prize had been dropped by its rightful owner. This I noticed on more occasions than one. As a rule, however, the female was content to fish for herself. Several Dominican gulls in immature plumage were seen amongst the crowd, and were easily distinguished from the adults by the mottled brown plumage, and by the colour of the mandibles being green instead of orange, as in the males, and black as in the females. Now and then the whole flock of gulls and shags would rise on the wing, as they lost the run of the shoal of fish. They would then be directed to the new position of the shoal by the success of some straggling bird, when a general rush would be made to the new hunting ground. It was most amusing to witness the widely different fishing powers of the shags and gulls, and the consequently unequal competition in the struggle for food. The shag in flight, on observing a fish beneath him, at once checks himself by presenting the concave side of his wings to the direction in which he has been moving, and then, flapping legs foremost into the water, turns and dives; whereas the gull has

CUBAN "GORTAIL," FOR TRANSPORTING CARGO OVERLAND.

first to settle himself carefully as he alights on the water, and has then to trust to the chance of some unsophisticated fish coming within reach of his bill. It was impossible to avoid noticing the mortified appearance of the poor gulls as they looked eagerly about, but yet caught only an odd fish, whilst their comrades, the shags, were enjoying abundant sport.

It is odd that the silly gull manages at all to survive in the struggle for existence. Here is another instance of his incapacity. A piece of meat, weighing a few ounces, drifted astern of the ship one day, and for its possession a struggle took place between a dominican gull and a brown hawk. The gull had picked up the meat, and was flying away with it in his bill, when he was pursued by the hawk—a much smaller bird—who made him drop it. Again the gull picked it up, and for a second time was compelled by the hawk to relinquish it. The latter now swooped down upon the tempting morsel, as it floated on the water, and seizing it with his claws, flew off rapidly into an adjoining thicket, to the edge of which he was followed by the disappointed gull.

Steamer-ducks (*Tachyeres cinereus*) are very abundant at Tom Bay, as indeed they are throughout all the western channels. Their English name, " steamer-duck," has reference to their habit of moving rapidly along the surface of the water by means of a paddling motion of the wings, and leaving a wake of foam which resembles, on a small scale, that of a paddle-steamer. A great deal has been written about these remarkable birds, and I shall not therefore attempt any general description, which at the best would only involve useless repetition. There are a few remarks about them, however, which I should like to make. Although aware of the careful investigations made by Dr. Cunningham in 1866-9, and his conclusion as to their being but one species, I have yet some reason to believe that the fliers and the non-flying birds which I have seen belong to two distinct species, and my impression is—though I am by no means sure—that the volant species frequents the fresh waters in the interior of Patagonia, and in the western channels is only represented by an odd straggler. Mr. Cox, of Talcahuano, who has travelled in Araucania and central Patagonia, mentions in his narrative, that in the fresh-water lakes of the latter district there are two different species of steamer-ducks, one of which possesses the power of flight. Immature specimens, although differing in the colour of the bill, and somewhat in plumage, from the adult birds, need not be confounded with a second species. The largest steamer-duck which I have come across weighed only 14 lbs., and although text books assign a much greater weight as the extreme limit, I think I am right in saying that few heavier birds are met with either in the Straits of Magellan or in the western channels. The female forms a low, oval-shaped nest of twigs, lined with a thick coating of down, and deposits therein six large cream-coloured eggs, $3\frac{3}{8}$ in. long, by $2\frac{1}{8}$ in. width. The nest is usually placed on the ground, at the foot of an old tree, some few yards from the beach, but in a place where the bush is almost impenetrable to a human being.

Land shells must be exceedingly scarce. I met with representatives of only four species, of which one, a specimen of *Helix*, I found on the frond of a *Hymenophyllum* at Tom Bay. Two others of the same genus were taken from the rotten trunk of a tree in the same locality. At Port Henry, in the Trinidad Channel, and other parts in the neighbourhood, I collected several specimens of a species of *Succinea*, which clings to dead leaves and decayed pieces of driftwood lying on the shore just above high-water mark. These four species of shells have since been described by Mr. Edgar Smith, of the British Museum, as new to science. In a fresh-water lake, where I made some casts of a light dredge, I obtained from the bottom of stinking mud several examples of a large *Unio* shell, and some small shells of the genus *Chilinia*. I afterwards found species of *Unio* in a stream issuing from the lake. North of the English Narrows, many pond snails of the genus *Chilinia* were also found abundantly in the stream beds.

I have found only two species of fresh-water fish, *Haplochiton zebra*, and a small *Galaxias;* and they inhabit most of the upland lakes which are of any considerable extent. The former is a smooth-skinned fish, with the general shape and fin arrangement of a grayling, but with a dark scaleless skin. It averages half a pound in weight, ranging up to three-quarters; and although it rose like a trout, we could not succeed in making it take the artificial fly, but caught it readily with worm-bait. These fish were also met with in mountain lakes far removed from the sea, whither their ova were probably, in the first instance, conveyed by cormorants. On one occasion Sir George Nares caught a specimen of this fish in a brackish lagoon, which communicated with the sea at high tide, so that it may have been derived from a marine progenitor which possessed the power of adapting itself to a fresh-water existence.

In the course of our survey of Concepcion Strait, we stopped for six days, in the month of March, at Portland Bay, an anchorage on the east side of the strait, and nearly opposite to Tom Bay. On the forenoon of our third day, a party of natives pulled in from the westward, with their canoe well-provisioned with shell-fish, as if they were about making a long voyage. There were three men, four women, three children, and four dogs. They were provided with a good iron axe, bone-pointed spears, a boat-rope made of plaited rushes, and other rude implements. It was evident that this party had previously met with some friendly vessel, for they readily came on board, and poked about the ship. Two of us went on a visit to their camp on the following day, but were received very ungraciously by a villainous-looking old hag armed with a club, who deprecated any attempt at landing on our part. We could only examine the canoe, which we found to be twenty-two feet long, four feet in beam amidships, and in other respects of the usual construction. On the next day we pulled over again, but only to find the hut deserted, and the party gone. We inferred, from various circumstances connected with their disappearance, that they must have penetrated up the Bay to the eastward, where there are unexplored channels which are supposed to extend towards the base of the Cordillera.

On the next day (March 24), a strong westerly breeze, with occasional rain-squalls, induced most of us to remain on board, and we were not a little surprised when, about 10 a.m., a boat under sail was reported standing across the Strait towards our anchorage. On nearer approach it turned out to be a native canoe, with a large sealskin hoisted in the forepart of the boat, so as to form a sort of square sail. As the natives came alongside to beg for biscuit and tobacco, we found that the wretched-looking boat contained three men, five women, eleven children (mostly very young), and five dogs. They had shipped a good deal of water on the passage, as might be expected, and all the wretched creatures looked as wet as fishes; indeed, to say that they were wet to the skin would be simply a truism in the case of the Fuegians. We had not previously noticed so prolific a family, the proportion of children being usually one for each woman. I use the word "family," because each of these canoe parties appears to constitute a sort of complicated family. One young mother did not appear to be more than sixteen years of age. I now inclined to the opinion, which subsequent experience gave me no reason to alter, that the Channel Fuegians are a migratory tribe, passing the summer months about the outer islands, where at that time of the year they may get seals, and the eggs and young of sea-birds, and in the autumn migrating up some of the fiords of the mainland, when the deer, driven down the hills by the winter snows, would be within their reach. There is no doubt that deer (probably the *Cervus chilensis*) have been seen from time to time on this coast. A few years ago the officers of one of the German steamers of the "Kosmos" line, stopping at Puerto Bueno about mid-winter, captured three or four in the immediate vicinity of the anchorage. We ourselves never met with any, although we saw doubtful indications of their presence; but further south we obtained portions of a deer from a native canoe. I was led to form the above-mentioned idea from comparing the great number of deserted wigwams which we encountered in our wanderings about these channels, with the small number of natives actually seen. The huts alluded to, moreover, bore indications of having been in use not many months previously, when they were probably inhabited temporarily by parties of natives on their way to the outer coasts. Fitzroy would seem to have entertained the same belief with reference to tribes about Smyth's Channel, from the fact that a party of men from his ship, when surveying Obstruction Sound in the *summer-time*, discovered a large deserted encampment containing many huts and canoes, and showing signs of its being the site of a great periodical gathering of the clans.

FUEGIANS OFFERING THEIR CHILDREN FOR BARTER (*p.* 74).

CHAPTER III.

EXPLORATIONS IN THE TRINIDAD CHANNEL.

IN prosecuting the survey of the Trinidad Channel, we anchored, for short periods each time, at a great many ports on its northern and southern shores; and in crossing and re-crossing the channel we ran lines of soundings which enabled us to ascertain roughly the general conformation of its bed. Across the seaward entrance of the channel, *i.e.*, from Cape Gamboa on the north to Port Henry on the south, the soundings gave a mean depth of thirty fathoms, showing the existence of a sort of bar, while one mile inside of this the depth increased to two and three hundred fathoms. This was just as we expected; the bar across the entrance representing the terminal moraine of the huge glacier which originally gouged out the channel, and whose denuding action is abundantly recorded in the scorings, planings, and striations so palpable on all the hard rocks of these inhospitable shores.

At Port Henry, on the southern side of the entrance to the channel, we anchored several times. The scenery here is very grand. A clay-slate rock enters largely into the formation of the hills, its highly inclined strata forming jagged peaks and ridges of great height; while the low-lying rock about the coast is a friable syenite traversed with dikes of greenstone. Immediately to the south of our anchorage was a lofty ridge of clay-slate hills, terminating above in a multitude of vertical columns of rock, which from our position on board reminded us of a cluster of organ pipes, and suggested the name which now appears on the chart, of the "Organ-pipe Range." The aspect of the vegetation is also different from that of other ports in these wâters, owing to the abundance of a veronica (*V. decussata*), which forms large glossy-green bushes, covered with a profusion of snow-white flowers, and so varies the otherwise monotonously green appearance of the beech forest.

Only one party of natives was here seen. They at first approached us very stealthily, paddling between the small islands off the eastern entrance of the harbour, and after the usual interchange of signals (waving of green boughs and caps), they came alongside. The boat was similar in construction and size to those already examined at Tom Bay and elsewhere; but we were now greatly struck at perceiving what a load it could accommodate; for there were in it sixteen natives and six dogs, besides provisions, weapons, and camp furniture. The party consisted of three men, five women, and eight children; and although they pulled only three oars (the women never taking part in this work), yet they managed to get along at a fair pace. On their arrival they were partially clad in seal skins; but in their eagerness to barter with our seamen, for knives, tobacco, and such treasures, they soon divested themselves of all artificial garb, and appeared in a state of nature. It was noticed that the males, who conducted the barter, compelled the women to give up their scanty covering. In the way of provisions, the boat contained a supply of large trumpet shells (*Concholepas*) in rush baskets, and the drinking water was carried in little bark buckets. They encamped near us for the night, but disappeared unaccountably the next day.

On our exploring the islets just mentioned, we found a large deserted encampment, in which we counted the remains of nine native huts. The refuse-heaps contained a good many seal and whale bones, besides echinoderms, limpet and trumpet shells, the latter shell here taking the place of the mussel. The trumpet shell (*Concholepas*) is found about the entrance of the

Trinidad Channel, inhabiting rocky places immediately below low water mark on the weather (*i.e.* the west) side of islets which are exposed to the heavy wash of the outer ocean. I have not seen the shell south of this latitude. The brown duck (*Anas cristata*) was here tolerably abundant, and with the ashy-headed Brent goose, and the two species of oyster-catcher, were in great request with our sportsmen, being the only edible birds worth mentioning in the western channels.

From Port Henry we shifted our base of operations to Wolsey Sound, the next inlet to the eastward. Here we anchored in an apparently well-sheltered cove, surrounded by lofty hills, but which we soon found to our cost to be a sort of aerial maelstrom. A strong westerly gale was blowing over the hilltops, as we could see by the fast-flying clouds; while below at the anchorage we experienced a succession of fierce squalls (williwaws) from various quarters, with intervals of complete calm; so that the ship kept swinging to and fro, and circling round her anchors in a most erratic manner. Eventually one of the cables parted; but with the other, aided by steam, we managed to ride out the gale, and to thoroughly satisfy ourselves that Wolsey Sound was not one of the anchorages to be recommended to passing vessels. From the translation given in "Burney's Voyages," (vol. ii., p. 10), of the journal of Pedro Sarmiento de Gamboa, who discovered the Trinidad Channel in the year 1580, it would appear that this is the same anchorage which his sailors named "Cache Diablo" (devil's box-on-the-ear), from the boisterous nature of the reception which they experienced.

On the east side of Wolsey Sound the rock of the mountain masses is for the most part a hard grey unfossiliferous limestone, irregularly stratified, but sometimes showing a dip of 10° or 15° to the westward. The most striking peculiarity of this rock consists in its solubility under the influence of both fresh and salt water, and it is this property that so often causes it to present a jagged honey-combed appearance. I noticed that in many places fresh water streams, running over bare patches of this rock, had eaten away narrow gutter channels, and that in other places where a broad sheet of water flowed slowly—as from a turf bank—over a long gently-sloping table of rock, an incrustation of hard calcareous matter had been deposited, presenting a sort of "ripple-marked" appearance, and reminding one of the effect produced when a film of slowly-moving water is submitted to the influence of intense cold. When viewed from a distance, the limestone hills presented a whitish bleached appearance, which contrasted strangely with the sombre hues of the other greenstone and syenite hills. Of this description was "Silvertop," a lofty and conspicuous mountain on the south side of the Trinidad Channel, which was frequently used by our surveyors as a landmark.

The next port to the eastward is Rosario Bay. It was named by Sarmiento "Puerto de Nuestra Señora Del Rosario." The rock formation here is limestone, and of the kind above mentioned, but the effects of frequent rain in washing away the more soluble parts of the rock were not only manifested by the honeycombed appearance of exposed surfaces, but also by the prevalence of caves of most irregular shape. Soon after we had anchored, Sub-lieutenant Beresford and I, who had gone away in the skiff, were paddling around an islet with lofty and precipitous sides, when we noticed in the face of a bare rocky cliff a suspicious-looking dark opening, partly blocked up with stones, and situated about thirty feet above the sea level. We ran the boat alongside the rocks, and Beresford kept her from bumping while I climbed up the cliff to reconnoitre. On clearing away a heap of stones and rubbish, I laid bare a sort of niche in the rock, in which were portions of a human skeleton, the long bones lying together in a compact bundle, as if they had been so placed there when in the dried state. Not many yards from this crevice we soon discovered a small cave in the rock, and partly imbedded in the soil which formed its floor were a human jaw-bone and fragments of smaller bones. On excavating the floor of the cave we found it to consist of a stiff pasty greyish-white marlclay, abounding in small shells, amongst which were species of the genera *Patella, Fissurella, Chiton,* and *Calyptræa.* On reaching a depth of about one foot, we came upon a nearly complete human skull of immature age, an otter skull with bones of the same, and the tooth of an *Echinus.* The human bones obtained were part of the skeletons of two individuals, one of whom must have been young, for the epithyses of the long bones were not quite cemented to the shafts. I noticed that the skull presented a completely ossified frontal suture, although, from the nature of the teeth and alveoli, the person to whom it belonged could not have lived for more than twelve years or thereabouts. A tibia found in the first depôt bore marks of having been chopped by some sharp cutting instrument. From the fact of these bones being found interbedded with marine deposits, coupled with what we know of these islands having been elevated within recent times—I here refer to the evidence afforded by raised beaches and old highwater marks in the faces of cliffs—there is reason to believe that these bones were deposited in the cave at a time when it was under water, that they thus became surrounded by and imbedded in an ordinary marine shallow water deposit, and that eventually, on the island being elevated so as to raise the cave to its present position—thirty feet above sea level—the surface deposit was reinforced by the percolation of lime-charged water from the rock above, thus resulting in the formation of the marlclay surface-layer above mentioned.

We made different attempts at dredging, but as the bottom was everywhere very rocky and the dredge in consequence continually getting foul, we were not successful in obtaining many objects of interest. However, among them there were specimens of a hydroid stony coral representing two species of the genus

Labiopora—one of which Mr. Stuart Ridley of the British Museum has ascertained to be a species new to science—and a fine orange-coloured *Astrophyton* of a new species, recently described by Mr. F. J. Bell as *A. Lymani*.

On the north side of the Trinidad Channel we stopped for a time at an anchorage near Cape Gamboa, which forms the north headland of the entrance. At Cape Gamboa the rock is a clay-slate showing distinct stratification, containing concretions of a whitish sandstone, and dipping to the N. E. at an angle of about 45°. To the eastward of Cape Gamboa is a limestone similar to that of the south shore. We did some dredging here on a smooth sandy bottom, the principal results of which were specimens of the *Chimæra* (*Callorhynchus australis*), and some curious Isopod Crustaceans of the genus *Serolis*. Another day (March 28th) when sounding across the entrance of the Channel, we made a heave of the trawl in thirty fathoms with most fruitful results, obtaining a magnificent specimen of the orange-coloured Astrophyton (*A. Lymani*), several small rays and flat fish, large *Actinia*, a new Crustacean of the genus *Arcturus*, starfishes, and a Cephalopod Mollusc of the genus *Rossia*. On the evening of this day we were fortunate enough to witness a most beautiful sunset effect. As the sun disappeared from a western olive-tinted sky it seemed to be followed in its descent by several horizontal bands of delicate rose-tinted stratus clouds, which extended themselves in parallel lines over an arc of 45°, and finally tapered away into the most delicate threads of silvery light. In the east the dark purple-tinted clouds melted upwards into the grey gloom of approaching night, and foreshadowed to us the advent of another day of sunshine in this the only really fine and summer month in these western channels.

At the head of Francisco Bay—which was the name subsequently given to this anchorage—at the outlet of a small river, we one day made a very large "take" of fish in a somewhat singular manner. A trammel net had been placed across the mouth of the stream at high tide, and on the tide falling had been examined and found to contain a fair number of fish (mackerel). Some hours later two of our people were wading up the river, and on coming to a depression in its bed, which was at about the limit to which the tidal salt-water reached, they found an immense collection of half-dead and living mackerel in a pool, in which—the tide being then rather low—the water was almost entirely fresh. Here they caught, with their hands, fish enough to fill a boat, amounting to a gross weight of 4 cwt. The probable explanation of this lucky "take" seems to be that the fish entered the mouth of the river with the flood tide—as is their wont—and on attempting to retreat with the ebb found their return to the sea barred by our net, and instead of endeavouring to pass through the meshes preferred to move back into the brackish water of the river. Here, as the tide fell still further and laid bare banks of sand stretching across the stream, they became shut off altogether from the sea, and at dead low tide the flow of fresh water so predominated over the salt as to render them helplessly stupid, so that they fell an easy prey to our sailors.

On the shores of this bay I came across a magnificent Winter's bark tree, the largest which I have ever seen in the channels. Its smooth and almost cylindrical stem was nine feet in circumference, and ran up without branching to a height of thirty feet from the ground.

In cruising to and fro about the channel we frequently came across whales. They were usually either "finners" or "sperms"; more commonly the former. I saw only one one "right" whale during the many months which we spent in these waters. On the 17th of February we steamed by a school of about twenty "finner" whales, and shortly after we passed through a shoal of small red shrimps (*Galatheas*), which were so densely clustered together as to give the water quite a scarlet appearance. This accounted for the great gathering of Cetaceans. Skeletons of whales in a very imperfect state were abundant about the shores of this channel, and many were of large size. On the shore of Francisco Bay I saw lower jaw bones which measured eleven feet from condyle to symphysis. I looked, but in vain, for remains of the Ziphioid Whales.

Some few miles to the eastward of Francisco Bay a deep inlet pierced Wellington Island in a northerly direction. We were anxious to explore it, as we thought it not unlikely that it might prove to be a navigable passage, connecting Trinidad Channel with the Gulf of Peñas. At length an opportunity occurred, and on a fine morning in the month of March we steamed into this unsurveyed inlet. On fairly passing the southern entrance, we found ourselves traversing a lane of water of such glassy smoothness, and bordered by such straight running shores, which were not more than half-a-mile apart, as to seem more like an inland canal than (which it eventually proved to be) a strait leading through a nest of breakers to an inhospitable ocean. Its eastern shore exhibited the kind of scenery prevailing about the Guia Narrows; viz., round-topped hills with great bare patches of rain-worn rock extending from the summits to a talus, which was covered with an uniform mantle of evergreen forest, the latter encroaching upon the sea-beach. But the country to the west presented a more pleasing variety, being composed of low undulating slopes of grassy-looking land, with here and there fissures or landslips exhibiting what seemed to us, as we scrutinized them with our glasses, to be sections of a sedimentary formation. We had hitherto seen nothing like this anywhere among the western channels, and consequently I for one was extremely anxious to land. However, the captain had to make the most of daylight for the surveying work in hand, so that our conjectures as to the nature of this formation remained unverified. When we had attained a distance of twenty-five miles from the southern entrance of the Strait, the western shore was found to be broken up into a chain of low islets, which in time dwindled away into a great arc of submerged rocks, over which the swell of the broad Pacific broke with great fury.

This then was the end of what is now known as the Picton Channel, and bold would be the mariner who would attempt to traverse it, and thread his way through such a maze of reefs and breakers. Among the islets at this, its northern extremity, we found an anchorage, where we decided on stopping for the night. As we cast anchor, a native boat approached, carrying no less than twenty-three inmates, most of whom were males, and of a most savage and treacherous appearance. They had with them several young fur seals, recently killed, which they were glad to barter for tobacco or biscuit. After stopping alongside for about half-an-hour, they paddled away and were seen no more. On the following day we steamed back.

The rocky shores and islets of the Trinidad Channel bear abundant indications of old ice action. These marks are not very apparent on the coarse-grained friable syenite which is the common rock of the district, but on the dikes of hard greenstone, with which the syenite is frequently intersected, scorings and striations of typical character may be seen. Close to the anchorage in Port Charrua, on the north side of the channel, there is a broad band of greenstone on which I observed very perfect examples of "crosshatchings," where the prevailing east to west striæ were intersected by those of another system at an angle of about 40°. These rock erosions, coupled with what we know from the sounding-lead as to the contour of the sea-bottom, lead us to infer that the Trinidad Channel was at some remote period the bed of a huge glacier, which flowed westward from the Cordillera. That most, indeed, of the other straits and channels of Western Patagonia were also at one time occupied by glaciers is clearly testified by the markings on the rocks.

There is a peculiar form of syenite rock not uncommon in exposed situations on the hilltops, which is composed of quartz, felspar, and hornblende, the quartz occurring in crystals of about the size of large peas. The felspar, being of a very friable nature, rapidly succumbs to the disintegrating influence of the weather, and crumbles away, taking with it the small particles of hornblende, so that the big quartz crystals, when in the last stage prior to being dislodged, are seen standing out in bold relief from the matrix. When this rock is seen projecting in round bosses, through the turfy soil of a hilltop, it looks at a short distance as if strewn with hailstones; and the illusion is heightened on .observing on its leeward side heaps of loose quartz crystals, which have been completely weathered out from the parent rock, and have been drifted by the wind into this comparatively sheltered situation, as would be the case with hailstones under similar circumstances.

But the most characteristic feature in the scenery of the western shores of Patagonia is owing to the phenomenon of "soil motion," an occurrence which is here in a great measure due to the exceptionally wet nature of the climate. This slippage of the soilcap seems in this region to be continually taking place wherever the basement rock presents a moderately inclined surface. Some of the effects of this "soil motion" are apt to be confounded with those due to glacial action, for the soilcap takes with it in its downward progress not only its clothing of trees, ferns, and mosses, but also a "moraine profonde" of rock, stones, and stems of dead trees great and small, whereby the hills are being denuded, and the valleys, lakes, and channels gradually filled up. When we first entered the Western Channels my attention was at once directed to this subject on noticing that the lower branches of trees growing in immediate proximity to the sea-shore were in many places withering from immersion in the salt water, and that in some cases entire trees had perished prematurely, from their roots having become entirely submerged. On looking more closely into the matter, I noticed that sodden snags of dead trees, mingled with stones, were often to be seen on the bottom of the inshore waters, and that the beds of fresh water lakes were plentifully strewn with similar fragments of wood, the remains of bygone forests which had perished prematurely. These circumstances are fully explained by the occurrence of soil motion, for as the soilcap by its sliding motion, imparted by gravitation, and aided by expansion and contraction of the spongy mass, reaches the water's edge, the soluble portions are removed, while its more durable contents are left to accumulate at the foot of the incline. In this way rocks and stones may sometimes be seen balanced in odd situations near the sea beach, simulating the "roches perchées" which are dropped by a melting iceberg or a receding glacier. These circumstances are all the more interesting from their occurring in a region where the effects of old and recent glacial action are exhibited to a marked degree. Planings, scorings, striations, and "roches moutonnées" may, one or other, be almost invariably found wherever the rock is sufficiently impervious to the disintegrating action of the weather to retain these impressions. Thus they are nowhere to be seen on the coarse-grained friable syenite, which is the common rock of the district; but where this rock is intersected by dikes of the more durable greenstone, the above-mentioned signs of former glacial action may be seen well developed. I speak now of old glacial action, because we have not found any glacier existing in the neighbourhood of the Trinidad Channel, from whence they seem to have entirely receded; but they are yet to be seen in the fiords of the mainland further north; and in the main Straits of Magellan we had opportunities of studying fine examples of complete and incomplete glaciers, exhibiting in all its grandeur that wonderful denuding power which these ponderous masses of ice exercise as they move silently over their rocky beds. There are, therefore, in this region, ample opportunities of comparing and differentiating phenomena, which have resulted from former glacial action, and those which are due to soil-motion—a force now in operation.

Sir Wyville Thompson (vide "Voyage of Challenger," vol. ii., p. 245) attributes the origin of the celebrated "Stone Runs" of the Falkland Islands to the transporting action of the soilcap, which among other causes derives its motion from alternate expansion and contraction of the spongy mass of peat, due to varying conditions of moisture and comparative dryness; and this hypothesis is to a certain extent supported by the occurrences which I now endeavour to describe. Here, in Western Patagonia, an evergreen arboreal forest, rising through a dense undergrowth of brushwood and mosses, clothes the hill-sides to a height of about 1,000 feet, and this mass of vegetation, with its subjacent peaty, swampy soil, resting—as it frequently does—upon a hill-side already planed by old ice action, naturally tends, under the influence of gravitation, combined with that of expansion and contraction of the soil, to slide gradually downwards until it meets the sea, lake, or valley, as the case may be. In the two former cases the free edge of the mass is removed by the action of the water, in a manner somewhat analogous to the wasting of the submerged snout of a "complete glacier" in the summer time; whereas in the last instance a chaotic accumulation of all the constituents of the transported mass gradually takes place, thereby tending to an eventual obliteration of the valley. It appears to me that the conditions which are said to have resulted in the formation of the "Stone Runs" of the Falklands here exist in equal if not greater force. There is a thick spongy vegetable mass covering the hill-sides, and acted on by varying conditions of extreme moisture and comparative dryness; there are the loose blocks of disintegrating syenite to be transported; and there are mountain torrents, lakes, and sea-channels to remove the soil. That motion of the soilcap does actually take place we have at least strong presumptive evidence; but anything resembling a "stone run" remains yet to be discovered. It would naturally suggest itself to the reader that the above phenomenon attributed to soil motion might be accounted for by a slow and gradual depression of the land, and I have carefully sought for evidence favouring this view, but have found no reliable sign whatever of subsidence; while on the other hand one sees raised beaches and stones testifying to the ravages of stone-boring molluscs at heights above the present high-water marks, which indicate that even elevation of the land has taken place.

On May 6th, the winter season having then fairly set in, we bade adieu for a while to our surveying ground, and commenced our northern voyage to Valparaiso. Our course lay first through the sheltered channels which separate Wellington Island from the mainland. As we rounded Topar Islands and entered Wide Channel, the heavy mist which had been hanging around us all the morning, almost concealing the land from sight, lifted at intervals like a veil, and exposed to view the noble cliffs of bare greenstone rock which hemmed us in on either side,—here and there streaked down their faces by long slender cascades of water, extending from summit to base, and seeming to hang over us like glistening threads of silver. On passing the southern outlet of Icy Reach, we saw shining in the distance the sloping tongue-shaped extremity of one of the Eyre Sound glaciers, whose bergs float out through Icy Reach in the winter time and sometimes prove a serious obstruction to navigation in these gloomy and mysterious channels. In Chasm Reach, which we next traversed, the hills on either side rose nearly perpendicularly to a height of 1,500 feet, their snow-capped summits contrasting grandly with the sombre tints of their rocky sides; so scantily clad with vegetation as to seem at a distance mere sloping walls of rock.

In the narrowest part of this " reach," where the width was only about half-a-mile, three native huts were seen established on low projecting shelves of rock, and situated about a mile apart. To these our attention was attracted by the long curling wreaths of grey smoke ascending from their fires. As darkness was coming on,

The English Narrows.

we did not stop to examine them, but steamed on towards Port Grappler, where we anchored for the night.

We got under way early in the morning of the following day, and proceeded through the channel as far as Hoskyn Cove, an anchorage just to the northward of the famous English Narrows. The morning had been hazy and showery, but towards noon the mist cleared away, and as we passed the English Narrows, a burst of sunshine completed the dispersion of the hazy vapour and lighted up a scene of surpassing splendour. The scenery here contrasted strangely with that of Chasm Reach, for the steep hillsides now were richly clothed with a luxuriant growth of primeval forest, and rising to a greater altitude, had their summits capped with a broad mantle of snow, which showed to great advantage against the deep blue of the sky. In the narrowest part of the channel, where the flood tide was making southward in a rapid stream, numbers of fur seals were gambolling in the water, and the energetic movements of the cormorants testified to the abundance of the fish.

Formerly the vessels of the Pacific Steam Navigation Company were in the habit of running through these "Narrows," but of late years the practice has been discontinued, on account of the difficulty of managing the long vessels which are now in vogue. Therefore, excepting an occasional man-of-war, the only vessels which at the present day make use of the channels leading to the Gulf of Peñas are the steamers of the German "Kosmos" line. The deciduous beech (*Fagus antarctica*) here formed a great proportion of the forest growth, and as its leaves were now withering, their autumn tints gave a variegated character to the wooded scenery, a feature not observed farther south, where the evergreen beech (*Fagus betuloides*) predominates. The *Campsidium chilense*, a large trailing plant, was abundant and in full bloom, its flowering branches usually depending in rather inaccessible places from the upper parts of the trees to which it clung ; and here we obtained for the first time specimens of the loveliest of South American ferns, the *Hymenophyllum cruentum*.

The morning of the 8th May broke wet and gloomy as we got under way and initiated the next stage on our journey. All day long the rain fell in torrents, and a fresh northerly breeze, blowing right in our teeth, raised a heavy, chopping sea, which made the old ship heave uneasily, and gave us a sort of foretaste of what we should have to encounter next day on emerging from the Gulf of Peñas into the troubled waters of the Pacific. Steaming thus against wind and sea, we made such slow progress that night had fairly come on us when we crept under shelter of the lofty hills which overshadow Island Harbour.

On the following morning we entered the open sea, and steered for Valparaiso.

CHAPTER IV.

ON THE COAST OF CHILI.

ON anchoring at Valparaiso on the 16th May, the first news we heard was that the country was in a great state of excitement, anent the war in which Chili was then engaged with Peru and Bolivia. All the available troops and men-of-war had been despatched to the seat of war in the north, leaving the capital in almost a defenceless condition, so that great fears were entertained lest one of the Peruvian cruisers should take advantage of this to bombard the town. The last detachment sent off consisted of the town police, and at the time of our visit the maintenance of order in the streets, and the manning of the guns of the forts, had been entrusted to the corps of "Bomberos" (fire brigade).

The principal part of the town is built on a plateau about ten feet above high-water mark, which forms a margin to the curving shore of the bay, and reaches inland for a few hundred yards. Beyond this the outskirts of the town are disposed irregularly over a number of steep ridges, which converge radially on the town from the mountain range behind. There was one principal street running more or less parallel with the shore, and containing fine-looking shops well supplied with everything needful, but the second-rate ones were very dingy in comparison. Owing to the great stagnation of trade brought about by the war, and the consequent scarcity of money amongst consumers, the prices of provisions were very moderate, although under normal conditions Valparaiso is famous among Europeans for its high prices. Fruit also and vegetables were in great abundance, and large bunches of delicious grapes were to be had for almost a nominal price.

One remarkable feature of Valparaiso is that within the precincts of the town a considerable number of people of the very lowest grade live in a sort of gipsy encampment. The buildings which they here occupy are filthy nondescript hovels, constructed out of a patchwork of mud, bits of tin, old planks, discarded doors, pieces of sackcloth, etc., all stuck up together anyhow. Even in the respectable quarter of the town these filthy dens were sometimes to be seen occupying blind alleys, or the site of razed buildings.

Sir George Nares left us here to return home by mail-steamer, on appointment to the Marine and Harbour Department of the Board of Trade, and was relieved in command of the *Alert* by Captain J. F. L. P. Maclear.

After wishing him good-bye on the 18th of May, we got under way and steered for Coquimbo. On gaining an offing of about ten miles, and looking in towards the Chilian coast, to which we were then pursuing a parallel course, we saw the lowlands partially veiled in a thin stratum of mist, above which towered magnificently the snowy summit of Aconcagua, 23,220 feet in height. As we approached the Bay of Coquimbo, we passed through immense shoals of fishes, which sheered off in great confusion to either side of our bows with the parting waves. On subsequently hauling in the "patent log," it was found that the revolving blades had disappeared, the towing-line having been chopped in two just above its attachment. This was probably the work of some hungry and indiscriminating shark, whose stomach must have been put to a severe trial in endeavouring to digest this angular and unwholesome piece of metal.

The port of Coquimbo, where we stayed from the 19th of May

to the 16th of July, derives whatever importance it has got from being one of the best (if not the very best) of the anchorages on the Chilian coast, and from its connection with the copper trade. It is brought into communication with the mines and smelting works by means of a line of railway, which, independently of its collateral branches, pierces the copper-producing country to a distance of sixty miles. The copper, either in the form of ingots, bars, or regulus, is shipped to Europe—principally to England— in steamers or sailing vessels. The country, as far as the eye can reach from the anchorage, is a mere sandy desert, dotted here and there with an odd oasis of cultivated land, which has been rendered productive by means of artificial irrigation. Trees are rare; but within the last few years the eucalyptus has been introduced, and with great success. In properly irrigated localities it thrives and grows with great rapidity,—in half-a-dozen years rising to a height of sixty feet,—and forming masses of foliage, which, by the shade it affords, increases the productiveness of the neighbouring soil.

Coquimbo has been rendered celebrated for its shell terraces by the writings of Darwin, Basil Hall, and others. These are long plateaux of variable size, sometimes a couple of hundred yards, sometimes a mile in width, with their sharply defined free margins running more or less parallel to the curved outline of the sea beach, and extending inland by a series of gradations, like the tiers of boxes in a theatre. There are five or six of these terraces; that furthest inland being about 250 feet above the sea-level, and its free margin being about six miles from the beach. They are of entirely marine origin, and abound in shells of existing species, and they testify to the different periods of elevation to which this part of the continent has been subjected.

On the night of the 2nd of June we felt a slight shock of earthquake. The cable rattled in the hawse-pipe as if it were being violently shaken below by some giant who had got hold of the other end; and the ship vibrated and surged up and down as if she had been struck by a wave coming vertically from the bottom of the sea. The shock lasted about ten seconds, and then all was again silent. Earthquakes of this magnitude are of common occurrence in Chili.

One day a large party of us went on a shooting excursion to Las Cardas, an estate occupying a mountain valley thirty-six miles from Coquimbo, and belonging to Mr. Lambert, an English gentleman. For this trip we were indebted to Mr. Weir, the courteous manager of Mr. Lambert's mines, smelting works, and estate, who not only provided a special train to convey us to the shooting ground, but entertained us there most sumptuously. The estate of "Las Cardas" lies at the termination of the southernmost part of the two valleys which open into the Bay of Coquimbo, and beyond this station the railway pursues its further course over the brow of a hill called the "Cuesta," which it ascends by a series of zigzags. Although its route here appears, at first sight, circuitous enough, the gradient of the incline is an average of one in thirty feet, ranging as high as one in twenty-five. We found it interesting to stop for a while at the station and watch our departing train trailing along its zigzag course up the hillside, as it steamed on towards the inland terminus of the line, viz., "Rio Grande," which was some thirty miles further on. The "Rio Grande" station is 2,000 feet above the level of the Coquimbo terminus at the other end.

In the bed of a broad valley, and in the gullies communicating with it laterally from the hills, we expected to get a good many partridges; but owing to the thickness of the brushwood, and the absence of dogs, we saw very few, and shot fewer still. However, we were assured that the birds were there, and only wanted proper stirring up to make them visible; so that as we were every minute expecting that the next moment a great covey would start up from the bushes, and consequently kept our guns ready for action, we managed to keep up the requisite amount of excitement for several hours without materially violating the spirit of the regulations of the Prevention of Cruelty to Animals Society.

In the evening we assembled at a clump of trees, which seemed to be a favourite roosting-place for doves; and as the birds came down from the hills to take up their quarters for the night, they afforded us some very nice shooting while the daylight lasted. The most interesting birds which I noticed in the valley were two species of *pteroptochus*, the smaller of which was almost identical in general character with the *tapacola* of Coquimbo, where it inhabits the low rocky hills, and attracts attention by its barking noise, and by the odd manner in which it erects its tail. Although the barking noise is heard frequently, and sometimes within a few yards of one, yet the bird itself is seen comparatively rarely. The bird of Las Cardas, however, might with a little care be seen, whilst uttering its odd programme of noises, as it stood under the overhanging branches of some large bush. On being startled it makes off in a peculiar manner, taking long strides rather than hops, and moving in a series of sharp curves in and out among the bushes. In adapting itself to these curves, the body of the bird is inclined considerably to the inner side, so that in this position, with its long legs and great clumsy tail, it forms a truly grotesque object. Examples of the larger species of pteroptochus (*P. albicollis*) were generally to be seen in pairs, perched on the summit of a tall bush, the white throat and white stripes over the eye showing conspicuously.

We sailed from Coquimbo on the 16th of July, and shaped our course for the Islands Felix and Ambrose, which lie about five hundred miles to the north-west of Coquimbo. The object of this cruise was to take some deep-sea soundings between the mainland and the above-mentioned islands. The weather was, for the most part, very unfavourable, the ship rolling and kicking diabolically, and making our lives very miserable. On the afternoon of the 20th, St. Ambrose, the eastward island of the two, hove in sight, but as the day was too far advanced to admit of our landing, we "lay-to" about six miles to windward of it. Viewing the island at this distance from the eastward, it presented the appearance of a roughly cubical flat-topped mass of rock, leaning slightly to the northward, and bounded—so far as one could see—by perpendicular cliffs of a gloomy and forbidding aspect, which rose to an altitude of 1,500 feet. As we approached the island on the following morning its appearance by no means improved, and nowhere could be seen any break in the rampart of lofty cliffs, which seemed to forbid our disturbing their solitude. We looked in vain for the "sheltered cove," where, as the sailing instructions say, "there is good landing for boats at all times of the year." After making the circuit of the island, we "lay-to" about a mile from the N.E. cliff, and two boats were sent to reconnoitre, in one of which I took passage. After pulling a considerable distance along the foot of the cliffs, we at length succeeded, though with great difficulty, in landing at the foot of a spur of basaltic rock, which sloped down from the cliffs at a high angle. The first thing that attracted our attention was a grotesque-looking crab (*Grapsus variegatus*), of a reddish-brown colour, mottled on the carapace with yellow spots. It scuttled about in a most independent way, and seemed quite indifferent as to whether it trotted over the bottoms of the rock pools, or ran up the steep face of the rock to a height of forty feet above the water-line. Sea-birds innumerable flew about us in all directions, but on careful inspection we could only muster up three different species; viz., a large white-winged gannet (*Sula*), a plump dark-coloured petrel (*Aestrelata defilippiana*), and a slender white and grey tern (*Anous*).* The petrels were nesting in the rock crevices. The nest consisted of a few withered twigs and dirty feathers, forming a very scanty bed on the hard rock, and containing a solitary white egg. The birds stuck bravely to their nests, and would not relinquish their charge until, with bill and claws, they had given an account of themselves, calculated

---

* These and other birds collected during the cruise have been described and determined by Mr. R. Bowdler Sharpe, the distinguished ornithologist of the British Museum.

to rather astonish an incautious intruder. Nevertheless, I subsequently ascertained, by dissection of specimens taken from the nests, that both male and female birds take part in the duty of hatching. The rock in this locality was almost completely sterile; only three or four plants (stunted undershrubs) were found, which eked out a miserable existence among fragments of crumbling rock.

The island is of volcanic formation. The cliffs which we examined displayed a section, fully 1,000 feet deep, of various layers of tuff, laterite, and scoriæ, which, for the most part, stretched out horizontally, and were intersected in every conceivable direction by dykes of basalt. In some places ridges or spurs of rock projected like buttresses from the vertical cliff; and where we landed the spur was composed of a vertical dyke of basalt flanked by a crumbling scoriaceous rock, which latter was being worn away by the action of waves and weather much more rapidly than its core of basalt. The columnar blocks of which the basalt was composed were bedded horizontally; *i.e.*, at right angles to the plane of the dyke, so that the appearance of the whole was strikingly suggestive of an immense stone staircase. After a stay of an hour and a half we were signalled to return on board, as Captain Maclear was obliged to get under way, and accordingly at half-past twelve we were sailing away to the southward, leaving this comparatively unknown island as a prize for future explorers.

In the course of this cruise we were followed by great numbers of petrels, among which were the giant petrel (*Ossifraga gigantea*), the Cape pigeon (*Daption capensis*), and two species of *Thalassidroma* (I think *T. leucogaster* and *T. Wilsoni*). I noticed on this, as on several subsequent occasions, that the little storm petrel is in the habit of kicking the water with one leg when it is skimming the surface in searching for its food. This movement is usually seen most clearly when the sea presents a slightly undulating surface; and when the bird strikes the water in performing a slight curve in its flight, one can see that it is invariably the *outer* leg that is used. The object of this manœuvre seems to be to give the body sufficient upward impulse to prevent the wings from becoming wetted in rising from near the surface. I have often observed the Atlantic storm petrels steady themselves on the water with both legs together, but have never seen them perform this one-legged "kick," like their congeners of the Pacific. There are contradictory statements in natural history works as to whether petrels do or do not follow ships during the night time. Those who adopt the negative view of the question maintain that the birds' rest on the waves during the night and pick up the ship next morning by following her wake. For a long time I was in doubt as to which was the correct view to take, although I had often on dark nights, when sitting on the taffrail of the ship, fancied I had heard the chirp of the small petrels. At length I became provoked that after having spent so many years at sea I should still be in doubt about such a matter as this, so I began to make systematic observations, in which I was assisted by the officers of watches and quartermasters, who were also interested in the matter. The result is that I am now quite certain that the storm petrel and Cape pigeon *do* follow the ship by night as well as by day, and that, moreover, the night is the best time for catching them. Every night, for a time, I used to tow a long light thread from the stern of the ship; it was about sixty yards long, and fitted at the end with an anchor-shaped piece of bottle wire, which just skimmed along the surface of the water and yet allowed the thread to float freely in the air. I found this device a great improvement on the old-fashioned method of using several unarmed threads, and in this way I caught at night-time, and even on the darkest nights, both storm petrels and Cape pigeons; the latter, however, usually breaking my thread and escaping. If I sat down quietly and held the line lightly between my finger and thumb, I would feel every now and then a vibration as a bird collided with it. On moonlight nights, moreover, one could always, by watching carefully, see the big Cape pigeons flitting about the stern of the ship.

My experience of petrels and albatrosses is that whenever they are having a really good meal, they invariably sit down on the water. This is especially noticeable about noon, when mess garbage is thrown overboard, and in perfectly calm weather I have even seen a flock of storm petrels settle down on the surface as if meaning to rest themselves, and remain as still as ducks on a pond, basking in the sunshine. One day also in moderately fine weather I thought I saw a Cape pigeon dive. This surprised me so that I watched, and saw the manœuvre repeated again and again. Some refuse had been cast overboard which scarcely floated, and this petrel, being desirous of possessing some morsels of food which were submerged, dived bodily down, apparently without the least inconvenience.

Before quitting this subject, I shall say a few words on a somewhat hackneyed but still open question, viz.,—"the flight of the albatross." I have had many opportunities of watching the yellow-billed species (*D. Melanophrys*), and I have noticed that it sometimes uses its wings to raise or propel itself in such a manner that to a superficial observer it would then appear to be only soaring with wings stationary. It does not "flap" them, but depresses them rapidly towards the breast, so that it seems as if the body were being raised at the expense of the wings, whereas, in reality, the entire bird is elevated. The movement does not resemble a flap, simply because the return of the wings to the horizontal position is accomplished by a comparatively slow movement. By resorting to this manœuvre occasionally, it is able to maintain a soaring flight for periods which, without its aid, might be considered extraordinarily long. Of course, when it wants to gain a fresh stock of buoyancy and momentum, it gives three or four flaps like any other bird.

During our return stay at Valparaiso from the 1st to the 21st of August, I made a trip to Santiago, the capital of Chili. Santiago is built on the great plateau which lies between the coast range of hills and the Cordillera, and is 1,500 feet above the sea level. The distance by rail from Valparaiso is about 120 miles, but as the railroad makes the greater part of the ascent within a distance of 50 miles, the average gradient of the incline is considerable. The train follows the line of the seashore for a distance of about 3 miles to the northward of Valparaiso, when it reaches the mouth of a wide valley running inland, the windings of whose right bank it follows until a station called Llallai (pronounced "Yayai") is reached. It then makes a steep ascent along the side of a mountain, and here on one side a precipitous wall of conglomerate rock faces the carriage windows, while on the other the eye gazes into the depths of an ever-receding valley, above which the train seems poised as if by magic. While one is still lost in contemplation of this abyss, a short tunnel in a buttress of the mountain is traversed, and the train suddenly sweeps round a sharp corner, and crossing the valley by a light iron bridge which here spans a part of it, constricted to a narrow chasm, enters a highland defile on the opposite side. This place is known as the "Mequin Paso." The train now pursues a meandering track among the hills of Montenegro, where the summit level of the railway is reached, and then inclines gradually downwards to the great plain of Santiago.

After establishing ourselves in the Oddo Hotel, which is situated in the middle of the city, close to the "Plaza De Armas," we commenced our explorations, and first proceeded to the Natural History Museum. It lies on the outskirts of the town and occupies a spacious building which was originally constructed for the Exhibition of 1875, and to which the Natural History collections were transferred in 1877. Favoured by a letter of introduction, we were here fortunate enough to make the acquaintance of Dr. Phillipi, the distinguished naturalist, who has for many years had charge of the museum; and to whose courtesy and good nature we were much indebted. The collections illustrative of South American ornithology and ethnology were particularly fine. The herbarium seemed to be very extensive, and was so excellently arranged as to afford ready access to any groups of specimens. In the spacious hall devoted to this department, we saw a section of a beech tree from Magellan which was more than seven feet in diameter, and the silicified trunk of a tree fifty centimetres in diameter, which had been found near Santa Barbara. The mammalian collection included two specimens of the Huemul (*Cervus Chilensis*), one of which was said to be the original figured by Gay in his "Historia Physica y Politica de Chilé." Among the human crania were some very curious specimens illustrating the extremes of dolicocephaly and brachycephaly. It is to be regretted that the subsidy voted by the Chilian government for the maintenance of this admirable museum does not exceed £100 a year, and Dr. Phillipi may well be congratulated on the results of his self-sacrificing labours.

About the centre of the town of Santiago is a remarkable hill called Santa Lucia, whose summit affords a very extended view. It is a mass of columnar basalt rising abruptly from the plain to a height of about 300 feet, and presenting on all sides boldly scarped faces in which several flights of stone steps have been ingeniously cut, so as to lead by various labyrinthine routes to the summit. We made the ascent towards the close of day, and were well repaid for our trouble by the really magnificent view. The town lay extended at our feet with its various buildings and monuments standing up in bold relief. As we raised our eyes, its outskirts dwindled into the broad plain of Santiago valley, which here seemed to form an immense amphitheatre, surrounded in the distance by a chain of lofty hills whose snowcapped summits were at this hour illumined with the lovely roseate colours so characteristic of sunset in the Cordilleras.

On the following day we visited the site of the church of La Compania, where the fire took place in the year 1863, when some 2,000 people, mostly women, were burnt to death. The church was never rebuilt, but in its place now stands a handsome bronze monument to commemorate the victims of this dreadful calamity.

Immediately adjoining are the splendid buildings in which the sittings of congress are held.

The morning of our return was cold and frosty, and the plain of Santiago was enveloped in a dense mist, from which we did not emerge until the train had entered the mountain valleys, through which it wound towards the heights of Montenegro. Here we rose above the gloomy mists, and were gladdened by the bright and warm rays of a sun whose beams were as yet screened from the lowlands. Wild ducks were to be seen in the marshes near the railways, scarcely disturbed by the passage of the train; flocks of doves rose from the bushes here and there; owls hovered about in a scared sort of way, as if ashamed of being seen out in the honest sunlight; and on many a tree top was perched a solitary buzzard or vulture. Later in the forenoon small flocks of the military starlings were frequently sighted, their brilliant scarlet plumage showing to great advantage against the pale green bushes of the hill sides. After passing the summit level we rattled down the incline towards Llallai, at what seemed to me to be a very high speed. I kept looking out of the window at first, watching the engine disappearing from sight as it suddenly swept round an abrupt curve and entered a cutting, and admiring the wriggling of the train as it swiftly threaded its way in and out among the hills. Sometimes our route would seem to lead us into a *cul-de-sac* of the hills, and when apparently almost at the end of it, the engine would abruptly alter her course and sweep away in a direction nearly at right angles to its former course, dragging the docile and flexible chain of carriages away with it. I had missed all this on the upward journey—I suppose because our slower speed then made curves and cuttings look less alarming. After a while, I began to reflect on the probable consequences of our suddenly coming upon a flock of heavy cattle in one of these nasty cuttings, and the more I pondered the more I became convinced that although the cow-catcher of our engine was well able to cope with a single bullock or even two, yet that in the case of our colliding with a flock of half-a-dozen or so, something unpleasant must surely happen. This was not a cheering subject of thought, so I turned away from the window and tried to interest myself in the contents of a Chilian newspaper. A few days previously, I heard that a single bullock had been met with on this same incline, and had been satisfactorily accounted for by the "cow-catcher." The body was smashed to pieces and thrown off the track, but the people in the train (one of whom was my informant) experienced only a very slight shock. At Llallai station we stopped for breakfast, for which the cold air of the morning had sufficiently prepared us, and in the afternoon we arrived comfortably at Valparaiso.

We again stayed at Coquimbo from the 23rd to the 30th of August, having been obliged to return there on account of a court-martial. The appearance of the country had changed very much since our previous visit. Bare tracts of sand had given place to an uniform coating of verdure, and a great variety of flowering plants were visible in full bloom. There was a species of *Aristolochia* very common on the rocky hills, whose large pitcher-shaped perianth frequently imprisoned a number of flies of different species, and I found that I could add materially to my entomological collection by examining these plants, and despoiling them of their living prey, for most of the pitchers contained living flies, and some of them the remains of insects apparently in a half-digested state. This flower constitutes a very effectual fly-trap; and I once noticed a great bluebottle-fly endeavouring in vain to work his way over the "chevaux-de-frise" of white hairs, which, with their ends pointing inwards, studded the interior of the tube.

During this stay I made a trip to the copper mines of Brillador, which are worked in connection with the smelting houses at Compañia. Both establishments are the property of Mr. Lambert, an English gentleman residing at Swansea, whose Chilian manager is Mr. Weir, to whom I have already alluded. I went by train to Compañia, which is the terminus of that branch of the line, and spent the night at the residence of Mr. Weir, by whose kind invitation I was enabled to make this interesting excursion. On the following morning we started on horseback, and rode over the hills to Brillador. The mines are eight miles distant from Compañia, and are situated at an elevation of 1,500 feet above the sea level. Here we put ourselves under the guidance of Mr. Richards, the courteous engineer, who clothed us in canvas mining suits, and supplied each of us with an oil lamp hung on gimbals at the extremity of a long stick; and thus equipped we entered one of the adit levels opening on to a steep hillside, and bade adieu for some hours to the friendly daylight. One of the peculiarities of a Chilian mine is that the ordinary ladder of civilization is replaced by a notched pole, and that, by means of a succession of these poles, the descent and ascent of the shaft of the mine is accomplished. Another is that the ore is conveyed from the works at the bottom of the shaft in sacks of hide, each man thus carrying on his shoulders the enormous weight of 200 lbs. The miners whom I saw employed in this work were naked to the waist, and exhibited splendid muscular development of chest and arm. I examined one of the sacks of ore, and found that I could barely raise it off the ground. These fine athletic fellows are fed principally upon maize, figs, and bread, few of them eating meat. Three kinds of copper ore are found in this mine. Near the surface is a light green carbonate of copper which is easily smelted, and when rich in metal (*i.e.* free from extraneous mineral matter) is in much request; but even when of low percentage it can be advantageously used for the manufacture of sulphate of copper. Next in order of depth is found a purple ore, which is a double sulphide of copper and iron; and at the bottom of the lode is the yellow sulphide of copper, commonly known in Chili as "bronce." Here we saw a most ingenious "rock drill," working at the end of a new level cutting.

The apparatus, which is simple and most effective, consists of a solid piston working in a very strong cylinder and driven to and fro by compressed air, whose action is regulated by a slide valve. The drill is fitted directly into the end of the piston rod, and by an ingenious arrangement it is made to perform a partial movement of rotation during each backward motion, so that it may strike the rock in a new direction each time. The working pressure of air was 50 lbs. per square inch. We noted the time while a boring was being made, and found that it took exactly nine minutes to make a hole nine inches deep, through the hard rock. The power is originated by a double-acting steam-engine, situated at the inner extremity of the main adit level, from whence a supply of compressed air is conveyed in flexible pipes along the various tunnels in which boring is being done. In subsequently blasting the rock, gunpowder is used in preference to dynamite or other explosives, I believe on account of the toughness of the ore, which therefore yields more satisfactorily to a comparatively gradual explosive. In the evening we rode back to Mr. Weir's residence at Compañia, and on the following day I returned on board the ship, which weighed anchor the same afternoon, and proceeded southward towards Talcahuano.

Talcahuano, where we lay from the 4th of September to the 4th of October, is the most important seaport in southern Chili, and possesses an excellent and roomy anchorage. It is situated in a fertile and picturesque country; and it is in direct communication by rail, not only with Concepcion and all the more important towns of the south and central provinces, but also by branch line with an extensive grain-producing territory bordering on Araucania, whose produce it receives. Concepcion, which takes rank as the third city in the Republic, is nine miles from Talcahuano, and lies on the bank of the Bio Bio, a broad, shallow, and sluggish river. The houses and public buildings there have the appearance of considerable antiquity, although in reality the greater number must have been rebuilt since the great earthquake of 1835, when the city was reduced to ruins. Penco, the old Spanish capital of the province of Concepcion, was situated in the eastern extremity of the Bay of Concepcion; but when it was destroyed by a tidal wave in 1730, the people moved inland and established themselves near the site of the present city. However, by the cataclysm of 1751, the newly-founded city of Concepcion shared the fate of Penco, but was soon rebuilt, as it was again, in great part, after the earthquake of 1835.

We had intended to make only a short stay at Talcahuano, but on the day preceding our arrival there, a case of smallpox appeared among the crew, followed by a second and third, and we were therefore obliged to remain in this harbour until our patients should be sufficiently well to return on board.

There was a long, low, sandy island (Isla de los Reyes) lying across the head of Talcahuano Bay, and inhabited only by a couple of shepherds who were looking after a herd of cattle and horses. There being no available hospital to which our patients could be sent, we obtained leave from the Chilian authorities to establish a temporary quarantine station on the island. Accordingly, on the day of our arrival we set up tents on an unfrequented and particularly airy part of the island, and having supplied them with provisions and all the necessary appliances, we installed our patients in their new quarters. They made good recoveries. My medical duties required me to make frequent visits to this little establishment, and I found it convenient to make it the centre of my afternoon rambles. On the mainland immediately adjoining the island, I found a great marshy plain of many miles in extent, and intersected in various directions by deep muddy ditches which communicated with the sea, and at high tide brought supplies of sea water to a chain of broad, shallow lagoons, the home of multitudes of waterfowl. Pintail ducks, widgeon, herons, curlew, flamingoes, turkey-buzzards, gulls, lapwings, and sandpipers found here a congenial home. The shrill, harsh cry of the spur-winged lapwing (the "terotero" of the Pampas so graphically described by Darwin) was for ever scaring the other peacefully-disposed birds, and at the same time invoking maledictions from the sportsman. The plumage of this bird is very handsome, and the bright crimson colour of the iris and eyelid during life gave it a strange fascinating appearance, which can hardly be realized from a stuffed specimen.

When the first ebb of the tide left bare the mudbanks in the lagoons, the gulls and curlews collected in vast numbers for their diurnal meal. Of the gulls only three kinds were seen, viz., *L. Dominicanus, L. Glaucodes,* and *L. Maculipennis.* The latter were in various conditions of plumage ; some birds having a deep black hood, and others with a head almost entirely white, while between these two extremes, there was every gradation. The turkey-buzzards derived a plentiful supply of food from the bodies of fish stranded on the beach. For some reason or other dogfish were constantly coming to grief in this way, bodies of fish, two and three feet long, being met with sometimes, all along the beach, at average distances of about one hundred yards apart.

One day we made an excursion up the river Andalien, which flows into Talcahuano Bay, near the village of Penco, and which at high tide is navigable for boats to a distance of seven miles from its mouth. Our main object was to see something of the nutria—a large rodent (*Myopotamus coypu*), which is common in some of the rivers of southern Chili, and which the natives call "Coypo." In a deep, narrow, ditch-like tributary of the Andalien, we came across several of these animals, swimming and diving about, some half-immersed clumps of bushes. At first sight their manner of swimming and diving would lead one to imagine that they were otters, but on closer inspection the broad muzzle with its long bristly whiskers, and foxy-red hair, reveal their true character. The "coypo" is distinguished from its northern ally, the beaver, in having the scaly tail round instead of flat, and from the

Chilian river otter, the "huillin" (*Lutra huidobrio*), it is easily known by its dental characters as well as by its tail and feet. The hind feet are webbed as in the beaver. I dissected one which we shot, and found the stomach full of green vegetable matter, and in the abdominal cavity, which was a good deal injured by the shot, were fragments of a large tapeworm. This specimen weighed 10 lbs., and measured 2 ft. 10 in. from snout to extremity of tail.

Some days subsequently I accompanied Captain Maclear on a railway trip up the country, Mr. Lawrence, the superintendent of the line, having, with the courtesy so characteristic of English residents in Chili, invited the captain and one other officer to join him in a tour of inspection which he was about to make along the Angol branch of the South Chilian railway. We started from Concepcion at 9 a.m., on a small locomotive which was set apart for the use of the superintendent. It was a lightly built affair, partly "housed in" and partly open, and was fitted to accommodate two or three passengers besides the driver and fireman, so that it afforded us an exceedingly pleasant method of seeing something of the country. This swift little vehicle was called the "Quillapan," in commemoration of a distinguished native chief of that name. Our driver was a most intelligent and well-informed Englishman named Clark, who had lost his foot about three years previously in a railway accident, at which I understood that Lady Brassey, of the *Sunbeam*, had been present; and he spoke gratefully of the kind attention which she paid to him. His wooden leg did not seem to be much impediment to his engine-driving, for he rattled us along round curves and down inclines at a speed which, while possessing all the charms of novelty, had also in no small degree the excitement of danger. However, we soon got used to this, as well as to the jumping and jolting of the light little engine.

For the first ten miles after leaving Concepcion, our route lay along the right or northerly bank of the Bio Bio river. Here most of the railway cuttings were through a clayslate rock, which alternated with bands of black shale, and occasionally exhibited thin seams of coal. Further on, and throughout the rest of the journey to Angol, the cuttings were through banks of sand exhibiting horizontal stratification, and being apparently of fluviatile origin. A run of two hours brought us to the junction station of San Rosendo, from whence the northerly line to Chillan, Talca, and Santiago, and the S.E. line to Angol diverge. Here we breakfasted, and stretched our legs by a stroll. Immediately on resuming our journey we crossed the Lara,—a tributary of the Bio Bio,—and then continued our course along the right bank of the main river, until we had just passed the station of Santa Fé. Here the line made a short semicircular sweep, and crossed the Bio Bio by a low wooden bridge of about two hundred yards in length. Clark, the driver, told us that during freshets the water rose about fifteen feet above this bridge, completely stopping the traffic. On asking him why they did not build a strong high level bridge, he replied that a rude wooden structure such as the present one cost little, and when swept away could be readily and cheaply replaced; but that a bridge of durable style would take too long to pay the cost of its own construction. This explanation may not at first sight seem very lucid, but it is worthy of consideration, for the principle which it involves is, I fancy, applicable to many of the affairs of Chili.

We had now entered the great central valley of the country, a broad plateau interposed between the coast range and the Cordillera, and extending in one unbroken sheet of fertile land from here to Santiago. Before us now, as far as the eye could penetrate, lay a straight level track, so Mr. Clark turned the steam full on, and the "Quillapan" responded to the tune of forty-five miles an hour. When about a mile or two from a desolate station called "Robleria," we were rapidly approaching a long wooden bridge, when we saw a man appear on the track just on our side of the bridge, and step leisurely from sleeper to sleeper. On hearing our whistle he looked round in a startled attitude; but to our astonishment, instead of jumping to one side of the line, he lost his head, and passing on to the bridge made frantic efforts to cross before our engine came up. The bridge was an open framework, consisting simply of wooden piles, spanbeams, and sleepers, and was so narrow that there was no room for a foot-passenger at either side of a passing train. The wretched man's misery must have been extreme, for as he crossed the bridge he had to jump continually from sleeper to sleeper, and could not of course look back again behind him to see how things were going on. It was a moment of intense suspense to us also, for it was now too late to stop the engine, Clark not having calculated on the man attempting to cross before us. However, he gained the off buttress of the bridge just in time to throw himself down a bank on one side of the line, while the "Quillapan" sped on like a whirlwind.

We reached the Angol terminus at 1.30 p.m., and on coming to a standstill, found ourselves the centre of a small admiring crowd, consisting of Chilian peasants and Araucanian Indians. The latter wore very scanty clothing, in which the only distinctive feature which I noticed was a band of red cloth tied round the forehead and occiput. In stature and regular features they somewhat resembled the Chilians, but their distinctly coppery colour marked them out at once. Angol is now one of the frontier settlements established recently by the Chilian Government in Araucanian territory, and it is fortified against the marauding expeditions of these hardy warriors by a chain of forts which overlook the settlement, and are garrisoned by regular Chilian troops. The district is of great value, on account of the richness of the soil and its suitability for the cultivation of wheat, which has now become the staple article of commerce in the southern provinces of the Republic. Our stay at Angol was, unfortunately, very short, as the station-master told us that a train due at Angol that afternoon was even then telegraphed as waiting at one of the upper stations until our return, when the line would be clear for it to move on.

On our journey back we narrowly escaped colliding seriously with a herd of bullocks. We had just passed Robleria, when we noticed some distance ahead of us a solitary bullock standing quietly on the line. On the whistle being sounded he at once left the track, so that the steam, which had been momentarily turned off, was again put on, and the engine resumed her usual speed. We had now approached to within forty yards of the place where the animal had been, when suddenly from a dense clump of bushes to the right there emerged a herd of half-a-dozen bullocks, who with one accord began leisurely to cross the line. Quick as thought Clark with one hand turned on the whistle, while with the other he reversed the engine, leaving the steam valve wide open; and immediately there was a great rattle of machinery below the platform, and the engine checked her way considerably. And now at the last moment, and when the cattle seemed to be almost under the buffers of the engine, they, suddenly coming to a sense of their danger, scattered, and sheered off; but not quickly enough to prevent one unlucky animal being caught by the hind quarters and chucked off like a football, its body rolling down the embankment to the left in a cloud of dust as we whirled by. Clark coolly replaced the reversing lever, and let the engine rush ahead again as if nothing had happened. He remarked that if he had been on one of the regular big engines he would not have bothered himself about the beasts at all, but that half-a-dozen bullocks were rather too much for the little "Quillapan."

Another trip which we made was to the Island of Quiriquina, which lies in the entrance of the bay at about five miles' distance from the anchorage of Talcahuano. An hour's run in the steam cutter brought us near the northern extremity of the island, where we landed with difficulty in the Bay of Las Tablas. This name has reference to the tabular form of the blocks of sandstone which have fallen from the face of the cliffs and lie strewn on the beach, in which position they resembled the blocks of concrete which one often sees near a pier or breakwater in course of construction. Close to where we landed we found portions of the silicified trunk of a tree, resting on the *débris* at the foot of the cliff, its fractured ends exhibiting a jagged appearance, as if the fragment had not long previously been broken from the parent stem. It was two and a half feet long by a foot in diameter, and presented well-marked sections of the concentric rings of growth. In one of the rock pools closely adjoining we found also a smaller water-worn fragment, which we were able to annex as a specimen. The sandstone cliff above us exhibited well-marked lines of stratification, dipping to the southward at an angle of about $15°$, and in the talus at its base were several large globular masses, which consisted almost entirely of fossil shells, bound together by a matrix of soft clayey sandstone. Conspicuous among these shells were examples of the genera *Baculites* and *Cardium*. While the lowest rock in the series of strata was a hard grey sandstone, full of fossil shells, and forming a kind of level terrace skirting the beach, and a wash at high tide, on the north side of the bay this last-mentioned rock was continuous with another horizontal terrace, which ran at a somewhat higher level, as if introduced there by a fault in the strata. It was a coarse, unfossiliferous conglomerate, composed of angular pieces of shingle bound together by a hard but very scanty matrix.

CHAPTER V.

OUR SECOND SEASON IN PATAGONIAN WATERS.

ON the evening of the 4th October, our small-pox patients being then sufficiently well to return on board, we sailed from Talcahuano, and proceeded to the southward in order to resume our surveying work in the Trinidad and Concepcion channels.

We entered the Gulf of Peñas on the afternoon of the 9th October, and as it was a clear, bright, sunshiny day, we had a good view of Cape Tres Montes, which forms the northern horn of the gulf, while ahead of us, and towards the S.E. bight, lay the Sombrero, Wager, and Byron Islands, the first of which marks the entrance of the Messier Channel. When we had got fairly inside this channel, a Fuegian canoe of the customary pattern was seen approaching from the western shore. We stopped to allow her to communicate with us, and, of course, the usual bartering of skins for knives and tobacco took place between the natives and our seamen. There were about twelve persons in the canoe, all of whom looked more than usually plump in regard to their bodies, but had the characteristically stunted legs of this wandering race. On leaving us they appeared to be quite sold out, and were almost entirely naked, some of them completely so; however, they seemed well pleased with the bit of traffic which they had accomplished.

We anchored for the night in Island Harbour. On the following morning we got under way at an early hour, and steamed down the Messier Channel and through the English Narrows, reaching Eden Harbour about dusk.

We passed several small icebergs, which had probably reached the channels from a glacier in Iceberg Sound. The largest was about twenty yards across, and projected about six feet above the surface. Most of the hills in this latitude were snow-clad as far as the 1,000 feet line.

On the evening of the next day, the 11th October, we reached the Trinidad Channel, and established ourselves for a time at Cockle Cove, an anchorage on the south shore of this channel, of which the survey was as yet incomplete.

It was now spring time on the west coast of Patagonia, but the weather was as chilly and wet as it had been in the autumn of the previous year, when we were moving north towards our winter quarters; indeed, from the accounts furnished to us by the sealers, as well as from our own experience, I am inclined to think that there are no marked seasonal changes in the weather on the west coast, whither the constant westerly winds are continually delivering the burden of aqueous vapour which they accumulate in their passage over the Southern Ocean. On the other hand, the condition of the fauna and flora indicate the natural two-fold division of the year as decisively as it is observed in the same latitude in the northern hemisphere.

In the month of October at Cockle Cove the kelp geese and steamer-ducks were preparing their nests, and the cormorants were assembling at their rookeries; the holly-leaved berberry (*Berberis ilicifolia*) was already displaying its gorgeous clusters of globular orange flowers, and the giant creeper (*Campsidium chilense*) was also in bloom, its scarlet bell-shaped flowers peeping from aloft among the branches of the beech-trees, where they appear to seek a position in which they may flourish safe from intrusion. Many of the mosses and *jungermanniæ* were also now in full fruit.

OUR TEGUAN FRIENDS AT TILLY BAY, STRAITS OF MAGELLAN (*p.* 115).   [*To face p.* 104.

We dredged several times at Cockle Cove. The bottom was muddy, and abounded in a species of *Mactra*, which the men were fond of eating; and as they commonly called these shells "cockles," the anchorage was given a name which would recall the memory of these much-esteemed comestibles.

We also obtained numbers of a pale rose-coloured *Gephyrean* On placing one of these creatures in a globe of fresh sea-water it seemed to feel quite at home, protruding its tentacles and puffing out its worm-like body until it looked like a tiny jam-roll with a star-fish attached to one end. These tentacles, which are eight in number and surround the mouth, are each one provided with from eight to ten finger-like processes. When there is only the former number, the organ looks remarkably like a hand, and the resemblance is rendered more striking when the tentacle is extended, and grasps some minute particles in the water, which to all appearance it conveys to its mouth. The usual shape assumed by this protean animal is that of a long cylinder with rounded ends, but it sometimes shows an annular construction about the middle of the body, and sometimes the whole anterior half of the body is retracted so as to give the animal a telescopic appearance. These changes of shape are produced by the action of two distinct systems of contractile fibres, transverse and longitudinal, the fibres of the former being disposed closely together like minute hoops, and girding the body from end to end, while the longitudinal fibres are arranged in five broad and well-marked equidistant bands, which extend uninterruptedly from one end of the cylindrical body to the other.

One night a small petrel flew on board, into one of the hoisted-up boats, where it was found by one of the seamen in the usual apparently helpless state. It is odd that some species of the family of petrels should find such difficulty about rising on the wing from a ship's deck. A freshly-caught Cape pigeon, placed on its legs on the deck, seems to forget utterly that it possesses the power of flight, and does not even attempt to use its wings, but waddles about like an old farmyard duck. The petrel above referred to was the little diver (*Pelecanoides urinatrix*), a bird not uncommon in the channels, but yet very difficult to obtain. During the previous season on the surveying ground, Sir George Nares, who was the first to notice it, reported one day that he had seen one of his old arctic friends, the "little auk," which indeed in its habits it strongly resembles. It usually (at all events during the daytime) sits on the surface of the water, and on the least sign of danger takes a long dive like a grebe, and on rising to the surface again flies away some few hundred yards, keeping all the while close to the surface. Its flight is like that of the grebe, but more feeble. In the Falkland Islands the habits of this bird are somewhat different. The bill is peculiarly broad and of a dark horn colour, the breast and belly of a dull grey, and the upper parts black; the tarsi and feet lavender. The body is short and plump, and is provided with disproportionately short wings. Speaking of this bird, Mr. Darwin says that it "offers an example of those extraordinary cases of a bird evidently belonging to one well-marked family, yet both in its habits and its structure allied to a very distant tribe."

There was a "rookery" of the red-cered cormorant (*Phalacrocorax magellanicus*) near Cockle Cove, but the nests were placed on almost inaccessible ledges in the face of the rocky cliff, which was streaked all over with vertical white lines from the droppings of the birds. This species of cormorant is very abundant throughout all the channels. A second species, a jet black bird (*Phlacrocorax imperialis*), builds its nest in trees; and there was a characteristic "rookery" of this tree cormorant at Port Bermejo, where we anchored in the month of November. It was in a quiet sequestered place, where two old and leafless beech trees overhung the margin of an inland pond. The nests were constructed of dried grass, and were placed among the terminal branches of the trees. These funereal-looking birds, sitting on or perching by their scraggy nests on the bare superannuated trees, formed a truly dismal spectacle. They uttered, too, a peculiar cawing sound, which was not cheerful, and so remarkably like the grunting of a pig, that before I saw the rookery I was for some time peeping through the bushes and looking for tracks, imagining myself in the neighbourhood of some new pachydermatous animal. It seemed as if the birds took the grunting business by turns, only one at a time giving tongue.

I was surprised to see how neatly they alighted on the branches. There was none of the awkward shuffling motion of wings and feet which they exhibit when alighting on the ground or on the water; but, on the contrary, each fresh arrival soared on to its perching place as smoothly and cleverly as a hawk, and grasped the branch firmly with its claws. At another tree rookery in Swallow Bay I noticed that when some of the birds on flying in observed my presence, they would rise high above the tree, and remain soaring around in circles till I had gone away. The method of soaring was to all appearance as smooth, steady, and devoid of effort as that of a vulture. And yet the cormorant is a heavy short-winged bird, that rises from the ground with difficulty, and whose ordinary method of flight is most laborious.

The handsomest bird in this region is the kingfisher (*Ceryle stellata*). It is commonly to be seen perched on some withered branches overhanging the water, where it will remain in a huddled-up sleeping attitude, its head turned sideways, but with an eye all the time fixed intently on the water beneath, until it espies a fish, when it drops like a stone, cleaving the water with a short sharp splash, and a moment afterwards emerges with an upward impulse, which raises it clear of the water, and enables it to fly away at once without any preliminary shaking or fluttering. It is an exceedingly unsuspicious and fearless bird, and when perched on its place of observation, will often allow one in a boat to approach within arm's reach of it. Mossy banks overhanging low sea cliffs are its usual nesting places, and there it excavates a tunnel through the soft moss and turfy soil, and at a distance of more than two feet from the aperture forms its nest.

There is a very peculiar and constant feature in the scenery of the woodlands about the summits of the low hills, which has given rise to much speculation amongst us. It is that many of the rounded bosses of syenite rock, which project for a few feet above the level of the swampy land, exhibit on their highest parts isolated mossy tufts, which look at a little distance like small piles of rubbish placed artificially in prominent places as landmarks, or like the marks which mountain climbers are so fond of setting up on rocky pinnacles as records of their feats. The usual shape is that of a cylinder about eighteen inches high, and ten inches in diameter, with a rounded top ; and it adheres to the rock by a well-defined base of matted fibres. It is composed of a very compact moss (*Tetraplodon mnioides*), which is of a rich green colour on the summit of the tuft when it is in a flourishing condition, and whose decaying remains, converted into a peaty mould entangled in a fibrous network of roots, form the body and base of the tuft. When this moss is in fruit, its long spore-bearing stalks, which rise to a height of three inches above its surface, are of a dark-red colour where they emerge from the green surface, this colour gradually changing into a beautiful golden-yellow above, where the spore-cases are supported. It is then an exceedingly pretty object. If one of these tufts be torn away from its rocky foundation, which is very easily done, and is a most tempting work of destruction, a white scar is left on the rock which will catch the eye at the distance of a mile, and which strongly resembles the small white-washed marks set up on the coasts by our surveyors for shooting theodolite angles at. Now the question is, why does the moss establish itself in this peculiar position, on the otherwise bare and exposed rock ? It is all the same whether the rock be dome-shaped, as it most commonly is on the low hill-tops, or pyramidal, or wedge-shaped, the tuft—if there is one present—is invariably to be found perched on the highest part of it. I can only attribute this to the peculiar habit of growth of the moss, adapting it specially to this shape and this situation; a situation to which moreover it gives a decided preference, for I have not observed it growing elsewhere. Sometimes on climbing a rocky mountain hereabouts, one sees from afar off one of these tufts perched on a commanding pinnacle at the summit; then one thinks that surely this must be a cairn erected by some desolate traveller, and it is only on approaching closely that the delusion vanishes. It will then, perhaps, be found that the tuft stands alone, surrounded in all directions by a sloping surface of bare rock which isolates it by a radius of forty yards from all other vegetation; the little tuft bearing itself up bravely as if in obstinate defiance of the wind and rain, which one is at first inclined to think must have swept away an old uniform mantle of vegetation from the rocky surface, leaving the mossy tuft on the summit the sole survivor.

There is another peculiar form of vegetable growth which is a characteristic of the landscape in certain parts of this region, and which I have not noticed to the same extent elsewhere. It is this. Whenever a mass of bushes happens to be exposed to the prevailing westerly wind, as in the case of promontories which receive the unbroken blast on one of their sides, or of exposed islets in mid-channel, it will be seen that the bushes not only lean away permanently from the direction of the prevailing wind (as is usual everywhere), but that their summits are cut off evenly to a common plane which slopes gently upwards, and thus presents as trim an appearance as if the bushes had been carefully clipped to that shape with a gardening shears. Our surveying parties have sometimes been disappointed at finding that a headland, which seemed from a short distance to be covered with an inviting mantle of short grass, and which therefore looked a convenient place on which to establish an observing station, was in reality defended by a dense growth of bushes, which exhibited the phenomenon in question, and over, under, or through which it was almost impossible to get. Sometimes one could get over these bushes by lying down at full length and rolling sideways down the incline; but this method was objectionable, for it was sometimes ten or fifteen feet from the surface to the hard ground beneath. The reason of this curious growth is obvious enough. Each aspiring leafy twig that happens by a too luxuriant growth to shoot above its fellows, is cut down by the relentless blast before it can acquire strength enough to make good its footing; and those branches alone survive in the struggle which grow uniformly with their neighbours, and which thus present a sufficiently compact surface to withstand the blighting influence of the westerly gales.

One day, when we were lying at our old anchorage in Tom Bay, I saw a cormorant rise to the surface with a large fish in its mouth, which, for several minutes, it vainly attempted to swallow. I noticed it chucking the fish about until it had got hold of it by the head, but even then it seemed unable to "strike down" the savoury morsel. A flock of dominican gulls now appeared on the scene, and seeing the state of affairs at once swooped down on the unlucky cormorant, but the wily bird discomfited them by diving and carrying the fish with it. It was now most ludicrous to witness the disappointed appearance of the gulls, as they sat in a group on the water looking foolishly about, and apparently overcome with grief at their inability to follow up the chase by diving. After an interval of about half-a-minute the cormorant reappeared some distance off with the fish still in its mouth, and now one of the gulls succeeded at last in snatching the fish from its grasp, and flew away with it rapidly up a long winding arm of the sea. At this critical moment a skua (*Stercorarius chilensis*), hove in sight, and gave chase to the fugitive gull, until, unfortunately, a turn in the creek concealed both birds from our sight, but left us to safely conjecture that the last comer had ultimately the satisfaction of consuming the wretched fish.

I have often wondered at the apparently stupid manner in

which long files of cormorants will continue on their course over the surface of the water without deviating so as to avoid a dangerous locality until they are close to the place or object to be avoided. Many persons are doubtless familiar with the appearance of these birds as they fly towards a boat which happens to lie in their route, and may remember the startled way in which, when about twenty or thirty yards off, they will alter their course with a vigorous swish of the tail and sheer off confusedly from the danger. Again, how eager they are to take advantage of the (probably) acuter vision of terns and gulls, when they observe that either of the latter have discovered a shoal of fish. Is it not therefore probable that cormorants are naturally short-sighted?—a disadvantage for which they are amply compensated by their superior diving powers.

The required survey of the Trinidad Channel was completed by the middle of the month of December; but before leaving this part of the coast, one day was devoted to an exploration of the "Brazo del Norte," a sound running in a northerly direction from the Trinidad Channel, and piercing the so-called Wellington Island. We got under way from Tom Bay early in the morning, and steaming across the Trinidad Channel, entered "Brazo del Norte," and explored it to a distance of twenty-six miles from the entrance. We were then obliged to turn back in order to reach Tom Bay before nightfall. It was a great pity that time did not permit us to trace this magnificent Sound to its northern extremity; for so far as we could judge there seemed every probability of its communicating directly with the Fallos Channel, which is known to extend southwards from the Gulf of Peñas to within a few miles of the place where we turned back. In this event it would prove a good sheltered route for vessels using the Straits of Magellan, and if free from the objectionable restrictions which close the Messier Channel route to large steamers, would be used not only in preference to it but to Trinidad Channel itself, whose approach from seaward is at least uninviting, if not hazardous.

On leaving Tom Bay we moved gradually down the Concepcion

and Inocentes Channels, always anchoring for the night, and sometimes stopping for a day or two in order to examine some new port.

At Latitude Cove a black-necked swan (*Cygnus nigricollis*)—besides which only one other was ever seen by us in the western channels—was shot. It proved to be a male bird, weighing only seven pounds, and was in poor condition, having strayed far from its own happy hunting grounds among the lagoons of central Patagonia.

We anchored at Sandy Point in the Strait of Magellan on the 2nd January, and remained there eleven days in order to provision the ship, and to give the crew a change of air.

Here I made the acquaintance of the master of a sealing schooner, an intelligent man named John Stole—a Norwegian by birth—from whom we obtained much interesting information about the natives of Tierra del Fuego. At the time of our visit he was laid up with a bad leg, on account of which he had had to relinquish the command of his vessel the *Rescue* for this season's cruise. His favourite sealing ground was among the rocky islets about the S. W. parts of Tierra del Fuego; but in the course of his wanderings he had visited most of the islets and coasts extending from the mouth of the river Plate on the eastern coast to the Gulf of Peñas in the westward. During his last cruise, he had the misfortune to be attacked by a party of natives in the Beagle Channel, at a place not far from the missionary station of Ushuwia. He gave us a most graphic description of the affair. His schooner had been lying quietly at anchor in a rather desolate part of the channel, having at the time only five men, including himself, on board, when a canoe containing ten Fuegians—eight men and two women—came alongside. Not suspecting any treachery, he went below to have his tea, leaving one man on the forecastle to look after the vessel. Presently hearing a scuffle on deck, he put up his head through the small hatch of his cabin, when a native standing above made a blow at him with a canoe paddle. The blow failed to take effect, as he had just time to duck his head under the boom of the mainsail which was secured amidships over the hatchway. He now retreated to his cabin, snatched up a revolver which was lying ready loaded, and returning to the hatch quietly shot the native who was waiting to strike another blow at his head. Two others now followed up the attack, armed with heavy stones, but they were shot in quick succession, one of them falling overboard and capsizing the canoe. As Stole now raised himself through the hatch, a fourth native attacked him from behind, but he turned half round, rested the barrel of the revolver on his left arm, and fired into his assailant's eye, the entire charge passing through the wretched creature's head. In the meantime the crew were successful in expelling the four natives who had attacked the fore part of the vessel, and all of whom were killed. The two women in the boat had been passing up stones as ammunition for their male companions, and when the canoe capsized one of them was drowned. When the fight was over, the deck presented a ghastly sight, being sloppy all over with blood in which were lying the bodies of the dead and dying savages, as well as quantities of stones which before the attack began had been passed up from the canoe to be expended in storming the hold of the vessel. Of the ten natives, eight men had been killed, and one woman drowned, the surviving woman being taken prisoner. The sealers now got under way, and proceeded to the mission of Ushuwia, where they reported the matter to Mr. Bridges, the manager of the station. He investigated the case, and on finding that the account given by the sealers was corroborated by the evidence of the surviving woman, exonerated the former of any misconduct in the energetic measures which they had taken to defend their lives, and to defeat the object of the natives, which of course was to obtain the possession of the schooner.

The first of the small sealing fleet to arrive at Sandy Point this season was the *Felis*, of Stanley, a small rakish schooner, commanded by an Irishman named Buckley. He had a cargo of

500 sealskins, which he sold to a German dealer on shore, at the rate of 30s. a skin, this being considered a good price for Sandy Point, and generally only given for the first arrivals in port; cargoes arriving late in the season not realizing more than 25s. a skin. In the present state of the home market, furs being in request, these skins, on being landed in England, whither they are conveyed by the mail-steamers, are bought by the furriers for about £4 apiece; so that the dealers at Sandy Point make a large profit by their share in the trade. Sealers fitting out at Sandy Point also usually get their stores and provisions on credit, and at an exorbitant valuation, from the same dealer to whom they subsequently sell their skins. The produce of the skins, moreover, as they are sold to the dealers at Sandy Point, is divided into three equal lots, of which one is divided among the crew, while the remaining two go to the owner, out of which he has to pay for the provisions and stores consumed on the cruise. It is calculated that the outlay on the stores swallows up about one-third of the entire sum, so that eventually about one-third of the value of the skins remains as the profit of the owner. In a very good season, the master and owner of a sealing schooner of thirty tons will make a clear profit of as much as £2,000, while each man of the crew (usually twelve in number) would get a share amounting to £80, on which to spend the blank eleven months of the off-season in idleness and debauchery.

The Magellan sealing season extends over the months of December and January. In or about the last week of November, the fur seal (*Arctocephalus Falklandicus*) and the sea lion (*Otaria jubata*) "haul up" on the rocks of the outer coasts, and bring forth their young. The breeding places, or "rookeries," which they usually select, are small, low-lying, rocky islets, which are exposed to the swell of the great ocean, and over which, in heavy weather, the sea makes a more or less clean sweep. Situated as these rocks are, it is often a very difficult and dangerous matter to effect a landing, so that, to make sure of it, a sealing master usually arranges his cruise so that he may reach the vicinity of the rookery about a month before the breeding time. He then takes advantage of the first fine day to land a party of men on the rock with fuel, camping arrangements, and a large supply of provisions. The latter is essential, for it may be two or three months after the season is over before he can get a favourable day for embarking the men and the stock of skins. Cases have occurred where men have been weather-bound on the rocks for months, and reduced to the brink of starvation, although making use of seal-flesh and shell-fish as long as they could get them. The different sealing captains are, of course, very careful to conceal from each other the position of the "rookeries" of which they know; and they have got so much into the habit of deceiving each other in this respect, that it may be laid down as a safe rule, that if a sealing master says he has landed his men on some rocks to the northward, it is more than probable that the real locality is somewhere in a southerly direction. After the camping parties have been established at the "rookeries," the sealing vessel with the crew, now reduced to a very small number, is employed for the next month or two in cruising in search of new hunting-grounds. In this pursuit they sometimes wander for hundreds of miles from the place where the men have been landed, traversing unsurveyed channels and islets, trusting confidently that at night time they can always find some sheltered place where they can either anchor close in shore, or, if the water be too deep, as it generally is, make fast to a tree. When cruising in this way, they kill numbers of the Magellan sea-otter (*Lutra felina*), an animal which they include in their line of business, although not at all to the same extent as the fur seal. The fur of the otter when dressed is of great beauty; but as it is not now in fashion in Europe, it commands a very small price in the market, the salted skins, on delivery in England, only realizing about 2*s*. apiece. When the long brown hairs which form the animal's apparent coat have been removed, the underlying fur is seen to be of a beautiful golden yellow colour. The otters are obtained by sealers in a great measure by bartering with native canoes (the Fuegians catching them with dogs), and also by shooting them, as they swim through the kelp close to the beach. Both the otter and seal-skin are salted dry,—that is to say, each skin is spread out flat, salt is sprinkled plentifully over the inside, and the skin is then rolled up with the hair outside, and tied up into a round bundle. The old fur seals are killed just as they are met with, and without any regard to the preservation of the stock. The sealers commonly call the females "claphatches," and the males "wigs;" the skin of the former is much the more valuable of the two. The sea lions (another species of seal) are seldom meddled with; but occasionally a sealer, in default of the regular article, will kill them for the sake of the oil, and take some of the hides, for which there is a certain demand for making "machine belting."

Buckley, the master of the *Felis*, told us that he had observed that in the case of the fur seal there was an interval of only one or two weeks between the date of parturition and that of coupling, and that, in the case of the "hair seal," coupling took place almost immediately after the young were brought forth. If this be true, the period of gestation cannot be less than eleven months.

Buckley presented the captain with a young fur seal—a male, six weeks old—which had been caught on the rocks, and nursed carefully by one of his crew, an Italian seaman, who had been 'bottle-feeding" it with milk, and had taught it to answer to the call of a whistle. It trotted about our decks in a most lively manner, its hind feet, when trotting or walking, being turned forwards and outwards in the manner peculiar to seals of its genus. On whistling to it, it uttered a strange cry—half wail, half bark—and came to the call like a dog. When taken up in the arms and petted like a child, it lay quite still, closed its eyes and seemed to go off into a gentle sleep. It, unfortunately, died on the following day—perhaps through fretting for its Italian nurse—and its body then came into my hands as a zoological specimen.

Dr. Fenton, whose acquaintance we had made on our first visit just a year previously, was still residing at Sandy Point as medical officer of the settlement, and, with great good nature, put his house and horses at our disposal. He told me of an experiment he had been trying on the flying powers of a condor, which had been caught alive. He perforated the quills of the wing and tail feathers, so as to allow the ingress and egress of air, and on then throwing the bird up in the air found that it could neither fly nor soar. The inference is that the bird derives its buoyancy in a great measure from the formation of a vacuum in the quills of these feathers, and consequently, on air being admitted, the flapping of the wings, unaided by the buoyancy derived from the rarefied air, was insufficient either to raise or support the bird's weight. If this theory be correct, it is probable that the mechanism by which this vacuum is produced is actuated by the wing muscles, which thus discharge a twofold office.

From the 13th of January to the 25th of March, after leaving Sandy Point, we proceeded to the western part of Magellan Straits, where we were for about nine weeks, occupied in making additions to the old surveys, principally in the narrow and tortuous part of the Strait which is called the "Crooked Reach." The scenery here is remarkably fine, and on a dry clear day—an event, however, of rare occurrence—one can fully realize the truth of old Pigafetta's remark, that "there is not in the world a more beautiful country, or better strait, than this one."

We made several stays, each of a day's duration, at Tilly Bay, a small land-locked anchorage on the north shore of Santa Ines Island, and immediately opposite to the mouth of the Jerome Channel, which leads into the Otway water. At the head of the bay a stretch of open moorland, dotted here and there with clumps of cedar trees, led by a gentle ascent to a sort of upland plateau, formed of moss-covered undulating land with sheets of still water occupying the hollows. Not a trace of a bird was to be seen, and I was never more struck with the extreme paucity of animal life in the interior of these islands than when standing on the shore of one of these desolate lakes in Santa Ines Island.

We frequently noticed, in the deep spongy moss over which we walked, the nests of a Trap-door Spider. They appeared externally as round apertures in the surface of the moss, about an inch and a half in diameter, which were covered over with a closely woven disc of web. On removing the cover from one of them, and clearing away the surrounding moss, I found that the burrow descended vertically for a distance of about eight inches, and was lined throughout with a silky network of spider web, so that the entire web structure, *i.e.*, the tube and lid combined, resembled in general shape some of the commoner forms of *Aspergillum*. At the bottom of the hole lay a great spider, embracing with its legs a spherical cocoon, three-eighths of an inch in diameter, which it seemed resolved on defending to the last extremity. I examined other nests with similar results.

While we were at Tilly Bay, a small party of Fuegians came in and took up their quarters in an old camping place close to the ship. They were a comparatively friendly lot, and had no hesitation about coming on board, especially about our meal hours, which they very soon got to understand. The party consisted of one adult man, a boy aged about seventeen, a woman about nineteen, with four small children, and two or three dogs of the usual kind. The canoe was made of planks, and was of the same build as those which we had seen about the Trinidad Channel. Lying in the bottom of the canoe were the putrid remains of two seals, a sea lion, and a fur-seal, whose heads I obtained. We got on such intimate terms with this family, that little by little we induced them to show us all their properties, even to the much-cherished materials for producing fire. These were kept in a wooden box somewhat of the shape of a small band-box, and made of Winter's bark sewn together roughly with strips of hide. The tinder, which seemed to consist of dried moss, was stowed away carefully in little bags formed of dried seal's intestines tied up at the ends.

I also obtained by barter two very dirty bits of iron pyrites which they used for igniting the tinder, and on striking them together they certainly emitted showers of sparks. The box also contained glass arrow-heads, glass spear-heads, bone harpoon-heads, a noose made of a strip of baleen and apparently intended for trapping otters, and a very strong net made out of seal-hide, which the old man gave us to understand was used for catching seals. The net was nearly square, measuring about six feet both ways, and the meshes were about eight inches across. This last was evidently considered a great work of art, for as the old man displayed it his eyes glittered with pride, and he assumed an air of importance, as if to imply—"See that and die!"

Subsequently two more canoes turned up, bringing a large party of natives, and as I was curious to ascertain the method by which they fashioned their glass implements, I visited the encampment one day, bringing with me an empty pickle bottle, and intimated by signs that I wished to have it broken up and to see a spear-head or arrow-head made. They understood readily enough what was required, and one of the men, coming forward, took hold of the bottle, smashed it against the stones, and selecting a suitable fragment, set to work at it. He held the piece of glass firmly in his left hand, protecting the fingers with a bit of cloth, while, with his right, he grasped a chipping tool, which consisted of a large blunt-pointed iron nail fixed in a stout wooden handle, serving the double purpose of a chipping tool and a means of calking the seams of the canoe. Holding it with the iron point directed towards his waist, he made steady pressure against the fractured edge of the glass, so as to make small chips flake off from the edge towards the smooth side surface. In effecting this he was able to use great force, because, while the left hand, which held the glass, was supported rigidly against his chest, the manner in which he held the fashioning tool enabled him to bring the whole strength of his wrist to bear upon the edge of the glass. After having bevelled off one side of the edge, he turned the glass round and bevelled the other side in a similar manner. Having once imparted a double bevel to the edge, he was easily able, by operating on each side alternately, to reduce the substance of the margin in any one place until the glass had assumed the outline required. Proceeding in this way, the formation of the barbs and the recessing of the base for the ligature which would secure it to the shaft, were effected to all appearance with the greatest facility. The most difficult part of the business was now the formation of the fine point, as the chipping and flaking had to be conducted with the greatest nicety. However, after half-an-hour's steady work, he triumphantly produced a spear-head two and a half inches long, and of the form shown in the annexed sketch. The arrow-heads are made in the same way, and are about one inch in length.

We had the chipping operation repeated on many subsequent occasions, and by various individuals, and found that all adopted the same method; the essential feature of which was that the fashioning of the glass was effected entirely by *pressure*, and that no *striking* implement was used. I induced one of the men to try an old flat file, instead of his own chipping instrument, but he soon discarded it; however he found a blunt-edged ship's knife very convenient for giving the finishing touches to the point of the spear-head. With the experience gained from the Fuegians, I soon learnt to turn out very fair imitations of their work; and after practising on various kinds of glass, I found that the easiest to work with was black bottle-glass, and the most difficult plate-glass. Green pickle bottle-glass is about a mean between the

two, and as it is tolerably thick the natives prefer it for their spear-heads; but for the arrow-heads they use the black glass. Crown-glass was easy to work, but flaked off in rather short pieces. I also experimented with some black flint, which happened to be on board, and found it could be worked in precisely the same way as the glass, but was certainly more difficult to fashion into shape. Then I tried different kinds of working tools, and soon found, to my surprise, that hard steel was the worst of all, for it scratched and slipped off the edge of the glass without chipping it at all; whereas soft iron, which was much preferable, could be manipulated so that it would bite only the extreme edge of the glass, and by this means very thin and broad flakes could be detached. Even an old bone harpoon-head answered very well indeed, but of course was worn away more rapidly than the soft iron.

One day, when the old man of the first canoe party was on board, and in an amiable mood, I succeeded in getting some Fuegian words from him, a matter often previously attempted in vain. As a rule, they merely repeat—and that most accurately—the gestures or ejaculations which one makes in drawing their attention to any particular object. I brought this old fellow into my workshop, and pointed out to him several objects which I had collected in the straits, and which were sure to be familiar to him. After some time he got fairly hold of the idea, and then became very communicative, eventually giving me the names for all the familiar objects which I could at the time command. I subsequently checked the vocabulary thus obtained, by reversing the process and repeating the words to him, and making him indicate their meaning, and in this way I made certain that my list, small though it was, had at all events the merit of being accurate. In fact, I tested some of the words afterwards on another party of natives, whom we met at Port Gallant, and found that they went off all right.

VOCABULARY OF FUEGIAN WORDS.

Obtained from natives at Tilly Bay, Straits of Magellan.

Basket (netted)	= cheebass.	Mussel	= chaloux.
,, (plaited)	,, dawyer.	Necklace	,, heskouna.
Beard	,, port.	Nose	,, los.
Bottle	,, kushki.	Nutria-skull	,, theerkusthads.
Breast	,, poan.	Otter-skin	,, lalthers.
Calf	,, kutchoice.	Paddle	,, chetarias.
Canoe	,, ayoux.	Paroquet	,, parabas.
Crab	,, karabous-kalpers.	Sea-egg	,, kawotchi.
Deer	,, halchun.	Seal-skull	,, arougsis.
Dog	,, sharkiss.	Ship's boat	,, sherroux.
Ear	,, hawish.	Skin of seal	,, harkusis-hushkei
Eye	,, sthole.	Spear (for fish)	,, kip-thatharsh
Eyebrow	,, thescoux.	Spear (for seals)	,, uäakutsh.
Eyelash	,, thesscriss.	Starfish	,, hiapparoux.
Fingers	,, sthœn.	Steamer-duck	,, karawus-poug.
Finger-nails	,, tharsh.	Stomach	,, kutshiss.
Fish	,, areous-arcersh.	Stone axe	,, kesaoux.
Flint	,, kosil.	Teeth	,, pathers.
Foot	,, kadthakous.	Thigh	,, athursh.
Hair	,, therkous.	Tongue	,, lekiss.
Hand	,, therrawaus.	Tooth (of seal)	,, sheriquish.
Head	,, iakalus.	Trumpetshell	,, tharagskar.
Ironstone	,, luksthaads.	Upland Goose	,, harrawaloux.
Limpet	,, ithashaquash.	Volute shell	,, tharaquakorass.
Mouse	,, akraceps.	Water	,, nupp.

NAMES OF FUEGIAN CHILDREN AT TILLY BAY.

Alkeress.
Ilchabesakodotis.
Kelchuarkuss.

Gounaco.
Gounaco Chikachikis.

We anchored at Port Gallant for three days in the latter end of January, and while we were there a bark canoe came alongside. It was of the kind which King describes as peculiar to the tribe inhabiting the western part of the Magellan Straits, and to whom he assigned the name "Pecherai," from their habit of frequently using that word. The canoe was much smaller and lighter than the plank canoes of the western channels, and was propelled entirely by paddles instead of oars. Two old women, who sat in the stern end, wore cloaks of deer skin, and were very noisy and talkative, so that we did not encourage them to come on board. The basket, in which they carried their stock of shellfish, was much more elaborately plaited than were those of the "Channel Fuegians." We did not observe any difference in their hunting implements, except that bows and arrows were more abundant with them.

On the 25th, a large iron steamship, the *Maranhense*, came in from the westward and anchored near us. It appeared that about six months previously she had come out from Antwerp, bringing a cargo of arms for the Chilian Government, and that she was now homeward bound, carrying a general cargo. As she was coming down the Messier Channel, she had touched the ground in the English Narrows, and been so much injured in the bows that her collision compartment was full of water. Captain Leadbetter came on board to solicit the services of our diver, which were of course granted; and on an examination being made, it was found that there was a hole in her bows big enough for a man to crawl through. For several days subsequently ineffectual attempts were made to stop it up, and on the 30th of January both vessels moved up to Sandy Point. Here we met a German man-of-war, the *Freia*, whose crew rendered further assistance to the disabled vessel, but all in vain. At length, our diver was sent down to make a complete examination of her bottom, and he came up with the unpleasant news that there was another great hole in her bottom, $7\frac{1}{2}$ feet in length, under the after-hold, that the iron skin and part of the keel had been torn away, and that the cement alone, with which her bottom was lined, prevented the water from coming in. In view now of the possibility of the cement suddenly giving way, and the vessel sinking, steam was got up, the anchor was raised, and she was moved into shallower water further inshore, so that in the event of her sinking, the hull might not be entirely submerged. The master of the *Maranhense* now decided on sending to Monte

Video for artificers and material to repair the bottom, and for a new crank-shaft for her engines, which had also recently come to grief.

On the 9th of February we bade good-bye to the officers of the *Maranhense*, and steamed back to Port Gallant.

Some days subsequently we moved westward to Playa Parda Cove in Crooked Reach, our boats having been meanwhile engaged in charting the coastline.

On February 18th a small party of us made a trip in the steam cutter from Playa Parda Cove to visit a glacier which is situated about six miles to the eastward. We steamed round to the inlet, which is marked on the chart as Glacier Bay, and moored the cutter under a lofty cliff near the head of the bay. The land here was low and flat, covered with a dense forest, and bounded on either side by precipitous lofty cliffs, whose smooth faces exhibited planings and scorings due to the abrading action of old glaciers. I landed about the middle of the low muddy beach, which extended from cliff to cliff, and proceeded to penetrate the forest in the direction of the glacier. Here I at first found some difficulty in advancing, for after tearing my way through a dense prickly scrub of barberry bushes, I came upon an even more serious obstacle, in the shape of a broad and rapid torrent of mud-coloured water, which it was absolutely necessary to cross. This was one of the streams which flowed from under the glacier. Cautiously feeling my way, and steadying myself against the rushing water, I just managed to get across, finding the process rather cold; and now, after traversing a belt of forest, which was only half a mile in width, but which gave me forty-five minutes hard work, I emerged all at once from the gloomy shade of the beech trees to find my eyes dazzled by a glare of white light, and the foot of the glacier straight before me. The line of trees was separated from the snout of the glacier by a freshly-accumulating terminal moraine, of about one hundred yards in width; and where this moraine adjoined the sharply-defined edge of the forest,

FOOT OF GLACIER AT GLACIER BAY, STRAITS OF MAGELLAN.

[To face p. 124.

its advancing condition was evident from the piles of rubble which were in places shot in among the green trees, and from the overturned condition of many of those on the margin of the forest, as they gave way before the advancing piles of rubbish. It was a strange sight, standing in the middle of this terminal moraine, to see, on the one hand, a fresh evergreen forest abounding in the most delicate ferns and mosses; and, on the other, a huge mass of cold blue-veined ice, which was slowly and irresistibly gouging its passage downwards to the sea. The stones of the moraine were composed of syenite and greenstone, the former predominating, and mixed up with them I saw many trunks of trees, which were crushed, torn, and distorted out of all shape. These were probably the remains of a portion of the forest, which had at one time extended further up the valley, and which had been annihilated by the advance of the glacier; and this circumstance, with the other which I have mentioned, showed clearly that the glacier was now extending its limits and approaching the sea. A few days afterwards, we paid a second visit to Glacier Bay, when a good photo was obtained.

We stayed for a fortnight at Swallow Bay, a port in Crooked Reach, a few miles to the westward of Tilly Bay. It would seem that this locality had been greatly resorted to by the natives for catching fish, for we found several of their "stone weirs," in a more or less perfect state. The places selected for these weirs were usually small smooth-bottomed coves, and the weir, which consists of a sort of dam built of loose stones about three feet high, is placed across the mouth of one of these coves in such a manner, that when it is complete, any fish which may be inside it will be imprisoned. When it is low water, and the cove is almost dry, a gap is left in the centre of the weir through which the fish may enter with the rising tide; at high tide the gap is closed up, so that when the water flows away through the interstices of the dam with the falling tide, the fish remain imprisoned in a shallow pool where they can easily be caught.

These shallow mud-bottomed coves are the favourite haunts of the grey mullets, who collect there in great numbers, and who sometimes on bright fine days may be seen resting on the mud with only a few inches of water over them, as they lie apparently basking in the sunshine.

Here, at Swallow Bay, a party of our men captured and brought to me a male specimen of the Magellan nutria, an animal which is abundant throughout the straits and western channels, but which is nevertheless very rarely seen. We had often previously seen its bones in the Fuegian midden heaps, where its skull, with the long curved orange-coloured incisors, was a conspicuous object; but this was the first recent specimen we succeeded in getting hold of. It was started from the brushwood by a retriever dog belonging to the ship, and on taking to the water was killed after a most exciting chase on the part of our bluejackets. It proved to be identical with the Chilian species, *Myopotamus Coypu*.

CHAPTER VI.

EXPLORATIONS IN SKYRING WATER.

ON the occasion of our last visit to Sandy Point, the captain received despatches from the Admiralty, which authorised him to proceed to Skyring Water in order to investigate the nature of the coal which was then being worked on the north-east of that basin, and to ascertain if it could be made available for the use of men-of-war or merchant vessels, passing through the Straits of Magellan. A favourable opportunity occurring on March 5th, the *Alert* accordingly got under way from her anchorage at Tilly Bay, and steaming northwards across the Strait, entered the Jerome Channel. Here we experienced a strong current from the northward, which was attributed by Mr. Petley, our navigating officer, to the ebb tide flowing from the Otway Water. This channel is twenty miles in length, from its southern opening opposite Tilly Bay to its northern extremity abreast of Corona Island, where it dilates into the wide expanse of Otway Water. Its shores are lined by precipitous mountains of an average height of 1,000 feet, and clothed to their summits with the dense evergreen forest which characterizes the scenery of the western half of the Magellan Straits. Behind, and towering above this coast range, were hills of a still greater altitude, whose summits were clothed with a mantle of snow and ice— the source of the glaciers flowing to the southward into the main straits. As we entered Otway Water, we saw on our starboard hand a broad expanse of rippling water, limited in the distance by a coastline of comparatively low land, while on our port side there was a marked transition from the lofty mountains of the Cordillera to an upland plain of undulating hills covered with forest, and sloping gradually downwards into low flat land as it extended to the eastward. In fact, we had passed through the backbone of the Cordillera, and were now approaching the alluvial plains of Patagonia; and it was also clear to us that we were crossing the line of demarcation between two climatic zones, for we found that we were exchanging the cloudy sky of the Magellan region for brilliant sunshine and a clear blue sky, a change only to be fully appreciated by those who have spent many months in the damp, cloud-collecting region of the Western Straits.

The north shore of Otway Water was low and shelving, presenting a glistening margin of sandy beach, and fringed by a wide belt of very shallow water. In the afternoon we entered the Canal of Fitzroy, where we encountered a strong current from the northward (*i.e.* from Skyring Water), which considerably impeded our progress. Indeed, at 4 p.m. we grounded on a sandbank, getting off, however, without much difficulty, and in an hour afterwards we dropped anchor in a bight where an S-shaped curvature in the canal afforded us shelter from the current.

Both shores of the canal are low, and formed of alluvial soil, of which the crumbling banks in places exhibited good sections. Well-marked terrace-levels bore testimony to the fact that the land must have been subjected to upheaval, with reference to the sea-level, at some period in the world's history. The country on the western side of the canal is covered with thick scrubby bush, while that on the eastern side, where we landed for a few hours, was a sort of open park-land disposed in undulating hills, covered with a luxuriant growth of grass, and studded here and there with isolated clumps of trees and bushes, among which we noticed the antarctic beech, an embothrium, a barberry, and a cheilobothrium. The ground in the middle of these clumps was worn bare from having been used as a resting-place by the wild cattle. Herbaceous composite plants grew in great profusion, and many specimens of a lychnis were seen, but unfortunately the season was too far advanced for our obtaining useful specimens of flowering plants. I was surprised at the great variety of grasses which flourished on the dark loamy soil. We saw countless tracks of wild cattle and horses, and a few deer tracks, but in the course of our ramble failed to meet with any of these animals. The existence of a species of *Ctenomys* was evident from the way in which the ground was in many places so riddled with holes as to be exceedingly dangerous for incautious horsemen; and while walking through the long grass I stumbled over the skull of a puma. We did not see many species of birds. Finches were abundant, and some flocks of the black starling, and also of the military starling, were seen. I got a specimen of a pteroptochus, which resembled the tapacola of Chili, but differed from it in having a red iris; and on the beach I shot a cinclodes, which seemed to be of a different species from the common kelp-bird of the straits. A fine buzzard (I think *Buteo erythronotus*) soared above my head, but out of range; and the tiny wren of Magellan (*Troglodytes*), completed the list of birds which we saw. During our absence great numbers of black-necked swans and brown ducks were seen in the vicinity of the ship.

At five o'clock on the following morning, we got under way and continued our course through the Canal of Fitzroy, steaming for hours through a dense interminable flock of black-necked swans, that paddled lazily to either side as we advanced, as yet in happy ignorance of the thirst for blood which characterizes the British sportsman. As we emerged from the canal, and skirted along the eastern shore of Skyring Water, we noticed two men on foot, walking along the beach. We afterwards learned that they had a day or two previously left the coal mine where they had been employed, and were now attempting the precarious task of travelling on foot to the Chilian settlement, Punta Arenas, in the Straits of Magellan, a distance of ninety miles.

At 10.30 a.m. we reached the bay of the mines (Rada de las Minas), and came to an anchor about half-a-mile from the shore. The settlement was larger than we had expected, and exhibited fair signs of activity, several shingle-built houses, large store sheds, and a steam sawmill, showing out conspicuously against the dark background of forest which spreads for a few miles to either side, and is seen extending inland to near the summit of Mount Rogers, a hill to the northward which reaches an elevation of 1,000 feet.

For information concerning Skyring Water, we are mainly indebted to Fitzroy's account of the short survey he made in the year 1829, when in command of H.M.S. *Beagle* (which account comprises information obtained from a sealer named Low, who visited these waters in pursuit of his trade), and to some papers published by the Chilian Government in the *Anuario Hydrografico*, detailing the results of two visits made by Chilian men-of-war. In November 1877 the Chilian gun-boat *Magellanes* visited Skyring Water, making a stay of three weeks, during which time her boats were mainly employed in making a survey of the eastern part of the basin. The results of this survey, so far as it went, favoured the idea of there being a channel connecting Skyring Water with Smyth's Channel to the westward. It was brought to an abrupt termination by the terrible mutiny which took place at Sandy Point in November 1877; however, in the months of December 1878, and January and February 1879, Captain Latorre, of the corvette *Magellanes*, made a second incomplete examination of Skyring Water. One of his boat parties penetrated a considerable distance to the westward, where the basin is continuous with a number of long, narrow, winding inlets or channels, which enter the hills of the coast range. Here they met with a party of Fuegians, who were in all respects similar to those of the western channels, possessing the usual canoe and hunting implements. They also found numerous traces of Fuegians in all the sheltered coves which they examined among the inlets towards the western part of Skyring Water. This would seem to indicate a direct water communication with Smyth's Channel, but on the other hand, the range of tide being found to be exceedingly small, would tend to prove that its connection with the ocean was at all events remote. This survey was brought to a close in a most unsatisfactory way when almost on the eve of clearing up the doubtful question as to the existence of through communication; the *Magellanes* having been ordered north on the outbreak of the war between Chili and Peru.

The Skyring coal-mines were originally started in the year 1877 by an enterprising German named Haase, who opened the seam, extracted some coal, and erected sheds, but soon afterwards (I believe through want of funds) abandoned the undertaking, so that when the Chilian corvette *Magellanes* arrived here in October 1877, the settlement was found to be in a deserted condition. Captain Latorre then made a trial of some coal which he found lying in a heap near the pit's mouth, and after executing a partial survey of Skyring Water was recalled to Sandy Point, on receiving news of a disastrous mutiny in that colony.

The settlement remained uninhabited from a few months before the *Magellanes*' first visit until the 15th of November, 1879, when the mine was reopened by Mr. Haase, provided with money, furnished by a company which had been formed at Buenos Ayres. Since that time the work has progressed steadily, so that the mine and adjoining works are now in a tolerably efficient state. At the time of our visit, the mines and the settlement were in charge of Monsieur Arnaud, a French engineer, Mr. Haase having some days previously gone on a trip to Buenos Ayres. The people numbered about twenty altogether; but as there were as yet no customers to buy the coal, and as consequently no wages had been paid for a long time back, the miners were gradually deserting and making tracks for Sandy Point.

The edge of the coal seam, which is now being worked, was visible in the face of a low cliff on the north-west promontory south of the bay of the mines. The outcrop of the seam is in a north and south direction, and it dips to the south-east at an angle of about 45°. From a cursory examination which I made of sections afforded by the cliffs adjoining the mines, I ascertained that the coal was overlain by a bed of clayey sandstone, overlying which was a stratum of hard limestone containing fossil shells, among which large Ostrœas were the most conspicuous. Above this, and lying conformably to it, was a layer of soft sandstone containing numerous comminuted fragments of shells in a subfossil state. The coal seam itself was about twelve feet thick.

The mine seemed to be in a most efficient state. A pit, sunk obliquely, descended to a depth of thirty-six feet, where it communicated with a horizontal cutting about sixty yards in length. At the end of this gallery the coal was being worked, whence it was conveyed in trolleys to the foot of the pit, and then hauled up the incline by means of a stationary engine working at the pit's mouth. From there a line of tram rails extended about 150 yards to the end of a strong wooden mole, where the water was deep enough to float heavy barges, and where a large pile was stored under a shed, and ready for shipment. It was of good black colour, but light and friable; very much resembling the Lota coal, to which it was little inferior in quality. A sample was taken on board, and submitted to various practical tests, by Mr. Dinwoodie, our chief engineer. It was of jet-black colour, and glistening appearance; leaving a faint black mark on rubbing. S. G. = 1·3. It contained sulphur and iron, burned with very little smoke, and produced a rust-coloured ash, which formed a proportion of 18 per cent. When used in the furnace, it formed large caky masses of a hard tenacious clinker, which adhered to the fire-bars, and so clogged the fires that it was found impossible to raise steam to more than thirty pounds' pressure. In an open grate it burnt freely enough, but without giving out much heat. It was, therefore, unsuited for engines using high pressure steam such as ours.

We were much disappointed on learning that game was now very scarce in the immediate vicinity of the settlement, and that as a matter of fact the miners were victualled on salt and preserved meats. Beyond a range of five miles, deer, guanacoes, ostriches, and wild cattle might be had, but could not be taken without the aid of horses, with which useful animals the settlers were at present (apparently through pecuniary embarrassments) unprovided. Foxes were abundant in the forest, and at night time prowled about the settlement, while recently a puma had paid it a nocturnal visit, to the great alarm of the pigs and other domestic animals. We walked into the "camp," to a distance of about five miles from the settlement, and were surprised at the scarcity of birds. We saw, however, a flock of black-necked swans, numbering about sixty, in the water near the seashore, but found them too wary for us. A paroquet, a few starlings, a finch, a wren, a buzzard, and the ubiquitous cinclodes were the only land-birds seen. On subsequently penetrating into the forest in the rear of the settlement, I saw many examples of a bird of the "tree-creeper" family, which the Chilians call "carpintero," from its habit of making a "tap-tap" sound when digging its bill against the bark of trees, in pursuit of the insect-larva on which it feeds. These birds behave in many respects like wood-peckers, producing a similar noise, using the same food, travelling over the boles of the trees in a spiral fashion, and creeping with ease along the under surface of horizontal branches. I shot two of them when in the position last-mentioned, and noticed that for some seconds after they had been shot they remained suspended by the legs, with the heads hanging vertically downwards, until the complete relaxation of the muscles allowed them to fall. The toes, of which there are three directed forwards and one backwards, are furnished with long and sharp claws. The bill is long, stout, and pyramidal, and the shafts of the tail-feathers project beyond the webs.

On the 7th of March, a small party of us got the use of one of the steam-cutters, and made a trip to Altamirano Bay, an anchorage about seven miles to the westward of the "bay of the mines," which was originally explored and surveyed by the Chilian vessel *Magellanes*. We reached the bay after steaming for two hours against a westerly breeze and chopping sea, and landed on its western shore. Here we found an open grassland interspersed with clumps of low trees and bushes, among which the most abundant were an embothrium, a panax, an escallonia, a berberis, a cheilobothrium, and the black currant of Magellan—the *Ribes Magellanica*. The tree-clumps showed evident signs of their being the resting-places of wild cattle and horses, of which we saw also numerous tracks in the open; none, however, being of recent date. We could find no fresh water of any kind, and therefore concluded that the deer, guanacoes, ostriches, and horses, which were reported to be abundant here, had gone up the hills during this dry season, and only resorted to the lowlands hereabouts during the winter time. There was certainly splendid pasturage for them, and I was much struck by the abundance and variety of the grasses. The land-birds were similar to those noticed previously in the neighbourhood of the coal-mines. The plain of grass-covered land over which we walked seemed to extend for a long way to the westward, but from the head of the bay a dense forest of beech-trees stretched away to the northward.

Skirting the shore of the bay, although overgrown with scrub and forest, were two distinct terraced levels, which testified to an upraising of the land. The rock formation, as far as could be judged from the rock *in situ* visible on the foreshore, was a clayey sandstone, devoid of fossils, and bedded horizontally. Erratic boulders of syenite and gneiss—some of considerable size—lay scattered about the beach.

The shores of the bay indicated a scanty littoral marine fauna. Shells of a small mussel were sparsely strewn about, and were the only molluscan remains noticed. The *débris* of a small, reddish alga was strewn along the beach in undulating lines; but no kelp was seen at all, either on the shore or adhering to submerged rocks.

During our four hours' stay, very little change was noticed in the level of the tide, an argument rather against the likelihood of a channel existing to connect Skyring Water with the ocean to the westward.

In the meantime those on board the ship were engaged in coaling. We purchased twenty-five tons of the new coal at £1 a ton, a quantity quite sufficient to enable us to test practically its value. The mining engineer, Monsieur Arnaud, was of opinion that on sinking deeper into the coal-seam a better quality would be met with. The present workings are at a depth of only thirty-six feet from the surface, and as the angle of dip is about 45°, it is not improbable that on sinking a deeper shaft his expectations may be realized. Should this be the case, the long-cherished scheme of establishing tug-steamers in the straits to tow sailing vessels from ocean to ocean, will probably be revived, and a great impetus will thus be given to the Straits of Magellan as an avenue for commerce. Moreover, should a permanent settlement be established at the Skyring Water coal-mines, intending colonists will find in the surrounding country a splendid field for their energies. The soil of the pampas is of excellent quality, for from its proximity to the Cordillera, where the eastern drifting Pacific clouds deposit their watery contents, it receives enough moisture to remove from it that arid dryness which has rendered the eastern part of Patagonia unsuited for the agriculturist. There is at present excellent pasturage for cattle, and from all that we know of the climate, I see no reason why cereal crops should not flourish. The day, I trust, is not far distant when this part of Western Patagonia will prove a fertile field of labour for the stock farmer and the agriculturist.

On the afternoon of the 8th of March we again weighed anchor, and steamed over to the Fitzroy Channel, anchoring for the night at a place in the fairway about five miles from the north entrance. Some of our officers were now employed for an hour or two in sounding out the channel, while others, more fortunate, amused themselves by waging war against the brown ducks (*Anas cristata*), and black-necked swans (*Cygnus nigricollis*), which were abundant enough, but more wary than on our first meeting them. I did not see a single specimen of the *Cygnus coscoroba*. On the western, or Fuegian shore, the recent tracks of a deer were seen by one of our party.

We got under way early on the following morning, and after passing through the Fitzroy Channel, recrossed Otway Water, and re-entered the Jerome Channel. On the south shore of this latter we noticed a large fur seal "rookery" (*i.e.*, breeding place), and stopped to examine it for some minutes. There were about thirty large seals hauled up on the rocks, besides a large number that were swimming about in the adjoining water. Some of those on the rock were hauled up about thirty feet above the sea-level. We fired a shell into their midst at about 800 yards range, which had the effect of making them tumble off hurriedly into the water, where they made a great tumult, turning somersaults and jumping clear out of the water, after the usual manner of fur seals. The seals in this rookery were probably congregated for the hair-shedding season. Later in the evening we reached our former anchorage in Tilly Bay, where we came to an anchor for the night.

Swallow Bay, 11*th to* 24*th of March.*—We steamed over to this anchorage, which lies a few miles to the west of Tilly Bay, in continuation of our surveying work. A most curious and interesting fish (*Neophrynicthys latus*) was here obtained. It was brought to me by one of our seamen, who found it lying dead on the beach, and bearing marks of having been torn by vultures. Of this fish, which was discovered by Mr. Hutton a few years ago in New Zealand, Dr. Günther says that it only differs from the New Zealand specimen in colouration, and in the presence of small tentacles, which are developed over the eye and on some parts of the body.

One day, when paddling round a small rocky islet, we saw perched on a stone, and apparently sleeping, as it remained motionless with bill resting on the stone, a large snipe (*Gallinago stricklandi*), one of the very few examples of the species which were observed during our cruise. It was shot and preserved.

Two mammalians were also obtained at Swallow Bay. One was the common Magellan otter (*Lutra felina*), the other a nutria (*Myopotamus coypu*).

On March 25th, our supply of coal running short, it was decided to conclude our survey of Magellan Straits, and to proceed northwards, *viâ* Smyth's Channel, to Puerto Bueno. There we took on board the residue of a depôt of coal which had been made for us during the previous season, and continued to pursue our way northwards, stopping for the nights at various anchorages. On April 2nd, we passed our old cruising ground in the Trinidad Channel, and entered Wide Channel, proceeding from thence *viâ* Indian Reach.

As we passed the entrance of Icy Inlet, we saw large patches of loose berg-ice floating tranquilly over its surface, and evidently derived from the glacier at its head. Contrary to our expectations, Eyre Sound was almost clear of ice, only a single small floating piece being seen; but to repay us for this disappointment we had a fine view of the magnificent glacier at its head.

Port Riofrio, 3rd to 10th of April.—We were detained for a week at this port, while our surveyors were occupied in examining the rocks and islets of the neighbouring "Covadonga

Group," of which the survey—commenced by the Chilians—was as yet incomplete. Port Riofrio is situated on the eastern side of Wellington Island, and derives its name from a large mountain torrent which pours its water into the bay nearly opposite to the entrance, for which it also forms one of the principal leading marks. On the western side of the anchorage, and forming a sort of mighty dam across the valley through which this torrent flows, is a remarkable raised beach, whose brow stretches horizontally from ridge to ridge, its continuity being only broken by a narrow fissure through which the torrent rushes, descending thence by a series of cascades to the sea. Inside this barrier the land slopes gradually but slightly downward to an extensive plateau, which forms the bed of the valley between the two mountain ranges. Opinions differed on board as to whether this barrier was a raised beach or an old terminal moraine; but I inclined to the former view, from the fact of its brow being so regular and horizontal, from its stretching evenly from hill to hill, from the absence of any vestige of lateral moraine on the hillsides, and from the slight difference in actual level between the brow of the barrier and the general surface of the plain within. It was covered with the usual swampy soil-cap, and the plain was for the most part occupied by an extensive swamp. Here I collected fine fruiting specimens of a handsome velvety moss, *Tetraplodon mnioides*, of a rich green colour, which I have before alluded to as forming curious tufts on the summits of boulders, on rocky pinnacles, and on the stumps of dead trees.

On the shores of this anchorage grew several plants which we had not previously seen in the Straits. Among these was the *Mitraria coccinea*, a climbing shrub, easily recognised by its dark-green glossy ovate-acute leaves, and short tubular scarlet flowers. Another was the *Weinmannia trichosperma*, a tall erect shrub with serrated pinnate leaves, and jointed petioles winged in a curious rhomboidal fashion. I was in hopes of finding here the beautiful *Hymenophyllum cruentum*, which we obtained last year at an island in the English Narrows, some miles to the northward, but was disappointed, its range probably not extending so far south.

Two animals new to science were here obtained, viz., a small frog of a dirty yellow colour, which has since been described by Dr. Günther as a new species of "*Cacotus*," and an Uncinated calamary, which has since been examined by Mr. Edgar Smith, and found to represent a new species, to which he assigns the name "*Onychoteuthis ingens.*" The last-mentioned specimen was found stranded on the beach. The body, from oral aperture to extremity of caudal appendage, measured fifteen inches, and the total length from caudal appendage to anterior extremity of tentacles was two feet nine inches. The tentacular hooks were very formidable. No other example of this species of squid was encountered.

Having completed the survey of the Covadonga Group, we again proceeded on our way northwards. On the first night we stopped at Gray Harbour, a port immediately to the northward of the English Narrows. As soon as we had anchored, Lieutenant Rooper and I took advantage of the few remaining hours of twilight and started off in the skiff, directing our course towards the head of the bay, where a fair-sized river entered the sea. We proceeded up the river for about a quarter of a mile, finding its banks composed of a bluish clay, and passing at its mouth a low triangular island, which seemed to be a delta formed of clay and sand washed down from the hills, and piled up here at the outlet where the fresh water flow was dammed up in a measure by its contact with the sea. On the pebbly shores of the river we picked up several specimens of a pond snail—a species of *Chilinia*, I believe; and on working a light dredge in mid-stream, we obtained many more specimens of the same. The location was one eminently suggestive of the haunts of otters, nutria, and water-fowl, but not a solitary animal of the kind was to be seen. The disappointment, however, was one which our experience of similar and equally tempting localities had taught us to be prepared for. The surrounding country bore recent signs of having been devastated by a great fire, the mountain sides for miles being covered with the charred remains of a dense forest.

Owing to its proximity to the English Narrows, Gray Harbour is probably frequently used as a stopping place by passing steamers, whose occupants amuse themselves by firing the forest. It is rarely indeed in this habitually wet region that the forest is sufficiently dry to allow a fire to spread over any great extent of country.

We got under way at an early hour on the following morning (April 11th). It was a fine clear day, and the channels showed to great advantage, so that we were able once more to confirm the remark of old Pigafetta, that in fine weather there is in no part of the world scenery more lovely. At about four o'clock in the afternoon we anchored at Hale Cove, a port situated close to the northern outlet of the Patagonian Channels, and here for the last time we anchored in Patagonian waters. Rain awnings were now stowed away, top-gallant masts were sent up, boats were topped and lashed, and all other requisite arrangements were made for our final departure from the Magellan region, and for encountering the long heavy ocean swell which we were sure to find awaiting us to seaward.

I had a run on shore for a few hours before nightfall, and was much gratified at finding two plants which I had not previously met with in these channels. One was a tall branching fern of the genus *Alsophila*, whose long slender woody stems, rising obliquely from the ground to a height of six feet, were crowned with a magnificent spray of dark-green glossy fronds. The other was a shrub of creeping habit, probably of the family *Vacciniaceæ*, with smooth ovate-acute leaves resembling those of the laurel, and bearing clusters of an egg-shaped fruit. No flowering specimens were seen. The trunks of the large trees were clothed with the beautiful fronds of the delicate *Hymenophyllum cruentum*, which here grows in great abundance. On the morning of the 12th of April we bade a final adieu to the Patagonian Channels.

During our passage northwards along the Chilian coast, sea-birds of various kinds hovered round us. Of these our most constant companions were the Cape pigeons (*Dapteon Capensis*), albatrosses of two species (*Diomedea fuliginosa* and *D. Melanophrys*), a small storm-petrel (*Oceanites grallaria*), a Fulmar petrel (*Thallasæca glacialoides*), and a white-breasted petrel (*Œstrelata defippiana*). A brown skua (*Lestris antarctica*) appeared on the scene now and then, creating consternation among the smaller petrels.

We arrived at Talcahuano, one of the most interesting of the Chilian ports, on the morning of the 20th of April, and were surprised and grieved to hear that a severe epidemic of small pox prevailed at the town of Concepcion, some nine miles inland. The epidemic had begun in January, and we were informed by Mr. Elton, the British Vice-Consul, that since then no less than 1,500 deaths had occurred, the mortality of those attacked having been at the extraordinarily high rate of 90 per cent. Ominous rumours reaching us as to the epidemic having already extended to Talcahuano, our stay was wisely cut short, and the vessel was moved on to Valparaiso, and subsequently after a short stay to Coquimbo.

The passage from Valparaiso to Coquimbo occupied two days. As we were sitting at dinner on the evening of the 3rd of May, the officer of the watch reported that the ship was moving through patches of light-coloured stuff resembling shoal water. On going on deck, we saw wavy bands of straw-coloured water, about one hundred yards in length by twenty in width, which were plainly visible through the gloom of the night, the light-coloured patches having distinctly circumscribed margins, which showed out clearly against the surrounding dark water. At the same time, the sea in our wake was brilliantly phosphorescent. On plying the tow-net for a few minutes, I obtained a quantity of entomostracous crustaceans, and mingled with them a number of milk-coloured annelids, a species of *tomopteris*, about one-eighth of an inch in length. A fringe of lateral appendages bordered its long, slender body, from whose anterior extremity projected two long antennæ, curving gracefully upwards and backwards. There were fifteen pairs of parapodia, the ends of which were furnished with tufts of cirri, which acted as swimming paddles for propulsion.

Our stay at Coquimbo this season extended from the 4th of May to the 14th of June, having been somewhat prolonged owing to the occurrence of a case of small-pox on board. Our principal amusement consisted in shooting excursions after the golden plover, or "pachuros," as the Chilians call them. These birds frequent the sandy plains, which form an elevated table-land, fringing the bases of the coast range of hills. One of our shooting-grounds was on a rather bare plain, encircling the base of a pyramidal hill called the Pan de Azucar, which lay at a distance of about eight miles from Coquimbo. It was a great undulating plain of waste sandy ground, with stunted shrubs growing here and there, but not affording any cover. Walking over it was laborious, for the ground was almost everywhere riddled with the burrows of the *upucerthia*, a sort of ant-thrush, which seems to make extensive underground tunnels in search of insect larvæ. I obtained a specimen, and found its stomach crammed full of insects. This bird is smaller than the *U. dumetoria*, and has a much shorter bill; moreover, in flying, the secondary feathers, which are of a brick-red colour, are very conspicuous. Sometimes, when walking over a riddled patch of ground, one heard a curious half-smothered "took, took," not unlike the cry of a ctenomys; and on treading firmly over the place from whence the noise seemed to issue, no sound would be audible for a minute or two, when the same noise would go on again from a place a yard or so away. The bird, of course, had moved along, for the tunnels communicate so that it is able to travel underground over a considerable area. The burrows of the ctenomys are larger and otherwise different from those now referred to. At the time of our visit the birds were not at all shy, allowing one to approach within a few yards of them. These are gregarious—at least at this time of the year—moving in flocks from place to place over the sandy plain; and it was sometimes rather astonishing to see a flock suddenly emerge from a number of burrow openings, and rise on the wing from a bare sandy patch of ground, where a moment previously there had been no sign of life.

FISH-HOOKS OF UNION ISLANDERS (*see p.* 157).

CHAPTER VII.

TAHITI.—NASSAU ISLAND.—UNION GROUP.

WE sailed from Coquimbo on the 14th of June; and after a somewhat uneventful voyage across the Pacific, which was considerably prolonged by sounding operations, and which lasted fifty-three days, we arrived at Tahiti.

Tahiti was discovered, in the year 1606, by a Spanish exploring expedition, which set out from Peru under the command of Pedro Fernandez de Quiros, a navigator who had previously acquired some renown in Mendaña's exploration of the New Hebrides group. One of his vessels anchored for a short time off the island; but as a landing could not be safely effected by means of the ship's boats, an adventurous young Spanish sailor stripped and swam to the shore, where he was well received by the natives; so that the honour of having discovered Tahiti and communicated with the natives is justly due to this expedition. The name then given to the island by Quiros was "La Sagittaria."

In 1767 Tahiti was visited by an English exploring ship, the *Dolphin*, commanded by Captain Wallis, who, unaware of the visit of Quiros, and imagining himself to be the original discoverer, set up an English flag at Matavai Bay, took possession in the name of King George III., and named the island "King George's Island." The account given by Wallis of this visit (published in Hawksworth's "Voyages") is full of most curious and interesting information, and perhaps in this respect equals the well-known

WOMAN OF TAHITI (p. 147).

[To face p. 144.

narrative subsequently given to the world by our greatest navigator, Cook.

In the following year (1768), M. de Bougainville, of the French frigate *Boudeuse*, arrived independently at Tahiti, and, being in ignorance of the priority of Spanish and English explorers, gave to the island its third name, " Nouvelle Cythére."

On the 12th of April, 1769, the expedition sent out from England under the command of Captain Cook, to observe the transit of Venus, arrived at Tahiti, and anchored at Matavai Bay. To protect the astronomers from the intrusion of the natives, a small fort was erected on the north shore of the bay, and from this position the transit was observed on the 3rd of June of the same year.

Through a misconception of the native pronunciation, the name of the island, " Otaheite," was now brought into general use by Cook; and although it was clearly pointed out by Ellis—the missionary who wrote in 1832—that Tahiti was really the native name, the term "Otaheite," erroneously assigned by Cook, remained in use for many years subsequent to the time of Ellis.

About the beginning of the present century the English missionaries, who had previously established themselves in Western Polynesia, extended their labours to Tahiti, where they met with great success in their efforts to Christianize the inhabitants. They retained their influence over the natives until the year 1838, when two French Catholic missionaries arrived at Tahiti, with the intention of preaching the doctrines of their Church. They were not, however, allowed to obtain a footing on the island, but were forcibly expelled. They accordingly sought the protection of the French admiral, Du Petit Thouars, then commanding the frigate *La Venus* in the Pacific, and in the year 1842 he demanded satisfaction in the name of his government; and on Queen Pomare of Tahiti refusing to accede to his demand, he declared war against the Tahitians. The islanders were compelled to submit to the superior power of the French; and on coming to terms with their conquerors, it was agreed that the Tahitians should be allowed to retain their own form of government, but under a French Protectorate, and that freedom should be given to all persons to practise or preach whatever religion they pleased.

The Protectorate continued in force until July 1880, when, at the request of King Pomare V. and the native chiefs, the island and its dependencies were definitely ceded to France, so that they now form an integral part of the French Republic.

Our visit to Tahiti took place a few weeks after the French annexation. At daybreak on the 6th August, 1880, we sighted the south-eastern extremity of the island, and on closing the land skirted along its north-east coast, having thus on our port hand a magnificent panoramic view of this lovely island. As we passed abreast of some of the deeper valleys, we got glimpses of the famous Diadem Peak, which rises to an altitude of 7,000 feet. Its summit is jagged, so as to present a very distinct resemblance to a royal crown, and hence the name "crown" or "diadem" so aptly assigned. I was much struck by the resemblance which the scenery here presented to that of Madeira. The conformation of the volcanic peaks and ridges is very similar, but the vegetable covering is of a sap green tint, whereas that of Madeira, seen from a similar distance, appears of a bronze hue. At the distance from the land which the barrier reef obliged us to maintain, the belt of cocoa-nut trees which covers the shore platform was only visible through the telescope.

In the harbour of Papiété, where we anchored, were the French flagship *Victorieuse*, an ironclad, and a wooden sloop the *Dayot*. Here we had abundant evidence of the extreme care taken by the French Government to render the harbour and its surroundings as perfect in every respect as a lavish expenditure of money could effect. A solidly-built seawall, alongside of which merchant vessels were landing and shipping cargoes, fronted the settlement; a neatly-kept alameda, shaded by the luxuriant foliage of large Hibiscus trees, covered what was formerly the coral foreshore ;

broad streets running in at right angles to the wharf traversed the town ; a dockyard with spacious sheds and storehouses covered a low point jutting out on the northern side of the harbour ; and on a small picturesque island lying near the entrance was a gun battery nestling under tall cocoa-nut trees, and yet so constructed as not to detract from the romantic appearance of this beautiful and marvellous work of nature. The Tahitians still retain and deserve their old reputation for great amiability of disposition and extraordinary good humour. One is greeted by almost every native passed on the road with the friendly salutation "Yoronha" (meaning "good-day"), accompanied by a merry smile. Indeed, one cannot help being struck by the number of smiling, laughing faces seen at Tahiti, and to my mind there is nothing more characteristic of the Tahitians, as distinguished from all other islanders, than the ever smiling face reflecting genuine good humour for which there is no apparent cause. In many respects, however, they seem to have improved but little since the time of Wallis. Morality is still at a very low ebb, and the abuse of intoxicating drinks is an evil which seems likely in time to create sad havoc among them. For unfortunately, since the French annexation, spirit shops have been thrown open to the natives, although, under the old missionary *régime*, the possession of spirit of any kind was forbidden by the command of Queen Pomare. Of late years the population has been increasing, owing to the abolition of infanticide, which was formerly the fashion of the country.

The principal products of the island are cotton, sugar, cocoa-nuts, oranges, and vanilla. These articles are sent to San Francisco, with which port there is monthly communication by means of sailing vessels ; the cocoa-nut trade being perhaps in this, as in most other Polynesian islands, the most reliable industry. Usually the sun-dried kernel, known commercially as "Copra," is exported, but sometimes the nuts are shipped entire. The cultivation of the cocoa-nut tree does not require much trouble. The ripe nuts, if exposed on the ground in places where they are free from the depredations of land crabs and centipedes, readily germinate, and on being planted at distances of about five yards apart, they take root and require no further care. However, those planted in good soil give, as might be expected, an earlier and more productive yield than is afforded by trees grown in the poor land which usually adjoins the coral sea-beach. A cocoanut planted in average soil commences to bear fruit in about the fifth year of its existence, and from that time until it has attained the age of a hundred years,—when it is probably blown down,—it yields about twelve dozen nuts per annum.

A large trade is also done in oranges. They are packed up in boxes and shipped to San Francisco, and although about half of the cargo decays during the voyage, the profit derived from the other half is found to yield a sufficient remuneration.

The cultivation of vanilla—an introduced plant—requires great care, artificial aid being necessary to ensure the proper fertilization of the flowers. Samples of the cured bean which we saw seemed to be of very fair quality, and likely to command high prices in the European markets. These are now sold at Tahiti at the rate of 4s. per pound;—I should rather have said at the rate of a dollar a pound, because, strange to say, the currency at Tahiti is in Chilian silver dollars, whereas in Chili itself the currency is now almost entirely in paper, a hard dollar being very rarely encountered there.

The great war canoes are now things of the past, even the single outrigger canoes being only used by the poorer classes who cannot afford to buy boats of European build. The manufacture of pandanus mats and native cloth is also becoming obsolete, and it is said that the art of making these things is almost unknown to the rising generation. At present the favourite occupation of the natives, if we exclude dancing and lolling in the sunshine, is fishing; and a well-to-do native, who can afford to provide himself with an European fishing net, makes plenty of dollars to spend in drink and gay-coloured clothes. The fishermen

FISHERMAN OF TAHITI. { p. 148.

of the poorer class paddle out on the reef at night, and spear fish by torchlight as of old, so that every night the reefs outside the harbour are gaily illumined by these torch fires.

A few days after our arrival at Papiété, I made an excursion to Point Venus, the northern extremity of Matavai Bay, in company with a party of our surveying officers, who wished to take sights at this station for chronometric measurements of longitude; Point Venus being one of the secondary meridians to which longitudes in the Pacific are referred. The distance from Papiété is about six miles. We went in one of the ship's steam cutters, taking a small boat in tow; and after a somewhat hazardous passage among the reefs, which here form an irregular barrier along the coast, we reached Matavai Bay. We landed easily upon a smooth sloping beach of black volcanic sand—the detritus brought down from the hills by a neighbouring stream; and while the observers established themselves and their instruments on a grass plot near the base of the lighthouse, I took a stroll into the surrounding country, having at my disposal about five hours.

The French keeper of the lighthouse, who was most obliging, pointed out to us a square slab of coral rock imbedded in the ground, and bearing on its surface a deeply-chiselled groove. It was placed there some ten years ago, to replace one which had been fixed there in the year 1839 by Captain Wilkes, of the United States Exploring Expedition, and was, I understand, intended to assist in determining the exact position of a submerged coral knoll, some 100 yards from the shore, on which measurements were made for determining the rate of growth of the coral. We were also shown a large and venerable tamarind tree near the lighthouse, which is said to have been planted more than 100 years ago by our own great navigator, Cook. Cocoanuts, breadfruit, oranges, bananas, and mangoes, grew in great profusion, and the greatest and most good-natured eagerness was shown by the natives in putting these delicious fruits at our disposal.

We also saw a large extent of cleared land devoted to the

cultivation of cotton plants, and near one of the native huts vanilla was growing successfully.

Nothing could exceed the civility of the natives in pressing food upon us, and in furnishing us with information. They know very little English, but many of them speak French, which the rising generation are taught in the government schools.

In one of the larger and more pretentious style of native huts, apparently that of a district chief, we read a proclamation, printed in French and Tahitian on opposite columns, announcing to the inhabitants the definitive annexation of the island and its dependencies; and, after pointing out in glowing colours the great advantages accruing to the natives from the complete establishment of French rule, it wound up with, "*Vive la France. Vive Tahiti.*"

One is much struck by the great scarcity of birds in Tahiti. There are, in fact, not more than six species of indigenous birds, and of these an average day's walk will only afford examples of the swallow; although in the mountain valleys, paroquets, pigeons, and kingfishers are met with, though rarely.

In the course of an afternoon's walk about the environs of Papiété, we were accosted by a portly native dressed in European clothes, who, sitting in a four-wheeled buggy, and accompanied by three native attendants, pulled up abreast of us. At his feet he had a large demijohn of wine, from which he had evidently been imbibing freely, for by way of salutation he greeted us with a volley of most disgusting oaths and imprecations. This seemed to be all the English he was acquainted with. A bystander informed us that the name of this native gentleman was "Tamitao," and that he was no less a personage than the brother of King Pomare V., the present monarch. The latter now only possesses a nominal sovereignty; for on ceding his possessions to the French, he relinquished all monarchical authority, and receives instead an annual stipend of 8,000 dollars, a pension which, we were told, would not be continued to his heir. It is said but

I know not with what truth, that one of the principal reasons which induced him to sell his birthright was a desire to exclude from the succession his nominal son, whom he believes to be illegitimate. Our conference with the royal brother was not an agreeable one, for he presently gathered up the reins, and amid a volley of imprecations delivered in the coarsest style of Billingsgate English, this tatterdemalion prince of an ancient dynasty flogged his horses into a gallop, and rattled away on his drunken career.

On the evening before our departure we were present at a ball which was given at the royal palace by the French inhabitants of Tahiti. It was intended to celebrate the annexation of the island by France, and was supposed to be the occasion for mutual congratulations between King Pomare and his chiefs on the one hand, and the Governor and French Admiral on the other. Pomare was attired in a gorgeous dress richly embroidered with gold lace, and the French officials appeared in full dress. The native chiefs were, however, very shabbily turned out in faded European clothes, and although for the most part very fine men, yet they looked very much as if they were ashamed of themselves, and were by no means at their ease in the richly-decorated ball-room. Among the quasi chiefs was "Paofai," an old gentleman who did duty as our washerman, wearing a black alpaca monkey-jacket, and carrying under his arm a large white sun-helmet, which he seemingly thought a becoming addition to his otherwise somewhat incongruous attire. He and his *confrères* would have shown to much more advantage in their ordinary native costume. Supper began about midnight, and it was then, and not till then, that the royal family and chiefs seemed to flourish in their proper element, the quantity of food and drink which they stowed away in their huge carcases being something prodigious.

A few days before the close of our visit to Tahiti, I received, through the kindness of Monsieur Parrayon, captain of the French man-of-war *Dayot*, a large coral of the Fungia group, which had just been removed from the bottom of his ship as the copper was being cleaned by native divers. The occurrence is interesting as illustrating the rapidity of the growth of coral in these waters There was the following history:—The *Dayot* had entered the tropical waters of the South Pacific about seven months previously, having come directly from the coast of Chili. She visited some of the islands, but made no long stay in harbour until she reached Manga Reva (Gambier Islands), where she remained for two months in the still waters of a coral basin. On entering this basin, she touched the reef slightly, and without sustaining any damage. From Manga Reva she sailed to Tahiti, where she arrived about the same time as the *Alert*.

Several specimens of living coral were found attached to the copper sheathing, that which I received being the largest. It was discoidal in shape, with its upper and under surfaces respectively convex and concave, and near the centre of the under surface there was a scar, where the pedicle by which it was attached to the copper sheathing appeared to have been broken through. The disc measured nine inches in diameter, and the weight of the specimen, when half dry, was two pounds fourteen ounces. On examining the under surface, another disc, three and three-quarter inches in diameter, was visible, partly embedded in the more recent coral growth. Of this old disc about one-sixth part was dead and uncovered by new coral, and was stained of a deep blue colour from contact with the copper, while the outline of the rest of this old disc was plainly discernible, although partially covered in by plates of new coral.

It is probable that on touching the reef at Manga Reva nine weeks previously, a young Fungia was jammed against the copper, became attached, and subsequently grew until it attained its present dimensions.

About midday of the 27th August we arrived off Nassau Island, in latitude 11° 31' S., longitude 165° 25' W. It is of coral formation, about half a mile long by a quarter of a mile broad, and somewhat elliptical in general outline. It was thickly wooded with tall screw pines, rising from a scrub of matted brushwood, and at the northern end of the island some cocoa-nuts were seen. It was discovered in the year 1835 by an American whale-ship, the *Nassau*, from which circumstance it derives its name. There were then no inhabitants on the island.

When about three miles off we lay to and sounded, getting bottom at 1,000 fathoms, on coral sand. At the same time a party of us started off in a whale boat to land, but this we soon found to be no easy matter, for the island was encircled by a broad fringing reef, on the sharp outer edge of which the surf everywhere broke heavily. Over our heads were flying and screaming great numbers of seabirds, among which I noticed a dusky brown tern with a white forehead patch, and a large brown gannet, of both of which I obtained specimens.

While we were vainly looking out for a landing-place, a white man, accompanied by two Polynesians, launched a small outrigger canoe from the reef edge, and paddled out to us. From the white man we learned that the island belonged to a Mr. Halicott, an American gentleman, for whom he had been acting as care-taker for the previous five years, and that he and his native assistants were engaged in planting cocoa-nuts, and hoped in time to do a remunerative trade in copra. There were, he said, only three or four trees bearing nuts, and the bread-fruit did not grow on the island. The present population amounted to six, viz.—the white man and his wife, and two natives from Danger Islands, with their wives. As for live stock, they had only two dogs and two pigs, and regarding the latter our informant remarked, with much concern, that they were not in a condition to multiply. For supplies of food, excepting fish, which was of course abundant, he depended on a sailing vessel, which visited the island once a year, bringing rice and meal. Water, fortunately, was plentiful.

Continuing on our course, on the following morning (August 28th), we sighted the Tema Reef, in latitude 10° 7′ S., longitude

165° 32·5′ W., and steaming up to and around it, we made a series of soundings, which occupied our surveyors for half the day. The reef, a submerged one, is indicated by a circular patch of breakers about a quarter of a mile in circumference, from one part of which a long tapering line of surf extends in a north-east direction, making the entire affair have some resemblance in outline to a tadpole. A cloud of white spray overhung this great mass of seething water, and the frightful tumble and confusion of the crests of the breakers as they uprose in pyramids twenty feet in height, made one shudder to think of the consequences to an ill-fated vessel striking on this reef. Its position is given correctly on the old charts.

On the same evening we passed about four miles to the northward of the Danger Islands, a low coral group, which is found to be about six miles to the eastward of the position assigned to it on the charts on the authority of the Tuscarora (U. S.) Expedition.

In the forenoon of the 3rd September we sighted Fakaata, or Bowditch Island, and some hours later Nukunono, which lies in latitude 9° 24′ S., longitude 171° 27′ W. These two islands, with Oatafu, which lies further to the westward, constitute the Union Group. They are all low lagoon-islands. At 3.30 p.m., when abreast of Nukunono, we altered course and stood in towards the land, and when about three miles off observed an outrigger canoe with three men in it, paddling towards us. The crew consisted of one white man and two Polynesian natives. The former came on board, and proved to be a Portuguese, in a very attenuated condition, and sadly in want of provisions. He told us in broken English that he had lived on the island for sixteen years, that he was the only white man there, and that the native population amounted to eighty. A conspicuous white building which we had noticed on the island was, he informed us, a church, presided over by a native missionary teacher, there being at present no clergyman on the island. He besought us to give some biscuit, salt meat, and nails, for which he tendered payment in dollars, which was of course refused ; but his heart was gladdened by a free gift of the stores he required, as well as other useful articles. He said that he very rarely saw any vessels—not more than once in ten months —and that no "labour ships" visited the island. The latter are small vessels whose owners make a living by conveying Polynesian natives to the Australian colonies, where they are employed as labourers, under—usually—a three years' contract.

The only native production was "copra," which was taken away by trading vessels that made visits at long intervals.

Fish were at times abundant, and they had a good many pigs, which were allowed to run wild. The natives, he said, were a very friendly, well-disposed people, of whom we saw two very promising examples in the canoe alongside.

We were obliged to get under way after only half an hour's stay, when our Portuguese friend shoved off, heavily laden with presents, and bidding us an affectionate farewell.

On the following morning (September 4th) we reached Oatáfu, the most westerly island of the group, and the ship was hove to at about three miles distance from that part of the island where the native settlement is situated. A boat was then sent in, from which a party landed, but not without some difficulty, it being found necessary to anchor the boat outside the line of breakers, and obtain the services of a native canoe to bring us through the surf.

We were received by the natives with every demonstration of good-will, and were at once conducted to the house of the native missionary teacher, who seemed to a great extent to occupy the position of a chief. We found the worthy old gentleman seated on a mat in the corner of his hut, a position from which he never stirred during the time of our visit. After drinking cocoa-nut milk, and exchanging some ceremonious remarks with the teacher through the imperfect medium of a native interpreter, we extricated ourselves from the crowd of natives that hemmed us in, and started on a stroll of inspection through the settlement.

The men are fine specimens of the Polynesian race, well-built, and with frank, open countenances; but the women are much inferior to them, both in good looks, and, as it seemed to me, in manners.

A great number of both sexes were affected with a rather unsightly skin-disease, evidently of a parasitic character, which they call "peeter." It begins on the chest and shoulders in small circular patches somewhat resembling "ringworm," and eventually extends over the entire cutaneous surface, causing desquamation of the cuticle, and giving rise to a very distressing itching. When the disease has become well established, the skin exhibits grooves of the "snail-track" pattern, which intersect each other in various directions; so that on examining at a few yards distance a man who is extensively diseased, he seems at first sight as if covered with artificial cicatrices, arranged so as to represent some hieroglyphic device. They possess no remedy for this disease, and were therefore extremely anxious to obtain from us some treatment for it. In other respects they seem to be a very healthy people.

We crossed the narrow strip of land—only a few hundred yards wide—on which lies the settlement, and then found ourselves on the margin of an extensive lagoon, on the smooth sandy beach of which outrigger canoes in great numbers were hauled up. The island is an irregular atoll, that portion on which we were being continuous for about three-fifths of the circle, while the remaining portion was made up by a straggling chain of islets.

During our subsequent stroll through the settlement, I obtained some information from an intelligent native who spoke a little English, and seemed to be one of the principal people. He seemed to be very proud of his small stock of knowledge concerning "Britannia," as he called Great Britain, and was very particular in explaining that he was a Protestant, and disapproved strongly of Catholicism, which he looked on as the height of infamy. He was therefore surprised and much crestfallen at hearing that *all* Englishmen were not Protestants.

TOTOONGA VALLEY, OVALAU, FIJI.

[To face p. 156.

We were unable to obtain many curiosities in the way of native implements, as according to the calendar of the island it was the Sabbath day, and was as such strictly observed; although with us, keeping eastern time and longitude, it was of course a Saturday. However, by a judicious distribution of a few plugs of tobacco, which I emphatically called "presents," and by bestowing on my native friend a surgical lancet, which he was very anxious to possess, I received—also as " presents"—a few implements, viz., a large wooden shark-hook with rope snooding made of cocoanut fibres, a small fish-hook, the stem of which was made of pearl shell and the hook of turtle shell, a fish-hook made of cocoanut husk, neatly carved, and the blade of an old native adze fashioned out of a clamshell. I was very glad to get these articles, for since the introduction of iron tools the ancient stone and shell implements have been thrown away and lost sight of, so that it is now exceedingly difficult to procure any of them. No weapons of any kind are used, and the spear is not used even for fishing. I entered one of the better class of native huts, and found it clean and neatly arranged ; and as in the hut of the missionary teacher, pictures cut from the London illustrated papers were stuck against the walls, and pointed out to us as objects of special pride. The entire population at this time numbered 260, and was presided over until a few weeks prior to our visit by a king. The late monarch, however, having shown himself to be a good-for-nothing sort of person, was deposed by his subjects, who now get on very well without any form of government excepting that of the missionaries.

There was one white man living on the island, a Scotchman named Adam Mayne, who collects cocoanut-oil on behalf of the firm of Henderson and Macfarlane, of Auckland. He receives supplies every three months or thereabouts from a trading vessel ; but as the latter was now three months overdue, he was very glad to receive from us a present of biscuit and medical stores.

The Christianizing of the island has been undertaken by the

London Missionary Society, who send at long intervals a missionary clergyman to inspect the settlement, and confer with their delegate, the native missionary.

The natural products are very limited, consisting solely of cocoanuts and fish. The latter commodity abounds. Pearl shell is obtained, but not in sufficient quantities to be an article of commerce.

Adam Mayne told us that sharks were very numerous, and were caught with the hook and line; but no case had ever occurred of a native being injured by them, although they were accustomed to swim in the open sea outside the reef, a fact of which we ourselves had ocular proof. At the same time, curiously enough, many instances had occurred at the Windward Islands, Nukunono and Fakaata, of natives being taken down by sharks. Turtle are ocasionally caught, and of these the shell of the carapace is used for making hooks for fishing, which native-made hooks are, by-the-bye, preferred to our English ones. Indeed, they say that the fish will not take our metal hooks at all.

On the afternoon of the same day (September 4th) we again got under way, and continued on our course to the westward, fixing the positions of islands and taking negative soundings frequently. On the 13th of September we obtained soundings on the Lalla Rookh bank in latitude 13° 5' S., longitude 175° 26' W., the depth ranging from twelve to seventeen fathoms. With the snap-lead a sample of the bottom was brought up, consisting of a lump of dead coral incrusted with red nullipores, and riddled in all directions by the borings of annelids,

CHAPTER VIII.

FIJI AND TONGA.

THE harbour of Levuka, in which we anchored on the 18th of September, is situated on the north-east side of the island of Ovalau, and from its central position in the Fiji Group has for several years been the principal seat of commercial activity and the favourite anchorage for men-of-war. Since the annexation in 1875, Levuka has been the seat of government for the colony, and the official residence of the High Commissioner for the Pacific. During our stay in harbour the ship was refitted and reprovisioned, and our boats were occupied in making some additions to the survey of the port.

A few days after our arrival I received a visit from the youngest son of the redoubted King Cacobau, a fine-looking man, twenty-three years old, whose proper designation is the "Ratu Joseph Celua" ("Ratu" meaning prince), but who is more generally known in Fiji as "Ratu Joe." It seems that soon after we had anchored, he came on board accompanied by some other native sight-seers, and as I had then shown him some slight civility, he now came to express his gratitude by presenting me with a large mat, made from the split leaves of the screw-pine. He surprised us all by speaking exceedingly good English, and possessing an intimate knowledge of the ways and manners of civilized life. It appears that when Fiji was ceded to Great Britain in 1875, he was taken to Sydney, in H.M.S. *Dido*, to be educated, and accordingly spent three years at the university there. There was no topic of general interest on which he did not possess a fair amount of knowledge. He wore his hair in the fashion of the country, *i.e.* in a mop frizzled out to an immense size, and in other respects he was got up as a native chief of distinction. He spoke favourably of British rule, although, as we were otherwise informed, he himself had recently acquired a practical experience of the unpleasant consequences attending the commission of an indictable offence, in having to undergo a sentence of three months' hard labour.

On the 25th of September a party of us made an excursion in one of the ship's steam-cutters to Bau, the old native capital of the Fiji Group. We started from Levuka harbour at nine o'clock in the morning, accompanied by our friend the Ratu Joe, who most kindly and hospitably volunteered to pilot us over, and to entertain us in his hut at Bau.

We steamed along in smooth water inside the barrier reef which protects the S. E. side of Ovalau for about three miles, when we passed out into the open sea through a narrow opening in the reef. We then steamed for about five miles through deep water, until we entered an intricate system of channels which wind among the submerged reefs extending across the Strait between Ovalau and Viti Levu. The distance from Levuka to Bau is about twenty-four miles, and after a pleasant passage of five hours we reached our destination and anchored the boat in smooth water at about forty yards from the shore. After depositing our baggage in Joe's hut, we went in a body to pay our respects to King Cacobau the "Vunivalu" (kingly title meaning the " Root of War "), to whom we were formally introduced by Joe, the latter also acting as interpreter, for Cacobau does not speak English at all. We were received in a small smoky hut, in which the aged monarch spends most of his time during this, the cold, season of Fiji. He seemed to be a feeble old man, aged about seventy, and almost entirely blind, yet evidently possessing

KING CACOBAU OF FIJI (*on right*), WIFE, AND RATU JOE (*on left*).

[*To face p.* 160.

his mental faculties in full vigour, for he put to us many shrewd questions concerning the work of our ship, and then, after a pause, during which he seemed to be pondering over her name, asked if we could give him some information regarding her previous work of exploration in the Arctic regions. On this subject he seemed to take much interest, and like many other people, did not fail to put the rather puzzling question as to what could be the use of exploring the uninhabited and inhospitable polar regions. During the conference he sat cross-legged on a large mat, crouching over a smoky wood fire. His hair was grey, and his upper teeth seemed to be gone. From time to time messengers came into the hut, who after assuming a respectful posture on the floor, asked for his orders concerning various municipal affairs. To these functionaries his replies were short, sharp, and decisive, and were acted upon with such alacrity that it was fully evident to us that he still retains no small part of his former control over his subjects.*

It happened, by chance, that on the day of our arrival at Bau, a feast was to be given by Cacobau to a tribe of natives who had just brought to him a tribute offering, consisting of eighteen large green turtle. As we were landing we saw the feast, which consisted of eight good-sized pigs roasted whole, and several huge piles of yams, spread out on a sort of common outside the enclosure of the native town; but on the king being apprised of our visit, he gave orders that the feast was to be transferred inside the town palisades, and it was accordingly removed and spread out on the grass in front of the small hut wherein he received us. Then, at a signal from him, conveyed in the form of a fierce growl delivered from his seat by the fire, the members of the stranger tribe assembled round the roasted pigs, which were quickly cut up into joints, and then carried by certain representatives of the tribe into various huts, to be there quietly consumed. During all this time the large trough-shaped wooden drums, called " Lalis,"

---

* The news of Cacobau's death has just reached England (April 1883). "Cacobau" is pronounced " Thackombow."

were being vigorously sounded to summon the people to the feast. Subsequently the old king shook himself together, came out from the hut, and standing in the open surrounded by a large and picturesque assemblage of his subjects, and assisted by his three big sons, distributed large rolls of "tapa" (native cloth made from the inner bark of the paper mulberry) to several leading personages of the strange tribe. These presents were valuable, for some of these pieces of "tapa" measured eighty yards in length by about one yard in width.

About two months before the time of our visit, there had been a great fire at Bau, which destroyed and reduced to ashes about one-third of the town, and compelled some of the inhabitants to move over to the main island of Viti Levu. Among the buildings destroyed by this fire was the great Bure Kalou, or native temple, where even so recently as thirty years ago the great cannibal feasts used to take place. Close to one angle of the square mass of earthwork on which the temple was raised, we saw a stone slab projecting from the ground in a nearly upright position. This was one of the famous stones—incorrectly styled "sacrificial" against which the unfortunate people who were to be cooked for "bakola" (human meat) had their brains dashed out. This interesting relic of cannibalism has not escaped the ravages of modern vandalism, numerous fragments having been chipped off as curios. Indeed, we were told that quite recently one of the white traders of Levuka had been endeavouring to carry off this stone altogether, with a view to making money by exhibiting it at Sydney and such places.

We saw another and somewhat similar stone near the water side, and close to the remains of the Bure Kalou of the tribe of fishermen, where the bodies of prisoners of war, brought in by the "Lasikaus," or fishermen, were landed and mutilated. The upright slab was worn quite smooth on one side, presumably by the friction of human heads.

Certain honeycombed slabs of coral here formed a pavement

of a few square yards in extent, and until recently it was usual to find human teeth imbedded in the pores of the coral. They have probably all been removed by curiosity hunters, for we looked in vain for a single specimen.

In a few years hence the old Fijian double canoe (consisting of two canoes placed side by side, and connected by a bridge) will be seen no more; but we were lucky in having an opportunity of seeing one good specimen at Bau. It was hauled up on a slip beneath a large thatched shed, and although by no means one of the largest of its kind, yet it greatly exceeded my expectations. The depth of hold was about five feet, so that standing on the bottom of either canoe, my neck was just on a level with the edge of the hatch, and the total length of each canoe was 72 feet; but what most surprised me was the enormous size of the mast, which lay alongside the vessel. It was about the size of the *Alert's* spanker boom. This canoe was intended to carry 250 men, and I have no doubt it would hold that number.

Single outrigger canoes are still largely used. We saw several in course of construction on the small recessed slips which indented the sea-wall of the island.

The genuine old native implements and weapons are now getting very scarce, the demand for these articles in Europe having created a trade which has almost exhausted the supplies of the country. I inquired for stone adzes, and, after some difficulty, obtained one, for which I paid a shilling; but on subsequently groping for myself amongst the ruins of the burnt huts, I succeeded in finding several perfect and imperfect specimens.

In the evening we witnessed the ceremony of *angona* drinking in the king's state residence, where our friend the Ratu Joe presided on this occasion instead of his father. The performance began with a long monotonous chant, which was maintained alternately by an elderly man, who seemed to hold the office of master of the ceremonies, and by a body of elderly men, amounting to forty or fifty, who squatted close together on the floor. In the meantime some boys were engaged in a gloomy corner of the hut in chewing the angona root, and in spitting the pulpy masticated mouthfuls of fibre into the large wooden bowl which was destined to contain the liquor. Suddenly the chant ended with a simultaneous and abrupt clapping of hands on the part of the singers; and now the angona bowl was brought forward into the clear space in the centre of the room, water was poured over the chewed pulp, and finally the liquor was rudely strained by sponging it up with a handful of hibiscus fibre, and filling the drinking cup with the squeezed contents. Great respect was throughout shown to Joe, the presiding chief; and on his emptying the bowl of angona, which was handed to him solemnly by the cupbearer, all the natives exclaimed in a loud voice, "*Amadtha*" (meaning, "It is emptied"). Subsequently similar draughts were politely handed to each of us guests by the official cupbearer, but notwithstanding the historic interest attaching to this famous South Sea beverage, and the impression made on us by the great concourse of native dignitaries gathered together in solemn awe, few of us were inclined to imitate the chief's example and do justice to the flowing bowl.

However, we tasted it, and thought it rather nasty, giving one the idea of a mixture of pepper and soapsuds.

The Fijians spoke very favourably of British rule, and it would seem that the Governor (Sir Arthur Gordon) had very wisely and successfully adopted the policy of retaining, so far as was practicable, the old native laws, only modifying them as much as was necessary for the establishment of a reasonable degree of civilization. Thus the old feudal power of the chiefs has been retained, and in many instances those among them who were well-behaved, and displayed a suitable amount of administrative ability, have been invested with magisterial power over the districts to which they belong.

We slept for the night in Joe's hut, stretching ourselves out on the mats which covered the floor, and excepting a little trouble from mosquitoes, were comfortable enough. Our return journey to Levuka on the following evening was accomplished without any incident worthy of note.

Some days later, I took part in a walking excursion across the island of Ovalau, accompanied by Mr. Parr, an English gentleman residing in the colony and the owner of a large plantation in the Rewa River district of Viti Levu, and under the guidance of two natives, who carried our small parcels of baggage. Starting from Levuka on the morning of the 30th of September, we proceeded up the Totoonga Valley, which stretches inland from the back of the settlement, and after about two hours' hard walking, discovered that our guides had lost their way, and had brought us up to the summit of a thickly-wooded conical hill. Here, however, we were compensated for our disappointment by finding several graves of the Kaicolos, an old hill-inhabiting tribe of Fijians, who for a long time held out against the aggressive policy of Cacobau, and struggled vainly to maintain their independence.

We had now to descend from this hill to the main valley below, from whence our guides made a fresh departure, by means of which we were enabled, after a stiffish climb up the face of a rather steep hillside, to attain a ridge 1,700 feet high, which separates the watersheds of the east and west sides of the island. After a brief stay here, we descended the other side by a steep and almost obliterated track for about three hours more, when we reached Livoni, the site of an old Kaicolo stronghold. Here, amid the ruins of the town, we found a farmhouse of recent construction, the property of a Mr. McCorkill, who had obtained a three years' lease of the land, and was about to try his hand at stock-farming. He had two hundred head of cattle, for which he obtained a ready sale at Levuka, but the difficulties of transit were considerable, and he did not seem hopeful as to the success of his enterprise. He was, moreover, apprehensive that his house, which was built close to the bank of a mountain torrent, was on a rather insecure site, and that the next heavy flood in the rainy season would sweep away all his household belongings.

He pointed out close to his own house the characteristic raised foundations of an old native temple (Bure Kalou), and told us that his workmen, in clearing the ground for his garden and paddock, frequently turned up human skulls and other bones. He also very kindly promised to send me some Kaicolo crania on the first opportunity; a promise which he amply redeemed some weeks later by presenting me with two excellent specimens.

After a short stay in his house, and refreshed by a drink of delicious milk, we continued our walk down this valley, following the course of the river, which, as we advanced, rapidly increased in size, and pursued so sinuous a course that we were obliged to cross and recross it five or six times before we arrived at Burĕta —a native village on the west side of Ovalau—which we gained just before nightfall. A further walk of about a mile brought us to the residence of a friend of Mr. Parr's (Captain Morne), a retired merchant captain, and now the owner of a large estate, by whom we were most hospitably entertained and lodged for the night.

This gentleman was doing a large trade in pine-apples, of which he has about twenty acres under cultivation. He sends the produce periodically to Sydney by steamer, packed in wooden boxes, where they fetch about 20s. per dozen. On the following morning we spent some hours in strolling about the estate, and in a creek near the outlet of the Livoni River we saw the curious mud-fish *Periophthalmus* jumping about on the moist beach in the ludicrous manner which has been so well described by Mr. Moseley in his "Notes of a Naturalist," its pectoral fins being used for terrestrial progression.

We made the return journey by the south side of the island, Captain Morne very considerately sending us on in one of his boats as far as the south-west extreme of Ovalau, from whence a three hours' walk along the seashore brought us back to Levuka.

On the morning of the 11th of October we got under way from Levuka, and spent the day in steaming over to Suva, a commodious harbour, situated on the south-east side of Viti Levu, where it was our intention to coal ship from a stationary hulk which supplies the steamers plying between Sydney and the Fijian ports. It is said that Suva, from the accommodation which its harbour affords, and from its position on an easily accessible part of the largest island of the group, is destined to become the seat of government and the future capital of Fiji; but at the time of our visit the settlement was very insignificant, and looked a mere speck in the great extent of wooded land which seemed from our anchorage to spread before us in a vast semicircle.

Leaving the ship on the morning of the following day, I started for a walk on shore, taking my gun, insect bottle, and collecting boxes. I at first directed my steps inland along the main road, and for about three miles proceeded over an upland plain of undulating land, thickly covered with tall reeds, and showing here and there patches of brush in the wet hollows. In the last-mentioned localities a good many birds, chiefly parrots, were to be heard screaming shrilly, but owing to the denseness of the foliage, few were visible.

In the afternoon I returned to the settlement, and from thence proceeded along the beach towards the low point which shelters the harbour from the north-east winds. Here, as the tide fell and laid bare broad flats of mud and coral, several flocks of sandpipers, whose general plumage resembled that of the snipe, came in from seaward, settled, and commenced to feed. A brace of duck and a large grey tern were the only other birds seen.

We learned that the country in the immediate vicinity of Suva was exceedingly unproductive. The soil was very thin, and the sub-soil was a stiff pasty clay of a grey colour—in places resembling soapstone—and so impervious to drainage as to render all attempts at agriculture hitherto abortive.

We left Suva on October 13th, and sailed for Tongatabu,

searching on the way for certain reefs and banks of doubtful existence, which it was desirable on proper evidence to expunge from the charts.

During the traverses which we made in sounding for these, I had a good opportunity of plying the tow-net. Among the forms thus obtained were a minute conferva, a brilliantly phosphorescent pyrosoma, measuring three inches in length, and a small shell-less pteropod, the *Eurybia gaudichaudi*. A specimen of the latter, which I examined in a glass trough, measured one-twelfth of an inch across the body. After giving it about half-an-hour's rest, it protruded its epipodia and tentacles, and commenced to swim about vigorously. The caudal portion of the body was furnished with cilia, and the digestive organs presented the appearance of a dark-red opaque mass, surrounded by a transparent envelope of a gelatinous consistency, whose surface exhibited a reticulated structure.

Tongatabu, Friendly Islands, 8th to 18th of November.—The credit of discovering the Tonga Islands rests with Tasman, who saw them on the 20th of January, 1643, and subsequently anchored his ship on the north-west side of the large island, Tongatabu. Cook saw the islands during his second voyage in October 1773, and on his third voyage in 1777 he made a stay of three months at the group, for more than a month of which time he was anchored at Tongatabu, the principal and most southward island of the group. The islands were subsequently visited by D'Entrecasteau, Maurelle (1781), Lieutenant Bligh of the *Bounty*, Captain Edwards of the *Pandora* (1791), and other explorers of the eighteenth century.

In the month of November 1806, an English privateer, the *Port-au-Prince*, arrived at Lifonga, one of the Hapai Islands, where the ship was seized by the natives, and most of the crew massacred. Among the few whose lives were spared was a young man named Mariner, who acquired the friendship of the chief, Finow, and lived peacefully with the natives for the space of four years, accumulating during that time a vast amount of information concerning their manners and habits. Mariner's narrative was subsequently published in a book written by Dr. John Martin, which is still regarded as the standard work on the Tonga Islands.

The Wesleyan missionaries established themselves here in the year 1822, and were well received; and some years subsequently a French Roman Catholic mission was also successfully established. At the time of our visit the entire population of the Tonga Islands, including Tongatabu, Hapai, and Vavau, amounted to 25,000, while that of Tongatabu alone was 12,000. Of the latter number, 8,000 belonged to the Wesleyan, and 4,000 to the Catholic, Church.

We anchored in the harbour of Tongatabu, off the town of Nukualofa, on the 8th of November, at about midday. The anchorage looked very bare indeed, there being only one vessel beside ours, a merchant barque belonging to Godeffroy and Co., of Hamburg, the well-known South Sea Island traders.

The most striking objects on shore, as viewed from our position in the anchorage, were the Wesleyan Church—an old dilapidated wooden building crowning the summit of a round topped hill, about sixty feet high, and said to be the highest point on the island—and the king's palace, a very neat-looking villa-edifice abounding in plate-glass windows, and surrounded by a low wall, in which remained two breaches, intended for the reception of massive iron gates, which, through a series of untoward circumstances, are not likely to be ever placed in position. It appears that some time ago the king gave a *carte blanche* order for two pairs of gates to be sent out from England, and when, after a long series of delays, owing to mistakes in the shipping arrangements, they at length reached Tongatabu, he was rather unpleasantly surprised to find that the excessive charges for freightage had run up the entire cost to the sum of £800. They were then found to be so large and massive as to be quite unsuited for the purpose for which they were intended, so they were thrown down on the ground in a disjointed condition, where they now lie, rusting and half-buried in weeds. Somewhat in the rear of the royal palace is seen a rather imposing private dwelling-house, the residence of Mr. Baker, formerly a Wesleyan minister, and now the political prime minister of the kingdom.

In the afternoon some of us walked out to see the old fortified town of Bea, which is distant from Nukualofa about four miles in a southerly direction, and is reached by a very good cart-road. This town—or, more properly speaking, village, for it is now but thinly populated—was formerly the stronghold of a party of Tongans, who objected to the introduction of Christianity, and were consequently obliged to defend themselves against the followers of the Wesleyan missionaries. The village is encircled by a rampart and moat, which have for many years past been allowed to go to decay, so that the moat is now partly obliterated with weeds and rubbish, and the strong palisades, which in former times added considerably to the defensive strength of the ramparts, have almost entirely disappeared.

As we entered the village by a cutting which pierced the ramparts on the north side, we saw the spot where Captain Croker, of H.M.S. *Favourite*, was shot down in 1848, when heading an armed party of bluejackets, with whom he was assisting the missionary party in an attack upon the irreconcilables. It seems to have been altogether a most disastrous and ill-advised undertaking, and of its effects some traces still remain in an assumption of physical superiority over their white fellow-creatures, which may be seen among some of the Tongans.

Nowhere have I seen the cocoanut-trees growing in such luxuriance as at Tongatabu. Here they grow over the whole interior of the island, as well as near the sea-shore; a circumstance which may be attributed to the mean level of the island being only a few feet above high-water mark, and to the coral subsoil extending over the entire island. The latter is everywhere penetrated to a greater or less degree by the sea-water, as evidenced by the brackish water which is reached on sinking a well to a depth of two or three yards.

We made shooting excursions for several miles to the eastward and westward of Nukualofa, and on one of the latter we met with an intelligent native, who excited in us hopes of obtaining some good duck-shooting, and undertook to bring us to the right place. Under his guidance we reached a series of extensive salt-water lagoons, which seemed likely places enough. However, on this occasion he proved to be a false prophet; and as he was anxious to make amends for our disappointment, he induced us to follow him into the bush in quest of pigeons. Of these, on reaching a thick part of the forest, we heard a good many; but owing to the dense foliage of the shrubs, which obscured our view aloft, we got very few glimpses of the birds, which, as a rule, keep to the summits of the tallest trees. Nevertheless, by dint of "cooing," to evoke responses from the birds and thus ascertain their whereabouts, we at length succeeded in shooting a good specimen of the great " fruit pigeon."

Our guide, "Davita," was most elaborately tattooed from the waist to the knees. He was a well-to-do man, and the chief of a district; and was also, as he informed us, a member of the "royal guard," whose duty it is to act as sentries in front of the door of the king's palace. "Davita" accompanied us back to the town, and after receiving his honorarium and bidding us good-bye, he went off to procure his military uniform, and subsequently, as we walked by the palace on our way to the boat, we saw our friend in full toggery doing sentry. He was a very fine man, but did not look half so well in a soldier's uniform as in his native garb, which consisted simply of a waistcloth, above and below which appeared the margins of his beautiful blue tattooing.

There are evidences of recent elevation of the land both to the eastward and westward of Nukualofa. I noticed above high-water mark extensive flats of almost barren land, composed of level patches of coral, the interstices of which were gradually getting filled up with coral detritus, and the decayed remains of stunted plants. The mangrove bushes here seemed with difficulty to eke out an existence, their roots being no longer bathed in seawater; but on the other hand a few Ivi trees (*Aleurites sp?*) had gained a footing. An amazing quantity of crabs of the genus *Gelasimus* inhabit these desolate flats, where they will have an opportunity of gradually adapting themselves to a terrestrial existence. I noticed two species, one of which was covered with a hairy brown integument, and was rather sluggish in its movements, waddling awkwardly into its burrow while it held aloft one of its hands in a most ridiculous fashion. The other was a smaller crab, with a greenish body, and having one of its pincer-claws, which was of a brilliant orange colour, of a huge size compared with its fellow. Probably, after the lapse of a few years, these flats will form part of the general forest land, when the crabs may undergo further adaptive changes.

We saw little of King George during our stay, as being now advanced in years he leads a retired life, passing his days in a small room in the rear of the palace, and only coming out of doors after sunset for a little airing. However, his grandson, "Wellington Gnu," who is governor of Nukualofa, and heir presumptive to the throne, was most civil and obliging. He is a remarkably fine-looking man, being six feet two inches in height, and stout in proportion; his face beams with amiability and intelligence; and he possesses all the manners and bearing of a polished gentleman. Although the lineal heir to the throne by direct descent, it is very doubtful whether he will succeed the present king, as Maafu, his cousin, and the son of a deceased brother of King George, is older in years, and is consequently by the Tongan laws the legitimate heir to the throne.[*]

Wellington entertained us most hospitably, and drove us in his buggies to various places of interest in the island. On one occa-

[*] Since the above was written I have heard of the death of Maafu.

sion he took three of our officers to Moa, a native town situated near the south-east extremity of the island. From there they went on to a place eight miles to the southward, where there is a famous megalithic structure of unknown origin, which has been described and figured by Brenchly in his "Voyage of the *Curaçoa*." As our experience differs somewhat from Brenchly's, I may be excused for making a few remarks thereon. The monument—if such it can be called—consists of three large slabs of coral rock, two of which are planted vertically in the ground at a distance of about fifteen feet apart, while the third forms a horizontal span, resting on its edges in slots made in the summits of the vertical slabs. The height of the structure, of which the picture gives a good idea, is about fifteen feet. We were, I regret to say, unable to obtain any information—legendary or otherwise—concerning the origin of this remarkable structure.

He also took us on a very pleasant excursion to a village called Hifo, which lies about eleven miles to the south-west of Nukualofa. The party consisted of Wellington Gnu (pronounced "Mou"), David Tonga, the principal of the native school, Captain Maclear, and myself. Our means of locomotion consisted of two buggies, in which we started on the outward journey by a circuitous route, so as to take in the village of Bea and four or five others on our way. On arriving at Hifo, we halted in the centre of the village, on an open patch of sward under the shade of several large vi trees (*Spondias dulcis*), on whose branches were hanging large numbers of fox bats (*Pteropus keraudrenii*), of which we obtained specimens. We were now formally introduced to the chief of Hifo, who at once announced that a feast would speedily be prepared in honour of our visit, and pending the necessary culinary arrangements, invited us to walk through his dominions. In an adjacent bay we were pointed out the place where Cook had formerly anchored his vessel, a matter of great interest to the Tongans, who are keenly alive to the fact that the period of Cook's visit formed the great turning-point in their history

As we returned to the village we found that the natives had collected in great numbers under the shade of the trees before mentioned; so we squatted down on the grass, taking up our places with the chief's party, so as to occupy the base-line of a large horseshoe-shaped gathering of natives. The ceremony began with the preparation of the kava, in which respect the Tongans now differ from the Fijians in reducing the root to a pulpy condition by pounding it between stones instead of the rather disgusting process of mastication. While the national beverage was being prepared, a large procession of women, gaily dressed, and bearing garlands, shells, and similar offerings, filed solemnly into the centre of the group, and deposited their presents at the feet of Captain Maclear and myself, who were the distinguished guests on this occasion. Sometimes a frolicsome girl would place a garland round one of our necks, and then trip away, laughing merrily. When the kava was ready, a fine-looking elderly man, the second in authority in the village, acted as master of the ceremonies, and gave the orders for carrying out the various details of the function. As the cup-bearer advanced with each successive bowl of liquor, this venerable functionary called out in order of precedence the names of the different persons who were to be served, beginning with the visitors, and continuing to indicate each one by name, until every one of the whole vast assemblage —men and women—had partaken. As soon as the kava drinking was over, a procession of young men advanced into the midst of the assemblage, bearing on their shoulders palm-leaf baskets which contained pigs roasted whole, large bunches of bananas, and cocoanuts, which they deposited *seriatim* at our feet. The district chief then made a short speech, informing us, through Wellington's interpretation, that these precious gifts were also at our disposal. Captain Maclear replied, to the effect that we gratefully accepted the present, and requested that it might be distributed for consumption among the villagers. Accordingly the feast was spread, and eating, drinking, and merry-making

ANCIENT STONE MONUMENT AT TONGATABU (p. 173).

[To face p. 174.

became general. Occasionally one of the girls would rise from her place, and after lighting a cigarette, of which the cylinder was composed of pandanus leaf instead of paper, would give a few puffs from her own swarthy lips, and then present it courteously to one of us. The act was looked on as a delicate way of paying a compliment, and was on each occasion loudly applauded, the damsel, as she returned among her friends, seeming as if overcome with confusion at her own temerity. When the time fixed for our departure arrived, a most affectionate shaking of hands took place, and we bade good-bye to the happy little village of Hifo, delighted with the kindness, hospitality, and good nature of these far-famed Friendly Islanders.

On the last day previous to our departure from Tongatabu, we made an excursion to the south side of the island, under the guidance of Mr. Symonds, the British Consul, and Mr. Hanslip, the consular interpreter, in order to examine some caves which were said to be of an unusually wonderful nature. They had, of course, never been thoroughly explored, and were consequently said to be of prodigious extent, forming long tunnels through the island. One story was to the effect that an adventurous woman had penetrated one branch of the cave, entering on the south side of the island, and threading its dark recesses for many days, until she finally emerged into the light of day somewhere near Nukualofa, on the north side of the island.

A pleasant drive of about ten miles brought us to the shore of a small bay exposed to the prevailing wind, and receiving on its beach the full fury of the swell of the main ocean. The foreshore was strewn with coral *débris*, and above high-water mark were quantities of pumice-stone, probably washed up from the sides of the neighbouring volcanic island of Uea. On either side, the bay was hemmed in by bold projecting crags of coral rock, whose faces indicated, by parallel tide erosions, that they had been elevated by sudden upheaval into their present position. About one hundred yards from the beach, and forty feet above the sea-level, was the entrance to the caves, a narrow aperture in the upraised coral rock, leading by a rapid incline into a spacious vaulted chamber, from whose gloomy recesses dark and forbidding passages led in various directions. In the floor of the chamber were deep pools of water, probably communicating with the sea, and said to be tenanted by a species of blind eel, about two feet long, which we were told the natives sometimes caught with hook and line, and fed upon. I was provided with fishing-tackle for capturing a specimen of this singular creature; but as several of our party were induced to relieve themselves of the intolerable heat of the cave by bathing in these pools, the fish were probably scared away, and I was unable to obtain a single specimen.

The rock pierced by the caverns was everywhere of coral formation, and as water freely penetrated through from the soilcap above, the roof and floor were abundantly decorated with stalactites and stalagmites in all their usual fantastic splendour. I noticed that many parts of the floor of the cave were speckled with white spots resembling bird-droppings, on which drops of water were frequently falling from the roof above, and I formed the opinion that the white colour of these spots was due to the drops of water which pattered on them having traversed a portion of the ground above, from which they did not receive a charge of lime salts, and consequently washing clean the portion of the coral floor on which they fell, instead of depositing thereon a calcareous stalagmite. This surmise was strengthened by observing the absence of stalactites depending from the roof in these situations.

Numbers of small swifts, apparently the same species which is common on the island (*Collocalia spodiopygia*), flitted about the vaulted parts of the cave, looking in the torchlight like bats, which at first sight I felt sure they must be, until our native guide succeeded in catching one specimen, which resolved our doubts. We traversed the more open parts of the cave to a distance of about one hundred yards from the entrance; but finding further progress all but impracticable, from the narrowness of the passages, and the quantity of water of uncertain depth to be encountered, we soon gave up the attempt, and were glad to return to the cool and clear atmosphere of the upper air.

During the voyage from Tonga to Fiji, we spent a good deal of time in hunting up the reputed positions of certain doubtful "banks," viz., the "Culebras" and "La Rance" banks, with a view to clearing up the question as to their having any real existence except in the too vivid imaginations of the discoverers. On the 24th of November, when in latitude $24° 25'$ S., longitude $184° 0'$ W., we steamed over the position assigned by the chart to the "La Rance" bank, and here our sounding line ran out to three hundred fathoms without touching bottom, thus sufficiently establishing the non-existence of any such "bank." Our position at this time may be roughly stated as some two hundred miles to the southward of Tongatabu. During the greater portion of the day, the sea-surface exhibited large patches of discoloured water, due to the presence of a fluffy substance of a dull brown colour, which in consistency and general arrangement resembled the vegetable scum commonly seen floating on the stagnant water of ditches. This matter floated on the surface in irregularly-shaped streaky patches, and also in finely-divided particles impregnated the sea-water to a depth of several feet. Samples were obtained by "dipping" with a bucket as well as with the tow-net, and when submitted to microscopic examination it proved to be composed of multitudes of minute *Confervoid algæ*. On slightly agitating the water in a glass jar, the fluffy masses broke up into small particles, which, under a magnifying power of sixty diameters, were seen to be composed of spindle-shaped bundles of filaments. Under a power of five hundred diameters, these filaments were further resolved into straight or slightly-curved rods, articulated but not branching, and divided by transverse septa into cylindrical cells, which contained irregularly-shaped masses of granular matter.

These rods, which seemed to represent the adult plant, measured $\frac{1}{2000}$ inch in width. On careful examination of many specimens, some filaments were observed, portions of which seemed to have undergone a sort of varicose enlargement, having a width two or three times that of the normal filaments. These propagating filaments (if I am right in so calling them) were invested by a delicate tubular membrane, and were filled with a granular semi-transparent matter, in which were imbedded a number of discoid bodies which were being discharged one by one from the ruptured extremity of the tube. These bodies measured $\frac{1}{1000}$ of an inch in diameter: when viewed edgewise they presented a lozenge-shaped appearance, and they were devoid of ciliæ or striæ. A jar full of the sea-water was put by until the following day, when it was found that the confervoid matter had all risen to the surface, forming a thick scum of a dull green colour, while the underlying water was of a pale purple colour, resembling the tint produced by a weak solution of permanganate of potash.

From the 24th to the 29th of November, during which time the ship traversed a distance of three hundred miles, we were surrounded by these organisms; during the first three days the large patches were frequently in sight, and for the rest of the time the sea presented a dusty appearance, from the presence of finely-divided particles. On the evening of the 25th an unusually dense patch was sighted, and mistaken for a reef, being reported as such by the look-out man aloft.

On the 28th November I encountered among the proceeds of the tow-net another minute alga, of quite a different appearance from that just described. It was composed of vermiform rods $\frac{1}{1000}$ inch in width, and breaking up into cylindrical segments with biconcave ends.

We returned to Levuka on the 4th of December, and stayed in harbour for ten days. At this time we had dismal wet weather, and consequently little was done in the way of exploration. I received a visit from a Mr. Boyd of Waidou, a colonist, who has resided for the last sixteen years in Fiji, and who has spent a great deal of his time in collecting natural history specimens. He very kindly presented me with some crania, three of natives of Mallicollo, New Hebrides, and two from Merilava in Bank's Group.

We anchored at Suva for part of a day, in order to fill up with coal, and then proceeded on our voyage to Sydney.

I made frequent use of the tow-net during this cruise, obtaining thereby a great quantity and variety of surface organisms. Among these were representatives of *Thalassicolla, Pyrocystis, Phyllosoma, Sagitta, Eurybia, Atlanta*, etc. I obtained one specimen of a curious Annelid. It was two inches in width, had two prominent ruby-coloured eyes, and was marked along its snakelike body by a double row of conspicuous black dots.

One day, as were lying almost becalmed, a few hundred miles from the Australian coast, we passed into the midst of a great flock of brown petrels, who were sitting on the water grouped in the form of a chain, and apparently feeding. I had the tow-net out, and after dragging it for about half a mile, brought it in, and found it to contain a mass of yellow-coloured cylindrical and oval bodies belonging to the group *Thalassicollidæ*. The cylindrical bodies were about one inch in long diameter, by $\frac{1}{8}$ of an inch in width, and those of an oval shape were about $\frac{3}{16}$ inch in long diameter. They proved to be mere gelatinous sacks, without any appearance of digestive or locomotary organs. The thin membranous wall was dotted over thickly with dark cells of a spherical or oval shape, each of which contained from three to nine light-coloured nuclei. On examining one of the oval bodies under a magnifying power of forty diameters, the clear transparent nature of the interior of the organism allowed the cells on the distal side to be seen out of focus with misty outlines, while the cells on the proximal wall, which was in focus, came out sharp and clear, and *vice versâ*.

CHAPTER IX.

THE EAST COAST OF AUSTRALIA.

WE remained at Sydney, refitting ship and enjoying the unaccustomed pleasures of civilized society, from the 23rd of January, 1881, until the 16th of April, 1881, but as little of general interest occurred during this period, and as Sydney with its surroundings is a place about which so much has been written by better pens than mine, I think I shall be exercising a judicious discretion by passing over this period in silence, and resuming the narrative from the time when we started on our next surveying cruise.

On leaving Sydney we received a welcome addition to our numbers in the person of Mr. W. A. Haswell, a professional zoologist, residing at Sydney, who expressed a wish to accompany us as far as Torres Straits, in order that he might have opportunities of studying the crustacean fauna of the east coast of Australia. He was consequently enrolled as an honorary member of our mess, and Captain Maclear kindly accommodated him with a sleeping place in his cabin. I am indebted to Mr. Haswell for much valuable information concerning the marine zoology of Australia.

Steaming northwards, along the east coast of Australia, the first place at which we anchored was Port Curtis, in Queensland, where we took up a berth in the outer roads close to the Gatcombe Head lighthouse. The place bore a rather desolate appearance. There was no building in sight except the lighthouse. The beach was lined with a dense fringe of mangrove bushes, behind which rose a straggling forest of gums and grass trees (*Xanthorrea*), and for a long time we saw no living thing excepting several large fish-eagles (*Haliætus leucogaster*), and an odd gull that hovered about our stern, picking up the garbage that drifted away from the ship.

On the following morning two of us landed and set to work to explore the mudflats, which, stretching out for a long distance from the beach, were laid bare by the ebb tide. As we ranged along in search of marine curiosities, we encountered a solitary individual attired in the light and airy costume of a pajama sleeping suit, and carrying a Westly-Richards rifle on his shoulder. We soon made his acquaintance, and found that he was in quest of wild goats, the descendants of some domestic animals originally let loose by the keeper of the lighthouse. He was an Englishman named Eastlake, and held the position of "government immigration agent" on board a ninety-ton schooner, the *Isabella*, which at the time was anchored just outside the lighthouse point, awaiting a favourable wind to enable her to put to sea. She was engaged in the "labour traffic" and was just then about to return to the Solomon Islands with some "time-expired" native labourers. The Queensland government compels every vessel engaged in the "labour traffic" to carry an immigration agent, who is accredited to and salaried by the government. His duty is to see that the natives who are shipped from the islands for transit to Queensland come of their own free will, and under a proper contract, and that during the voyage they are treated well and are furnished with proper accommodation, and are dieted according to a scale laid down by the government. In the afternoon I accompanied Mr. Eastlake on board. The *Isabella*, a vessel of ninety tons, was allowed to carry eighty-five natives besides her crew of some half-a-dozen hands. She had now on board about a dozen natives of New Hebrides, who had completed their time as contract labourers in Queensland, and were about to be returned to their island home.

The skipper of the vessel was an old Welshman, who, in the true spirit of hospitality, did the honours of the ship, and pressed me to partake of such luxuries as the stores in his cuddy afforded.

Among the articles which the New Hebrides men had purchased in Queensland with the proceeds of their labours were a number of old muskets, which they seemed to set great store by. These weapons are probably destined to be brought into action against some future "labour vessel," or "slaver," as they are commonly called by the Australians, which may violate the provision of the "Kidnapping Act" by forcible abduction of natives.

We worked the dredge from the ship as she swung round her anchor in seven fathoms of water, and also dragged it from a boat in shallower water inshore. Conspicuous by their abundance amongst the contents of the dredge, and by their curious habit of making a loud snapping noise with the large pincer-claw, were the shrimps of the genus *Alpheus*. When placed in water in a glass jar, the sound produced exactly resembles the snap which is heard when a tumbler is cracked from unequal expansion by hot water. We also obtained a good many whitish fleshy *Gorgoniæ*, and among Polyzoa the genera *Crisia* and *Eschara* afforded a good many specimens. A moderate-sized brownish *Asterophyton* was generally found entangled in the swabs, but in most cases some of its brittle limbs had parted company with the disc, so that we got scarcely a single perfect specimen. A good many crabs were found on the foreshore; among others were species of the genera *Ozius*, *Gelasimus*, and *Thalassina*; the latter a lobster-like crustacean which burrows deeply in the mud about the mangrove bushes, and throws up around the aperture of its burrow a conical pile of mud.

On April 23rd we got under way, and steamed for five miles further up the bay, anchoring immediately off the settlement of "Gladstone." Nothing could exceed the hospitality shown to us by the inhabitants of this quiet little Utopia. Our stay of five days was occupied by an almost continuous round of festivities, during which we were driven about the country, had a cricket-match, shooting expeditions, two balls in the Town Hall, and sundry other amusements. The settlement contains a population of only 300, and seems to have been of late years rather receding than advancing in numbers, as many of the settlers had moved on to other more promising centres of industry. There was the old story of a projected railway which was to open up the country, develop its hidden resources, connect it with the neighbouring town of Rockhampton—distant about eighty miles—and give a fresh impetus to trade; but the hopes of its construction were visionary.

We made several shooting excursions in quest of bird specimens, and found the pied grallina (*G. picata*), the butcher bird (a species of *Grauculus*), the garrulous honeyeater (*Myzantha garrula*), the laughing jackass (*Dacelo gigas*), and many doves and flycatchers abundant in the immediate vicinity of the settlement. Walking one day through the forest about two miles inland, we came upon a grove of tall eucalyptus trees, on the upper branches of which were myriads of paroquets, making an almost deafening noise as they flew hither and thither, feeding on the fragrant blossoms. Among them were three species of Trichoglossus, viz., *T. Novæ Hollandiæ*, *T. rubitorquis*, and *T. chrysocolla*. We also shot specimens of the friar bird (*Tropidorhyncus corniculatus*), and several honeyeaters, flycatchers, and shrikes; so that as a place for bird collecting it was exceedingly rich, both in numbers and species.

We got under way on the 30th of April, in the morning, and on the following day anchored off the largest and most northern of the Percy Islands. I landed with Haswell in the afternoon, and after exploring the beach in search of marine specimens, we directed our steps towards the interior of the island. We followed a narrow winding foot track, which led us to a rudely-built hut, in which dwelt an old Australian colonist named Captain Allen, to whom the island virtually belongs. He had a small kitchen garden in the bed of a valley, through which ran a tiny stream; and his live stock consisted of a herd of goats and a number of poultry. We understood that he intended eventually to undertake regular farming operations, but that he at present merely *occupied* the land in order to retain the "pre-emptive" right until the Queensland government should be in a position to sell or let it. It appeared that as yet it was not certain whether the colonial government had a clear title to the group of islands, or whether—being on the Great Barrier Reef, and detached from the mainland by a considerable distance—it was still under the control and jurisdiction of the imperial government.

We noticed very few birds: among these were a *Ptilotis*, a flycatcher, a crow, and a heron; but we were told that in the less frequented parts of the island there were brush turkeys, native pheasants, and black cockatoos.

Among the rocks bordering the shore, a large white-tailed rat—probably of the genus *Hydromys*—was said to be abundant. The only other mammal recorded was a large fox-bat, a skeleton of which was found hanging on a mangrove bush.

We left our anchorage at the Percy Islands on the morning of the 2nd of May, and on the forenoon of the 3rd steamed into the sheltered waters of Port Molle, *i.e.*, into the strait which separates Long Island from the main shore of Queensland; and we finally came to an anchor in a shallow bay on the west side of Long Island, where we lay at a distance of about half-a-mile from the shore.

The island presented the appearance of undulating hills, covered for the most part with a thick growth of tropical forms of vegetation, but exhibiting a few patches of land devoid of trees, and bearing a rich crop of long tangled grasses. On landing, we found that there was no soil, properly so-called, but that the forest trees, scrub, and grass sprung from a surface layer of shingle, which on close inspection contrasted strangely with the rich and verdant flora which it nourished. Small flocks of great white cockatoos flew around and above the summits of the tallest trees, and by the incessant screaming which they maintained, gave one the idea that the avifauna was more abundant than we eventually found it to be. On the beach we collected shells of the genera *Nerita, Terebra, Siliquaria,* and *Ostræa,* and among the dry hot stones above high water mark we found in great numbers an *Isopod Crustacean,* and as the females were bearing ova, Haswell took the opportunity to make some researches into the mode of development of the embryo.

I spent another day accompanying Navigating-Lieutenant Petley, who was then cruising from point to point in one of our whaleboats, determining on the positions for maintriangulation. In the course of the day we visited the lighthouse on Dean Island, and on arriving there found a large concourse of blacks on the hill above, looking on our intrusion with great consternation. The lighthouse people told us that the natives, from their different camps on the island, had observed our approach while we were yet a long distance off, and hastily concluding that we were a party of black police coming to disperse (*i.e.,* shoot) them, had fled with precipitation from all parts of the island, to seek the protection of the white inhabitants of the lighthouse. It appeared that some few years previously the natives of Port Molle had treacherously attacked and murdered the shipwrecked crew of a schooner, and in requital for this the Queensland Government had made an example of them by letting loose a party of " black police," who, with their rifles, had made fearful havoc among the comparatively unarmed natives. The " black police," or " black troopers," as they are more commonly called, are a gang of half-reclaimed aborigines, enrolled and armed as policemen, who are distributed over various parts of the colony, and are under the immediate direction of the white police inspectors. Their skill as bush "trackers" is too well known to need description, and the peculiar ferocity with which they behave towards their own countrymen is due to the fact that they are drawn from a part of the continent remote from the scene of their future labours, and from tribes hostile to those against which they are intended to act. Through their instrumentality the aborigines of Queensland are being gradually exterminated. In the official reports of their proceedings, when sent to operate against a troublesome party of natives, the verb "to disperse" is playfully substituted for the harsher term "to shoot."

But to return to our friends at Dean Island. Our peaceful aspect, and a satisfactory explanation on the part of the white people in charge of the lighthouse, soon set matters right, and the wretched blacks were now so delighted at finding their fears to be groundless, that they crowded about us—male and female —to the number of forty or fifty, brought us some boomerangs for barter, and finally shared our lunch of preserved meat and coffee, of which we partook on the rocks near where the boat was moored. I was surprised at noticing a large proportion of children, a circumstance which does not support one of the views put forward to account for the rapid decrease in numbers of the race.

Most of the men had a certain amount of clothing, scanty and ragged though it was, but the children were all stark naked, and some of the women were so scantily attired that the requirements of decency were not at all provided for. They seemed to be fairly well nourished, and from their cheerful disposition I should imagine that they were not undergoing any privations which to them would be irksome.

On re-embarking, we sailed along the western shore of the island, and again landed in a small bay about a mile to the northward of the lighthouse. We then proceeded to ascend a hill, on which Petley wished to erect a mark for surveying purposes. The natives, although quick enough about following us along the seashore, showed no inclination to follow us up the hill-side, and before we had gone a few hundred yards they had all dropped off. Possibly the fear of snakes was the deterring influence.

Port Molle proved to be an excellent place for obtaining

examples of the marine fauna of this part of the coast. A great extent of reefs was exposed at low spring tides, exhibiting Corals of the groups *Astræa, Meandrina, Porites, Tubipora, Orbicella,* and *Caryophyllia,* besides a profusion of soft Alcyonarian Polyps. Holothurians were abundant, as were also some large Tubicolous Annelids, with very long gelatinous thread-like tentacles. We also got a few *Polynöes,* and several other annelids of the family *Amphinomidæ.* A *Squilla,* with variegated greenish markings on the test, made itself remarkable by the vigour with which it resented one's attempts, for the most part unintentional, to invade the privacy of its retreat. An active black *Goniograpsus* was a common object on the reefs, and the widely distributed *Grapsus variegatus* was also met with. Haswell obtained from the interior of the large *Pinna* shells examples of a curious small lobster-like crustacean, which is of parasitic—or perhaps rather commensal— habit, like *Pinnotheres.* Not uncommon in the rock pools was a bivalve shell of the genus *Lima,* which on being disturbed swims about in a most lively manner by flapping its elongated valves, exhibiting at the same time a scarlet mantle fringed with a row of long prehensile tentacles. Shells of the genera *Arca, Tridacna,* and *Hippopus* were common, and three or four species of *Cypræa* were seen.

We dredged several times with one of the steam cutters in depths varying from twelve to twenty fathoms, obtaining several species of Comatulas, two or three Asterophytons, Starfishes, Ophiurids, Echini of the genera *Salmacis* and *Goniocidaris,* small Holothurians, many species of Annelids, two or three Sponges, a great variety of handsome Gorgoniæ, Hydroids of the group *Sertularia* and *Plumularia,* Polyzoa of the genera *Eschara, Retepora, Myriozoum, Cellepora, Biflustra, Salicornaria, Crisia, Scrupocellaria, Amathea,* etc., and Crustaceans of the genera *Myra, Hiastemis, Lambris, Alpheus, Huenia,* and many others. Among the Annelids was one with long glassy opalescent bristles surrounding the oral aperture, and projecting forwards to a distance of one and a half inches from the praestomium. Another Annelid (species unknown) was peculiar in having two long barb-like tentacles projecting backwards from the under part of the head. On examining the proboscis of the latter, while it was resting in sea-water in a glass trough, Haswell noticed a number of singular bodies being extruded from the mouth, which he eventually ascertained, to his great astonishment, were the partially developed young of the worm.

One of the large Asterophytons which came up with the dredge was seen to exhibit nodular swellings on several parts of the arms, but principally at the points of bifurcation. Each of these swellings was provided with one or more small apertures, and had the general appearance of being a morbid growth. On incising the dense cystwall a cavity was exposed, containing a tiny red gastropodous mollusc (of the genus *Stilifer*), enveloped in a mass of cheesy matter, which contained moreover one or two spherical white pellets of (probably) fœcal matter. Haswell obtained about a dozen specimens of the shell from a single asterophyton.

Port Denison is only forty miles to the northward of Port Molle, so that we accomplished the passage in about six hours, and before dusk took up a berth in the shallow bay about a mile and a half from the shore, and three-quarters from the end of a long wooden pier, which was built some years ago in the vain hope of developing the shipping trade of the port. The township of "Bowen" is built on a larger scale than "Gladstone"—of which we had such pleasant reminiscences—but did not appear to be in a more flourishing condition, a "gold rush" further to the northward having drawn off part of the population, and some of the trade which had previously gone through the port. On the outskirts of the town were some large encampments of the blacks, who lived in a primitive condition, and afforded an interesting study for an ethnologist. Like most of the Australian aborigines, their huts were little better than shelter screens to protect them from the wind and sun. In some instances the twigs on the lee side of a bush, rudely interlaced with a few leafy boughs torn from the neighbouring trees, afforded all the shelter that was required. Both men and women, especially the latter, seemed to be in a filthy, degraded state. They had just received their yearly gifts of blankets from the Queensland Government—I believe the only return which they receive for the appropriation of their land. It appears, however, that they do not much appreciate the donation, for soon after the general issue many of the blankets are bartered with the whites for tobacco and grog. Some of the young men are really fine-looking fellows, and seemed to feel all the pride of life and liberty as they strutted about encumbered with a variety of their native weapons, among which I saw the *nulla*, *waddy*, shield, huge wooden sword, spear without throwing-stick, and different patterns of boomerangs. They are very expert in the use of the latter. It was the first time that I had seen the boomerang thrown, and I can safely say that its performances, when manipulated by a skilful hand, fully realized my expectations. I noticed that whatever gyrations it was intended to execute, it was always delivered from the hand of the thrower with its concave side foremost—a circumstance I was not previously aware of. Some of the children were amusing themselves in practising the art, using instead of the regular boomerang short pieces of rounded stick bent to about the usual angle of the finished weapon; and I was surprised at noticing that even these rude substitutes could be made to dart forward, wheel in the air, and return to near the feet of the thrower. I had always imagined up to this time that the flat surface was an essential feature in the boomerang.

The foreshore at low-water afforded us examples of a great many flat Echinoderms of the genus *Peronella*, Starfishes of the genus *Asteracanthus*, and Crustaceans of the genera *Macrophthalmus*, *Matuta*, *Mycteris*, etc. We made several hauls of the dredge in four to five fathoms of water, obtaining a quantity of large Starfishes and Gorgonias, and Crustaceans of the family *Porcellanidæ*.

We left Port Denison on the 24th of May, and continued our

coasting voyage northward, anchoring successive nights off Cape Bowling Green, Hinchinbrook Island, Fitzroy Island, Cooktown, and Lizard Island. We landed at the island last mentioned for a few hours. On the shore of the bay in which we anchored was a "Beche-de-mer" establishment, belonging to a Cooktown firm, and worked by a party of two white men, three Chinese, and six Kanakas. The buildings consisted of two or three rudely-built dwelling huts, and a couple of sheds for curing and storing the trepangs. We learned from the "Boss" that his men had been working the district for the previous twelve months, and having now cleared off the trepangs from all the neighbouring reefs, he expected soon to move on to some other location further north.

The Beche-de-Mer industry seems simple enough to conduct. The sluggish animals are picked off the reefs at low tide, and at the close of each day the produce as soon as landed is transferred to a huge iron tank, propped up on stones, in which it is boiled. The trepangs are then slit open, cleaned, and spread out on gratings in a smoke-house until dry, when they are ready for shipping to the Chinese market. The best trepangs are the short stiff black ones with prominent tubercles.

Since the above notes were written, a horrible catastrophe occurred at Lizard Island. The bulk of the party had gone on a cruise among the islands to the northward, leaving the station in charge of a white woman—wife of one of the proprietors—and two Chinamen. A party of Queensland blacks came over from the mainland, massacred these three wretched people, and destroyed all the property on the station.

On the evening of the 29th of May we anchored off Flinders Island, in latitude 14° 8′ S., and before darkness came on we spent a few hours in exploring. The shore on which we landed was covered with large blocks of quartzite stained with oxide of iron, and disseminated among them were many large irregularly-shaped masses of hæmatite. Immediately above the beach, and among the familiar screw-pines, we saw a few fan palms, the first met with on our northern voyage.

Groping among the rocks of the foreshore, I encountered a multitude of crabs of the genera *Porcellana* and *Grapsus*, and caught after much trouble a large and uncommonly fierce specimen of the *Parampelia saxicola*. On anchoring, the dredge had been lowered from the ship, and when hauled up after the ship had swung somewhat with the tide, a curious species of *Spatangus*, a *Leucosia*, and a somewhat mutilated *Phlyxia*, were obtained.

Early on the following morning I accompanied Captain Maclear and Mr. Haswell on a boat trip to Clack Island (five miles from our anchorage). We were anxious to see and examine some drawings by the Australian aborigines, which were discovered in the year 1821 by Mr. Cunningham, of the *Beagle*, (see "King's Australia," vol. ii., p. 25), and since probably unvisited. After about an hour's sailing we reached the island—a bold mass of dark rock resembling in shape a gunner's quoin; but we now found it no easy matter to find a landing-place. On the southeast extremity was a precipitous rocky bluff about eighty feet in height, against whose base the sea broke heavily, while the rest of the island—low and fringed with mangroves—was fenced in by a broad zone of shallow water, strewn with boulders and coral knolls, over which the sea rose and fell in a manner dangerous to the integrity of the boat. After many trials and much risk to the boat, we at length succeeded in jumping ashore near the southeast or weather extremity of the island. Here we found abundant traces of its having been frequently visited by natives, but it did not appear as if they had been there during at least half-a-dozen years prior to the time of our visit. We saw the drawings, as described by Cunningham, covering the sides and roofs of galleries and grottoes, which seemed to have been excavated by atmospheric influences in a black fissile shale. This shale, which gave a banded appearance to the cliff, was disposed in strata of about five feet in thickness, and was interbedded with strata of pebbly conglomerate—the common rock of the islet. In these excavations, almost every available surface of smooth shale was covered with drawings, even including the roofs of low crevices where the artist must have worked lying prone on his back, and with his nose almost touching his work. Most of the drawings were executed in red ochre, and had their outlines accentuated by rows of white dots, which seemed to be composed of a sort of pipe-clay. Some, however, were executed in pale yellow on a brick-red ground, and in many instances the objects depicted were banded with rows of white dots crossing each other irregularly, and perhaps intended in a rudimentary way to convey the idea of light and shade. The objects delineated (of which I made such sketches as I was able) were sharks, dolphins, dugong, turtle, boomerangs, waddies, shields, woomerahs, pigs, dogs, birds, jelly-fish, etc. There was one well-defined sketch of a medusa, showing the position of the radiating canals and eight marginal tentacles. *Trochus* shells in great profusion were strewn about the old camping places, as well as bones of the dugong and turtle, the pursuit of the latter having been probably the main inducement to visit the island.

A careful hunting of the holes and crevices in the face of the cliff resulted in the acquisition of some portable specimens of native art in the shape of drawings on old pieces of driftwood, on *Melo* shells, turtle skulls, and tortoise shell. These luckily afforded us good examples of the style of art, and were accordingly, and without many conscientious scruples as to the sacred rights of ownership, carried off in triumph and deposited on board.

After leaving Flinders Island, we continued our voyage northward, anchoring each of the three following nights successively at Clairmont Island No. 6, Clairmont Island No. 10, and Bird Island. On each occasion we dredged to a small extent, and collected specimens from the reefs and beaches. On the evening of the 2nd of June we entered the narrow strait which separates

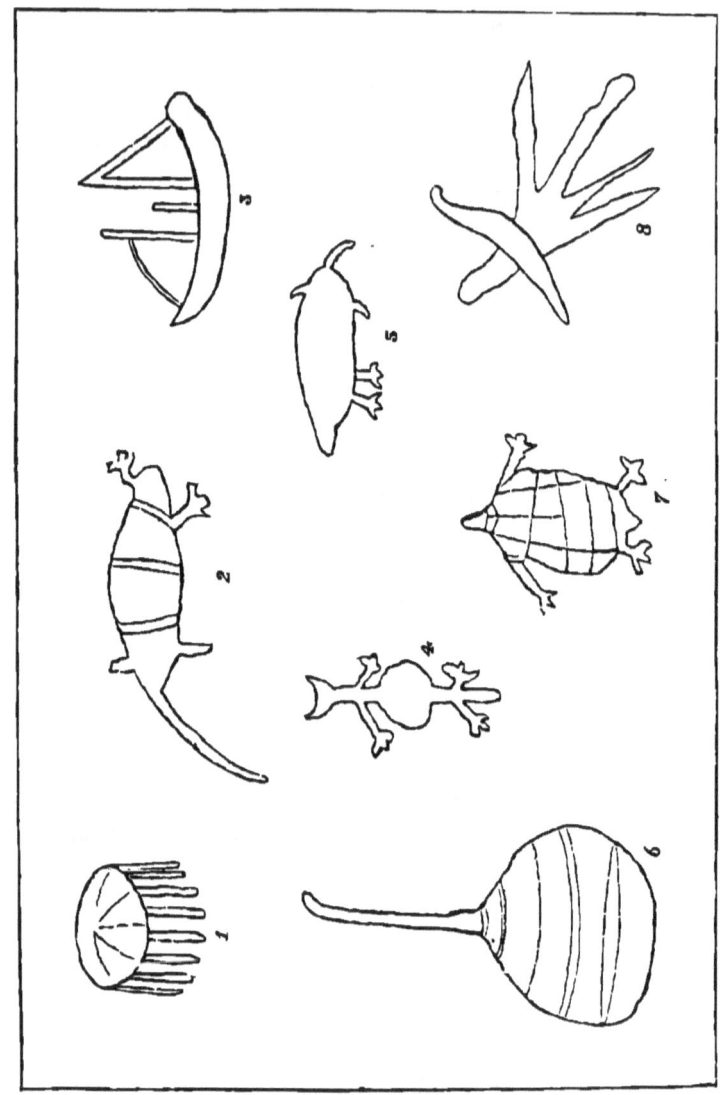

FACSIMILES OF DRAWINGS BY AUSTRALIAN ABORIGINES.

1. Medusa. 2. Lizard. 3. Steamship. 4. (?). 5. (?). 6. Gourd. 7. Turtle. 8. Bird on branch of tree.

[*To face p.* 192.]

Albany Island.

Albany Island from the mainland of north-east Australia, having the small settlement of Somerset on our port hand, and on our starboard side a pearl-shell station known as Port Albany. The anchorage at Somerset being of bad repute on account of the strong currents which sweep through it, we steamed on to the northern extremity of Albany Island, where at about 4 o'clock in the evening we dropped our anchor in six fathoms. A party of officers landed at once on the shore of the mainland, and while some wandered through the woods in search of birds, the boat was employed in dredging over the bottom of mud and sand in depths varying from three to five fathoms. Among the contents of several hauls were a large number of Comatulas, a few Ophiurids, several examples of a *Pentaceros*, a *Goniocidaris*, a spider-crab of the genus "*Egeria*," an *Alpheus*, a *Galathea* clinging to the feathered arms of a purple *Comatula*, and many specimens of an Isopod adhering to the oral surfaces of the comatular discs. There were also a few shrimps, two species of *Murex*, and a volute. Some small fishes were also brought up—apparently a species of *Platycephalus*.

On the following morning some of the boats were employed in searching for an uncharted rock which was reported by the pearl fishermen as existing somewhere near our anchorage, while Haswell and I had the use of a whaleboat for a couple of hours' dredging. We worked across the channel towards the mainland in eight fathoms over a bottom of mud and sand, obtaining a quantity of Comatulas and Gorgonias, a large grotesque *Murex*, several small *Synaptas*, and a large flat sponge.

CHAPTER X.

TORRES STRAITS ISLANDS.

WE remained for nearly four months anchored at or in the neighbourhood of Thursday Island. During this period our boats were employed in making a survey of the Prince of Wales Channel, which is now the route almost invariably used by steamers and sailing ships in passing through Torres Straits. There is a small settlement at Thursday Island consisting of about a dozen houses, wooden built, which are occupied by white families and their coloured domestics. There is a police magistrate, whose jurisdiction, as an official of the Queensland government, extends over all the islands in Torres Straits; an officer of customs, through whose hands passes all the trade of the Straits; a staff of white policemen to enforce the Queensland law; a prison for the incarceration of the refractory pearl shellers; a store for the supply of tinned provisions and all the miscellaneous requirements of the pearl shell trade; and, finally, there are two public-houses which do a flourishing business and supply ample material for the official ministration of the police. The entire population, white and coloured, does not exceed a hundred.

Thursday Island owes its importance to being the shipping port for the produce of all the pearl shell fisheries in Torres Straits. It is visited monthly by steamers of the "British India" and "Eastern and Australian" Steamship Companies, and also by a small coasting steamer, the *Corea*, belonging to an Australian firm. The latter plies regularly and constantly between Thursday Island

and Sydney, and does most of the business in connection with the fisheries, conveying the shell to Sydney, and returning with a cargo of tinned provisions, slops, and other stores for the use of the pearl shellers. The inhabitants of Thursday Island, and those belonging to the various pearl shell stations scattered through the group of islands, are dependent for support upon extraneous supplies of provisions. Cattle will not thrive on the islands, owing to the poisonous nature of the grass, and as yet all attempts at growing fruit and vegetables have in most cases proved unsuccessful.

The native inhabitants of the Torres Straits Islands are a small tribe of Papuan origin, who lead a wandering life, and show little inclination to hold intercourse with either white or coloured colonists. They have the frizzled hair, the aquiline hooked nose, and the wide curved lips of the Papuans; and among their implements are the long "hour-glass" drum, headed with lizard skin, the tortoise-shell mask worn at corrobories, and the pearl shell ornaments dangling from the neck; but their intercourse with the North Australian aborigines is shown by their having acquired the practice of using the "throwing sticks" for their spears. Their food being almost solely of marine origin, their camps are only found on the shores of the islands. At certain seasons in the year they catch the turtle and dugong, and apparently in great numbers, if one can judge by the quantity of bones of these animals seen by us in the midden-heaps. Fish they obtain in abundance by means of the hook and line, and the shore molluscs also supply them with food; so that it is not to be wondered at that we generally found them to be in a well-nourished condition, and not at all anxious to barter their fish for such a commodity as ship's biscuit. Their boats are long dug-out canoes, fitted with double outriggers, and very rudely constructed. Whether under sail or paddle, they manœuvred very badly, and were on the whole very poor specimens of naval architecture, even for a tribe of savages.

In 1879 the population of the shelling stations amounted to 720, while that of the settlement at Thursday Island was only 80. In 1880 the shelling population amounted to 815, showing an increase of nearly a hundred on that of the previous year. As far as I could ascertain, any change that has taken place during the last two years has been indicative of the increasing prosperity of the pearl shell industry. Indeed I was informed by a resident gentleman connected with the fisheries, that the shareholders in one of the stations had that year received a dividend of seventy per cent. on the capital invested. I made the acquaintance of several of the managers (or "bosses" as they are commonly called) of the pearl shell establishments, and through their civility had opportunities of visiting many stations within a range of twenty-five miles from our anchorage at Thursday Island. They are all constructed more or less on the same general model; consisting usually of one whitewashed house,—the residence of the white manager,—a store-house, and a couple of sheds for the stowage of boat appliances and pearl shell, and a few large grass built huts in which the labourers employed at the depôt are housed. These men, who are spoken of under the comprehensive term of "Kanakas," are for the most part Malays: the remainder being a motley collection of Manila men, Fijians, natives of New Hebrides, and brown-skinned Polynesians from various Pacific Islands. There is usually but one white man to each station, viz., the manager. The shelling boats—called "apparatus boats" —are entirely under the control of Kanakas. They are each of between five and eight tons burden, are rigged with standing lug-sails, and are provided with the most approved air pump diving apparatus. The crew of one of these boats usually consists of five men, one of whom is the diver; another steers, and the remaining three look after the air pump and signal rope. The time selected for diving operations is usually when there is a "weather tide"; the vessel is then hove-to under easy canvas, so that she may drift slowly to windward, while the diver, following her movements, gropes about the bottom in search of pearl shell. The work is carried on at depths varying between five and sixteen fathoms, and in order to provide against accidents from inequalities in the bottom, as well as to allow the diver greater freedom in his movements, the length of the pipes connecting his dress with the air pump is usually twice the mean depth of the water in which he is working. The signal rope is of a similar length, so that it may be used for hauling up the shell-bag which the diver fills from time to time, without his having to release the end attached to his body, or to make use of a second line. The bag is therefore attached about the middle of the line.

When diving apparatus was first used in Torres Straits, white divers were exclusively employed, and at the same time the Kanakas continued to work as "swimming divers" in the tedious old-fashioned way. As soon, however, as the Kanakas were tried in the diving dresses, it was found that they were far superior to any professional white divers, for not only could they remain much longer under water, but they were also able to move about on the bottom more independently, and to dispense altogether with the weighted rope ladder which the white divers used to look upon as essential. Since the introduction of boats fitted with diving apparatus, the pearl shell trade of Torres Straits has become highly remunerative, and the export of shells has increased enormously.

The shells obtained are classified into two qualities : firstly, young shells, known to the trade as "chicken shell," which are the most valuable, and average about 2,000 to the ton ; and secondly, adult shells, about 700 of which weigh one ton. It is calculated that the annual take of a single boat is about seven tons, of which five tons cover the outlay, and two tons may be reckoned as clear profit. The value per ton has a wide range, varying according to the state of the home market, and may be estimated at from £100 to £300. The number of boats employed last year was 100. In the year 1878, shells to the weight of

449 tons, and valued at £53,021, were exported; and during the same year pearls to the value of £230. Most of the pearls taken are of poor quality, and are so few as to be comparatively valueless; although a fairly good one, without a flaw, and about the size of a pea, is said to be worth £5. Coarse ones of extraordinary size are sometimes obtained. A proprietor and manager (Captain Tucker), who was considered exceptionally fortunate in obtaining pearls, once showed me the proceeds of nine tons of shell which he had just brought in from the fishing-ground. The pearls were of all sorts and sizes; one was as big as a large hazel nut, others were like millet seeds. Altogether they were just sufficient to fill a common match-box, in which indeed he carried them. Official statistics regarding the take of pearls are only to a small extent reliable, as many—probably most—never reach the hands of the proprietors, but are retained as perquisites by the Kanaka divers, who dispose of them secretly.

Most of the shell is sent to Sydney by the steamship *Corea*, where it is purchased by merchants, who send it to Europe for manufacture. Since the establishment of the Queensland Royal Mail steamers, which traverse Torres Straits, some of the shell has been by them conveyed direct to England, where it is consigned to the manufacturers, to the greater profit of the pearl shellers. Most of the shelling establishments in Torres Straits are the property of companies consisting of two or more capitalists, who for the most part reside in Sydney, and it is indeed a rather odd anomaly that a lucrative industry subject to the jurisdiction of the Queensland government should be worked by capital from New South Wales.

Much of my time was occupied in giving medical aid to the people of Thursday Island, and to the *employés* of the pearl-shell stations. My spare time, as opportunities offered, I spent in exploring the group of islands within reach, viz., Horn Island, Prince of Wales Island, Hammond Island, Fitzroy Island, Goode Island, Thursday Island, Possession Island, West Island, and

Natural Features of the Islands—Animal Life.

Booby Island. In geological formation they are all much alike, a quartzite or quartz porphyry being the prevailing form of rock. The land is covered with rank grass, and is for the most part lightly timbered with gum-trees. On the latter a parasitic plant, resembling mistletoe, is commonly met with. Water is scarce, and during a great part of the year some of the islands are practically without any. In searching for water-holes or for damp spots, where water has at some period of the year been present, *Pandanus* trees are in many instances considered to be a safe guide. The rule, however, seems to be that where moisture habitually collects, *Pandanus* trees will be found growing, and not the converse. Attached to rocky surfaces, and to the bark of trees in shady places, the eye is frequently arrested by the sight of most beautiful orchids, principally of the genus *Dendrobium*. These orchids are objects of much concern to the more enterprising colonists, as there is an oft-repeated story that some years ago a white-flowered *Dendrobium* was found on Goode Island, and on being sent to England was sold for £200. Consequently everyone collecting orchids is supposed to be in quest of the famous white species.

Lizards are abundant, especially a large *Monitor*, which, when disturbed, astonishes one by the noise which it makes in scampering over the stones and dead twigs to its burrow, or if this be not at hand, to seek the protection of some friendly tree, up which it climbs with extraordinary facility. They are easily shot. When first I saw their burrows, I considered them to be the work of some burrowing marsupial, and accordingly set a cage-trap opposite the entrance of one. On returning next day, I found, to my surprise, a large *Monitor* coiled up inside the trap, whose dimensions were so small in proportion to the size of the reptile, that the wonder was how he ever managed to stow himself inside. We encountered few snakes, and from inquiries were led to believe that few, if any, poisonous ones existed. However, they are said not to show themselves much during the dry season, which among these islands is supposed to be their time for hybernating.

One day, when exploring in company with Haswell, we found portions of the carapace and pincer-claw of a land-crab (most likely a species of *Geograpsus*), an animal not previously recorded from the islands. On examining the beds of dry mountain gullies, and digging into sand-choked crevices between spurs of rock, where a certain amount of moisture existed, I subsequently obtained several live specimens. No doubt, during the wet season they might be more easily obtained.

Thursday Island possesses six species of land shells. They are *Helix Krefftii, H. Delessertiana, H. Spaldingi, H. Buxtoni, Bulimus Beddomei,* and *Helicina reticulata.* During our stay the island was fired, in order to remove the "spear-grass," which is so destructive to cattle. The fire spread over the whole island, and continued to rage for several days, consuming not only all the grass, but also a great quantity of scrub, and laying bare a vast extent of arid stony surface. It was now an easy matter to collect land-shells, for they lay dead in prodigious numbers on the bare summits of the hills as well as in the hollows, gullies, and other more likely places.

This fire was a great blow to my hopes of collecting plants, almost all the herbaceous ones and many of the creepers having been consumed or shrivelled up by the heat of the conflagration. After much trouble I succeeded in obtaining five species of ferns, which I fancy is not far short of the entire number. Among these were the *Nephrolepis acuta, Pulœa nitida, Polypodium quercifolium, Lindsaya ensifolia,* and the common Australian form, *Lygodium scandens.*

The avifauna of the different islands is, as might be expected, of a similar character to, and differs very little, if at all, from that of the adjoining part of the mainland of Australia. The list of birds includes species of the genera *Campephaga, Ptilotis, Pachycephala, Myzomela, Nectarinia, Dicœum, Trichoglossus, Artamus,*

Mimeta, Halcyon, Nycticorax, Ptictolophus, Chalcophaps, Erythrauchena, Geopelia, Ptilinopus, Myiagra, Sauloprocta, Sphecotheres, Chibia, Centropus, Graucalus, Grallina, Donacola, Tropidorhyncus, Climacteris, Megapodius, Œdicnemus, Ægialitis, Merops, Dacelo, Bruchigavia, Sterna, Pelicanus, Hæmatopus, and others. At Booby Island, a small rocky islet in midchannel, affording no cover beyond a few bushes growing in a cleft in the rocks, we found no less than twelve species of land birds. These were the *Ptilinopus superbus, P. Swainsoni, Myiagra plumbea, Nectarinia Australis, Megapodius tumulus, Porphyrio melanotus, Halcyon sanctus, Nycticorax caledonicus,* a *Zosterops,* a yellow-breasted flycatcher, a landrail, and a quail. From the discrepancies between the different records of the birds found on this island, there is reason to believe that it is mainly used as a temporary resting-place for birds of passage. The "mound bird" (*Megapodius tumulus*) is probably, however, a regular inhabitant.

In examining the cliffs of this island, in quest of sea-birds' nests, I noticed, considerably above the reach of the highest tide, some smooth basin-shaped cavities in the rock containing rounded waterworn stones, such as one sees in the rock pools between tide marks. This circumstance would point to an upheaval of the island during recent geological times.

We sailed from Torres Straits on October 1st, and proceeded under steam towards Port Darwin, in North-West Australia, sounding and dredging on our way, and eventually coming to an anchor in Port Darwin on October 20th. The settlement of Palmerston, off which we lay, is the seat of government for the northern territory of the colony of South Australia, whose capital, Adelaide, is about 1,800 miles away on the south coast, and is separated from Port Darwin by an enormous patch of uncivilized country extending for about 1,500 miles in a north and south direction.

The foundation of a settlement at Port Darwin, which took place about ten years ago (1872), was practically due to the completion of the submarine cable and land telegraph lines, which have each got terminal stations at Port Darwin, where the "through" messages are transferred. Its subsequent progress, such as it has been, was encouraged and fostered by the trade in provisions and gold induced by the workers at the northern territory gold-fields. There are now two submarine cables connecting Port Darwin with Singapore, *viâ* Java, and thence with Europe. The first was laid in 1872, and was found most difficult to maintain on account of the ravages made in it by a boring mollusc, a species of *Teredo*, which in an amazingly short space of time pierced the galvanized iron-wire sheathing of the cable, and destroyed the insulation of the copper core. The repairs of this cable necessitated an outlay of £20,000 per annum, a circumstance contrasting strangely with the condition of a similar cable in the China and India seas, which is not attacked by the *Teredo*. Recently a duplicate cable has been laid, in the construction of which a tape of muntz metal was wound round in a spiral fashion between the insulating material and the twisted wire sheathing. By this provision the new cable has been rendered proof against the boring effects of the *Teredo*, and has hitherto worked successfully without the slightest hitch.

The land telegraph line stretches directly from Port Darwin to Adelaide, a distance of about 1,800 miles, and thus serves to connect all the principal towns of Australia with the station of the Cable Company at Port Darwin. It was at one time thought that there would have been much difficulty in inducing the aborigines to abstain from meddling with the overland wire, but experience has not justified this impression. . It appears that the black fellows hold it sacred, looking on it as a sort of boundary mark to separate the white man's territory from theirs.

Palmerston contains a police magistrate, who is the chief executive authority in the northern territory; a lands department, with its staff of surveyors ; a police inspector, with a detachment of white troopers ; a government doctor ; the two telegraph

Gold-Mining.

stations, with their separate staffs of telegraphists; and, of necessity, a jail.

Our acquaintances on shore spoke in sanguine terms of the prospects of the settlement, and the future greatness which is in store for the northern territory; but to us strangers the appearance of Port Darwin and the surrounding country was by no means indicative of progress, or suggestive of a superabundance of the elements of greatness. Indeed, although the settlement has been in existence since 1872, yet the white population of the whole northern territory does not exceed two hundred; and if it were not for the Chinamen, who have been attracted thither by the "gold-rush," and whose numbers—including those at Port Darwin, Southport, and the gold-fields—amount to 6,000, there would be almost no manual labour available for the white colonists.

The auriferous quartz reefs, which here constitute what are called the "gold-fields," are situated on the side of a range of hills beginning at a distance of about one hundred miles from Port Darwin, in a southerly direction. The usual route thither is by steamboat for twenty-five miles to Southport, a small settlement at the southern extremity of one of the arms of the inlet, and thence by cart track for eighty miles. Unfortunately, during the wet season this track is almost impassable. The gold is obtained from the ore by crushing and amalgamating with mercury in the usual way. In this country the crushing or stamping machines are known as "batteries," and I believe in the northern territory they are worked entirely by steam power. The average yield of gold from the reefs ranges from one and a quarter to one and a half ounces per ton of crushed material, although rock has been met with containing no less than twenty ounces per ton. The latter, however, is altogether exceptional. There are in the same localities alluvial diggings worked in a small way by Chinamen, but the yield of gold is insignificant compared with that from the reefs. I find it stated in the returns furnished by the customs officer at Port Darwin that during the year ending 31st of March, 1881, the northern territory exported 10,107½ ounces, valued at £36,227.

I was told that at the time of our visit there were only two genuine squatters in the whole northern territory. From their stations is drawn the beef supply for the people living at Port Darwin, Southport, and the gold-fields, and it would seem that the supply was quite equal to the demand. Most of the land in the territory is now held on lease by speculators, who pay to the South Australian Government an annual rental of sixpence per square mile, which gives them, under certain conditions, a right of pre-emption, and these speculators now hold on to the land with a view to ultimately disposing of their interest to *bonâ fide* settlers at a large profit to themselves. But until the Colonial Government takes the initiative in affording facilities for the conveyance of produce from the interior to Port Darwin, there seems little likelihood of the land being taken up for either agricultural or pastoral purposes.

The aboriginal inhabitants are numerous in this part of Australia. Those in the vicinity of Port Darwin are of the tribe of "Larikias." In company with Dr. Morice, the government medical officer, I visited two native encampments, which were situated a few hundred yards apart, and at a distance of about half-a-mile from the settlement. One of the camps was on an elevated plateau, covered with thin grass and a sprinkling of scraggy bushes, while the other was at the foot of a high cliff, and immediately adjoining the beach. We found in camp a large number of men, women, and children, most of whom were lolling about on the ground, smoking short wooden pipes, polishing their skins with red ochre, and producing a rude burlesque of music out of pieces of hollow reed about four feet long, which they blew like cowhorns. The stature of the men was much superior to that of the natives we had seen previously on the east coast; but although strong and active, they presented a slim lanky appearance, especially as regards their lower extremities. Their features

ABORIGINES OF NORTH-WEST AUSTRALIA.

were regular, and for the most part pleasing; the hair was long, black, and wavy, sometimes hanging in ringlets; the nose was aquiline, with broad alœ nasi, and having the septum perforated for the reception of a white stick like a pipe-stem; the upper lip, cheek, and chin were furnished with a moderate growth of hair; the teeth were regular—no incisors removed; trunk and extremities almost devoid of hair; the skin of the arms, chest, and abdomen was decorated with cicatrices which stood out from the skin in bold relief, having the form and consistency of cords. On the arms these scars were disposed in parallel vertical lines, while on the chest and abdomen they were in horizontal curves. Dr. Morice informed me that these ghastly decorations were produced in some way unknown by means of a sharp cutting instrument, and that no foreign substance is introduced into the wound. He had been unsuccessful in all his efforts to ascertain how the peculiar raised and indurated character of the sore is produced. The women had fewer scar decorations than the men, but had the same nasal perforation, in which they also wore sticks. All seemed cheerful, happy, and contented with their lot. Their huts were of the usual unsubstantial character, but were, however, an improvement on the "shelter-screens" of the eastern aborigines. They were constructed of boughs of trees supplemented with stray bits of iron sheeting, and other scraps of wood and iron gleaned from the settlement, and they were provided with an arched roof, so that the whole structure was of the shape of a half cylinder lying on its side. Many, however, were little more than "shelter screens," to protect them from the prevailing winds.

Their weapons consisted of spears and clubs. The spears were of different shapes and sizes, some being provided with two or three long slender tapering points of hard wood, deeply serrated along one side, while others were tipped with rudely chipped pieces of sandstone. The former is used for spearing fish, the latter for fighting purposes. The "woomerahs," or throwing sticks, which they always use in propelling their spears, are of two kinds. The most common is about four feet in length, flat and lathlike, and is peculiar in having the angular hook, which engages the butt of the spear, projecting in a plane at right angles to the flat surface of the stick. The other is a light cylindrical stick tapering from the handle end, and its hook consists of a conical-shaped piece of wood, which is secured at an oblique angle to the distal end by means of gum and fibre lashings. The clubs are about four feet long, are made of a hard heavy wood of a red colour, and are fashioned with double trenchant edges towards the striking end, so that a moderate blow from one of these formidable weapons would effectually cleave open any ordinary skull. The boomerang is not used in this part of Australia.

Small-pox has made sad ravages among this tribe of natives, and accounts for the large proportion whom we found to be wholly or partially blind.

The season of the north-east monsoon had just come to a close, and with it the drought and intermittent fever which render Port Darwin an undesirable residence for six months of the year. Calms usually prevail during the month of November, and in December the N.W. monsoon is ushered in by copious showers of rain, an event looked forward to with much satisfaction by the inhabitants of Port Darwin. The annual rainfall during the last half-a-dozen years has ranged from fifty-six to seventy-seven inches, nearly all of which is precipitated during the months of December, January, February, March, and April. Strange to say, during the rainy season the settlement is healthy and entirely free from malarial fever. But shortly before our arrival there had been an epidemic of beriberi—a disease not indigenous to Australia—which had probably been introduced by the Chinese immigrants.

I devoted one forenoon during low water springtides to an inspection of the beach between tide marks, but excepting a few sponges obtained nothing of particular interest. The beaches in the immediate vicinity of our anchorage were smothered with a thick coating of slimy mud, and were consequently not favourable to marine life. With the dredge I was more successful. About the centre of the harbour, in eleven fathoms, the bottom is of sand, and here the fauna is abundant. Of Polyzoa I obtained representatives of several genera, including *Retepora, Eschara, Crisia, Idmonea, Cellepora,* and *Lepralia ;* among Crustaceans the genera *Myra, Phlyxia, Hiastemis,* and *Lambris* afforded many specimens. Many silicious Sponges were also found ; among Shells, *Murex* and *Ranella* were the principal genera observed ; and in hauling the dredge over some muddy ground I got a *Virgularia* about eight inches long.

The commonest bird about the settlement was a brown kite (*Haliastur* sp. ?), which hovered about the refuse heaps on the lookout for garbage, or, perched on the leafless branch of some dying tree, remained huddled up in a lazy and unconcerned attitude, taking no more notice of passers-by than do the hideous Turkey-buzzards which act as scavengers in the towns of Central America. Our ship was all day long surrounded by a flock of these kites, who occupied themselves in picking up with their talons the morsels of food which from time to time were, amid other refuse, cast overboard. The thinly-wooded hollows in the immediate vicinity of the settlement were thronged with numbers of a black and white Grallina (*Grallina picata*) of about the size of a magpie, which, on being disturbed, rose from the ground in flocks to perch on the lower branches of the gum trees, and in company with them I saw many examples of the Drongo (*Chibia bracteata*). Amidst the foliage of the low bushes, a large black Shrike was frequently seen, also a Zosterops, a fly-catcher (*Piezorhynchus nitidus*), and examples of a small finch-like bird (*Donacola castaneothorax*). The latter were congregated in dense flocks, which shifted frequently from tree to tree, making a loud whirring noise with the rapid vibrations of so many tiny wings. When walking through the short grass, numbers of small ground doves (*Geopelia placida*) would start up from almost under one's feet, and alight again on the nearest tree, allowing one to approach them within a few yards. Along the inner or landward edge of the mangrove fringe I saw perched on the summits of the trees a large oriole (*Mimeta*), of which I obtained two female specimens in full plumage; and among some low prickly bushes which grew over the shell heaps of the inner beach, I had a long, and finally successful, chase of a goat-sucker, which had been dodging about under the bushes, without rising on the wing. Large flocks of the New Holland paroquet (*Trichoglossus Novæ Hollandiæ*) flew about the topmost branches of the large gum trees, screaming shrilly. I also saw and obtained a specimen of *S. rubitorquis*, just now a scarce bird, but at other times of the year said to be tolerably abundant. One day I joined a party on a shooting excursion to a fresh water lagoon about twelve miles from the settlement. We were driven to the ground by Mr. Gott, the superintendent of the British and Australian telegraph station, who not only afforded us a pleasant day's shooting, but on this and other occasions evinced the greatest kindness and hospitality. A large black and white goose (*Anseranas melanoleuca*) was met with in immense flocks in the lagoon; and when started from their feeding ground, these birds, to our surprise, betook themselves to the neighbouring gum trees, where they perched with an apparent ease which was astonishing in such great and unwieldy creatures. Although thus so easily circumstanced for pot-shots, it was no easy matter to bring them down, as they required very hard shooting to make any impression on them; so that, notwithstanding a liberal expenditure of ammunition, our united efforts did not produce at all so large a bag as we had at first anticipated. The country through which we drove on our way to and from the lagoon was of an extremely uninteresting nature, being flat and arid, and thinly wooded with stunted gums.

CHAPTER XI.

SEYCHELLE AND AMIRANTE ISLANDS.

OUR voyage from Port Darwin to Singapore took place during the interval of calms which separates the north-west and the south-east monsoons, so that we were enabled to steam the entire distance of 2,000 miles in smooth water. Our course lay among the islands of the Eastern Archipelago. On the 5th of November we sighted Timor Island, and on the following morning passed to the northward of its eastern extremity, and then steered westward, having Timor on our port hand, and the small island of Wetter to starboard. From that date, the chain of islands which extends in a north-west direction from Timor right up to the Malay Peninsula was continually in sight. After dusk on the 7th, we saw away on our port beam, and towering up into the blue and starlit sky, the conical mountain which forms the island of Komba. On the 10th, as we passed to the northward of Sumbawa, we had a fine view of Tambora, a great volcanic pile 9,040 feet in height. On the same day a handsome bird of the Gallinula tribe flew on board, and came into my possession. On the following day a large swift of the genus *Chætura* shared the same fate. On the morning of the 12th we passed through the strait which separates the islands of Sapodie and Madura, and as we emerged from its northern outlet found ourselves in the midst of a large fleet of Malay fishing boats, of which no less than seventy were in sight at one time. These boats were long narrow crafts, fitted with double outriggers, and having lofty curved bows and sterns. They carried a huge triangular sail, which, when going before the wind, is set right athwart-ships with the apex downwards, and when beating seemed to be used like a reversible Fiji sail. On November 17th we passed through the long strait which lays between the islands of Banka and Sumatra, and on the afternoon of the following day dropped our anchor in the roadstead of Singapore.

We made a stay of two and a half months at the great commercial city of Singapore, and for the greater part of the time our ship lay at the Tanjon Paggar dockyard, where she underwent a thorough overhaul, while officers and men had abundant opportunities for relaxation and amusements.

On February 5th, 1882, we again got under way, and quitting the eastern Archipelago by the Straits of Malacca, steered for Ceylon. On the 10th of February, in latitude $6° 15'$ N., longitude $93° 30'$ E., we passed through several remarkable patches of broken water, resembling "tiderips." There was a light northerly breeze, and the general surface of the sea was smooth, so that these curious patches could be distinctly seen when a couple of miles ahead of us, and as we entered each one the noise of tumbling foaming waters was so loud as to attract one's attention forcibly, even when sitting down below in the ward-room. The patches were for the most part disposed in curves and more or less complete circles of half-a-mile in diameter, so that at a distance they bore a strong resemblance to lines of breakers. Soundings were taken, but no inequality in the sea-bed was observed sufficient to account for them. They were most probably due to circular currents revolving in opposite directions, and producing the broken water at their points of contact.

We stopped for two days, February the 17th and 18th, at Colombo, the capital of Ceylon, and then steered for the "Eighth Degree Channel," north of the Maldive Islands, after passing through which we shaped a straight course for the Seychelle Islands.

On the morning of the 4th of March land was reported right

"TRAVELLERS' TREES" IN GARDENS AT SINGAPORE.

[*To face p.* 210.

ahead; but as we soon found out with our glasses, all that was really visible above the horizon was a big tree, which by an optical delusion appeared to be of a prodigious size, and on account of the absence of the usual appearance of land was thought by some of us to be only a sail. We were at this time about ten miles to the north-east of Bird Island, the most northerly of the Seychelle Group. About mid-day we anchored in seven fathoms off the western end of the island, some dozen or so large gannets coming off to meet us, and hovering inquisitively about the ship.

Soon after, a party of officers, including myself, proceeded to land. On touching the beach we were met by a pair of negroes, who, we learned, formed the entire human population of the island. They occupied some wretched huts which had been hitherto screened from our view by a dense thicket of bushes, which forms a fringe around the margin of the island, and gives it, from the anchorage, the delusive appearance of being well wooded.

Their occupation consisted in catching and drying fish, and in salting, for consumption at Mahé, the bodies of sea-birds, which breed on the island in vast numbers, and which are easily taken on their nests during the breeding season—now just coming to an end. The negroes spoke a French dialect, and, whether owing to their habitual taciturnity, or to linguistic difficulties on our part, we could not succeed in extracting much information from them. We gathered, however, that turtle visited the island for breeding purposes, but not at this time of the year.

Bird Island is half-a-mile long, and a quarter of a mile in width, being thus more or less oval in outline. It is formed entirely of coral, and is margined all round with white glistening beaches of calcareous sand. Outside this extends a fringing reef, which forms a submerged platform, on which there is some three or four fathoms of water, and which has a mean width radially of about a quarter of a mile. There is no encircling barrier reef, while the soundings are so regular as to exclude the existence of coral knolls. The general surface of the island is quite flat, and has a mean elevation above the sea-level of about eight feet. Immediately within the sandy beach above mentioned is a raised inner beach composed of blown sand and lumps of coral, on which flourishes a belt of low green *Tournefortia* bushes. After traversing this, one walks over a rugged plain of honey-combed coral rock, the interstices of which are in some places filled with sand and vegetable mould, which supports a more or less general mantle of scrubby grass, interspersed with several introduced plants gone wild. Among these were cotton, sugarcane, papaws, yams, gourds, cocoa-nuts, and perhaps a few others. It appeared that none of these had been found to thrive, which no doubt accounts for their present neglected state. We now ascertained that the large tree which had attracted our attention from the offing was a *Casuarina*, of which there were altogether two or perhaps three on the island.

There were no land birds. Sea birds, however, were very abundant, and seemed in many ways to have partially adapted themselves to the habits of their terrestrial congeners. The sand and light soil, which in some places occupied the cavities in the coral rock, were everywhere excavated by the burrows of petrels, so that within an area of four square yards one might count as many as a dozen. There were also smaller burrows—not admitting the hand—in one of which I captured a land-crab. Walking over the island—small as it was—proved to be very fatiguing and aggravating, for after one had extracted a bruised ankle from some treacherous hole in the coral, which the long grass concealed, the next step, taken with misplaced confidence on an inviting-looking patch of sand, would probably put the other foot through the frail roof of a petrel burrow, into which it would descend, to the alarm and indignation of its proper tenant, no less than to the mortification of the explorer.

Many gannets were breeding on the island. I approached

a large brown bird as it sat on its nest, and, being anxious to obtain a specimen of the egg, endeavoured to frighten it off by going within a couple of yards and shouting riotously. The bird, however, did not seem to heed me. I then tried stones, but with no better result. Eventually I had to resort to sterner measures, which I forbear to mention, but which proved satisfactory. The nest consisted of a few twigs and pieces of withered grass, placed on the surface of the hard coral.

The terns, of which there were great numbers, either standing quietly on the ground in flocks or perched singly on the low bushes, had just concluded their breeding labours, and I found a few abandoned eggs. Their nests were similar to those of the gannet above mentioned. Consorting with the terns and gannets were multitudes of white egrets, stalking about unconcernedly in the long dry grass, or perching in a dreamy sort of way on the topmost twigs of the bushes. All these birds, terns, gannets, and egrets, seemed to be quite as much at home when perching on the bushes or standing in the grass as in their usual attitude on the wing. They seemed indeed very loth to fly, and after being rudely disturbed soon settled down again. The beaches of the weather or east side of the island were studded with great flocks of turnstones and curlews, with which were a few oyster-catchers, and soaring high overhead was a great flock of frigate birds.

At an early hour on the following morning (March 5th) we were again under way, and steering towards Port Mahé, which lies sixty miles to the southward of Bird Island. The dredge had been laid out from the stern of the ship soon after anchoring, and on hauling it up just before waying, one of the tangles was found to have attached to it a large slab of dead coral, which contained a great variety of forms of life. There were on its surface several detached masses of growing Corals, comprising five or six different species, and an equal number of Polyzoa, besides some Nullipores and Millepores. In the interstices were several species of shells, worms, and Ophiurids, and two or three species of sponge.

At three o'clock in the afternoon we anchored at Mahé, the chief island of the Seychelle Group.

Seychelles, a term which is used to comprise the group of eighty islands, has been a British colony since the year 1794, when it was taken from the French by force of arms. Most of the land is in the possession of descendants of the old French settlers, men who have the reputation of being devoid of enterprise, and of squandering the produce of their land in habits of dissipation. We were told that among the upper classes there were only about six Englishmen in the group, including the governor, secretary, and doctor, etc. By a census taken in 1880, the total population was 14,035, of which 2,029 was represented by African negroes. The population of the chief island, Mahé, alone amounted to 11,393, so that there remains less than 3,000 to be divided among the remaining islands of the Group. The total has since been increasing, owing to a stream of immigration having set in from Mauritius, where there exists a commercial depression; so that at the time of our visit it was said to amount to 18,000.

I think that to most people Seychelles is principally known as the home of that eccentric palm, the double cocoa-nut, or " Coco de Mer." Its range is indeed very restricted, being, in fact, limited to Praslin,—one of the smaller islands of the Group,— and even there it only grows in one particular valley. A few have been introduced into Mahé, and great care is now being taken in order to promote their extension. There was a handsome specimen of the female tree growing in the grounds of Government House, which was shown to me by Mr. Brodie, the courteous Secretary to the Council. The tree being unisexual, isolated specimens can only be made fruitful by artificial means. In the present instance, the tree being over thirty years old, and in the proper condition for impregnation, Mr. Brodie had taken the trouble to obtain from Praslin the reproductive portion of a male plant, which he had placed over the immature fruits on the female tree. The male tree bears a long thick spike, studded with minute flowers, the pollen from which must be shaken over the female flowers, in order to insure impregnation. The tree at Mahé was about twenty feet high, but I was informed by Mr. Brodie that fully grown trees in the island of Praslin attain a height of a hundred feet. The mature nuts if left on the ground readily germinate. The outer hard covering splits at the sulcus of the nut, and from thence shoots out a rhizome, which after extending underground for a few feet gives origin to the future stem and rootlets, which proceed respectively upwards and downwards from the termination of the rhizome. The Coco de Mer is an article of trade, a good many being brought over annually to Mahé, where some are sold to visitors as curiosities, while the remainder are shipped to the Red Sea ports to be sold to the Arabs, who have a profound belief in their medicinal properties.

In the gardens of Government House were also two fine examples of the celebrated Land Tortoise of Aldabra, an animal which, although indigenous in Aldabra Island alone, has of late years been introduced into many of the neighbouring islands. The pair at Mahé were male and female, and weighed respectively about four hundred and five hundred pounds. The male seemed to have no difficulty in bearing a man upon his back. At the time of our visit the female had just commenced to lay, depositing her eggs in holes which she excavated in the damp soil, and carefully filled in.

From a commercial point of view, the Seychelle Islands are now in a transition state. The cocoa-nut industry has of late years been unprosperous, mainly owing to the ravages of a worm which invades the roots and stem of the cocoa-nut trees, and causes them to dwindle and perish. The produce of oil has consequently been so reduced, and the freight charges continue to be so high, on account of the absence of steamship competition, that only a small margin of profit is left to the planter. This failure of the cocoa-nuts has led to a revival of the old spice industry, which, under the early French settlers, was at one time deemed likely to vie with that of the Moluccas. On looking over the Blue Book Report, I find that in the year 1880 there were 12,000 acres of land planted with cocoa-nuts, which in spite of the recent blight continue to be the staple product of the Group. In the same year there were one hundred and fifty acres devoted to the growth of vanilla; a hundred acres were planted with cacao bushes, and a hundred and fifty were producing cloves; besides a large extent of land bearing coffee plantations. Both the Liberian and the common coffee plants have been introduced, and found to grow remarkably well. Vanilla, in particular, seems to find a congenial home in the Seychelle Islands, and, during our short visit to the colony, we gathered that the future hopes of the settlers were mainly centred upon the successful cultivation of this plant. It grows rapidly, and although the flowers require to be fertilized by hand, yet this process is so readily performed that beans of large size and excellent quality are produced. It is as yet only grown in a small way, most of the vanilleries, as these plantations are called, covering only an extent of about five acres. It is estimated that each plantation of this size represents an annual produce of two hundred and fifty pounds' weight of vanilla beans. We inspected some plants in the garden of Dr. Brookes, an old resident, and noticed that the beans averaged eight inches in length, and were otherwise well formed. He told us that he had been most successful in the curing of these beans, and expected that when they became well known they would command a large price in the European markets, and that eventually vanilla would became the staple produce of the Seychelle Islands.

The method employed at Seychelles for the expression of the oil from the internal white lining of the cocoa-nut struck me as being novel and primitive; and as it is said to be very efficient, I shall try to give an intelligible description of a crushing mill and its mode of construction. In principle it is a sort of gigantic pestle and mortar, in which the pestle is made to perform a movement of circumduction, and whilst doing so to rotate against the sides of the mortar, where the crushing process is effected. A large-stemmed tree of very hard wood having been cut down, so as to leave about three feet of the trunk projecting above the ground, a bucket-shaped cavity is excavated in the stump. A heavy round spar about ten feet in length is stepped into this cavity, and is made to incline forcibly to one side by means of a wooden outrigger, which is supported by a rope attached to the head of the spar, and is weighted with heavy stones placed at its outer extremity. The inner end of the outrigger is fitted with wide U-shaped jaws, which engage in a collar scored in the tree stump just above its point of emergence from the ground, while the rope-lift which supports its outer extremity is so attached to the head of the upright spar that the outrigger may be free to move radially about the stump at the same time that the upright spar rolls round on its long axis, as it presses heavily against the sides of the trough. Finally a small hole is bored laterally, so as to reach the bottom of the cavity in the tree stump, and into this is thrust a short bamboo tube to act as an oil-tap. The broken-up copra is thrown in around the lower extremity of the upright spar, and a bullock is set to work to drag round the outrigger arrangement. The only attendance required is that of a small boy to feed the wooden trough with copra, and occasionally to throw stones so as to accelerate the otherwise lazy motion of the bullock. In the mill which I examined the oil was flowing steadily from the bamboo tap in a clear limpid stream.

We dredged several times with the steam cutter in the channel between Mahé and St. Anne's Island, and also in St. Anne's Channel. The depth of water in these channels ranged from four to twelve fathoms, and the bottom consisted of sand and coral. The fauna was abundant, and comprised Shells of the genera *Murex, Arca*; large grey Holothurians; Echinoderms of four or five species; Crustacea of the genera *Thalamites, Galathea*,

Porcellana, Atergitus, Scilla, Alpheus, etc., and a large variety of Corals and Polyzoa.

One of the most conspicuous objects about the foreshore at Port Mahé is a curious fish of the genus *Periophthalmus*, which may be seen not only jumping about the dry mud flats at low water, but also climbing up the rugged vertical faces of the blocks of granite of which the sea-wall and pier are formed. It is very difficult indeed to catch one, as I have good reason to know. Associated with them were several species of crabs, among which I recognized representatives of the genera *Macrophthalmus, Gelasimus, Grapsus,* and *Ocypoda.*

The Seychelles are peculiar in being the only small tropical oceanic islands of granitic structure. All the others, excepting St. Paul's Rocks, are either of volcanic or coral formation. The rock about Port Mahé is a syenitic granite, in which the mica of ordinary granite is replaced by hornblende. In some cases the felspar is coloured blue, in others reddish, and in every instance it occurred in large coarse crystals. The soilcap was a reddish pasty clay, of great thickness. In one of the road cuttings near the settlement a section of this clay fully ten feet in depth was exposed.

We left Mahé on the 14th of March, and on the following day anchored off a small coral islet, the northernmost of the Amirante Group. This, with another similar islet adjoining, constitute the African Islands. A party of surveyors immediately landed in order to fix on a suitable place for taking midnight observations of the stars, and I had soon afterwards an opportunity of landing to explore. The islet is two hundred yards long, by about sixty yards in width, is more or less elliptical in outline, low, and flat, and for about three-fourths of its circumference is girt by a smooth beach of coral sand, on the surface of which I noticed a prodigious number of *Orbitolites* discs. The northern end of the islet is composed of upraised coral sandstone, which has been grooved and honeycombed into various fantastic shapes, so that

"COIRA" CRUSHING MILL IN USE AT SEYCHELLES (*p.* 217).

(*To face p.* 218.)

for walking over it presents quite as unsatisfactory a surface as volcanic clinker. All the central part of the islet within the inner drift beach is covered with scrubby grass and low bushes of the same character as those at Bird Island. There were one or two young shoots of a *Barringtonia*; but nothing else in the shape of an arborescent plant. Among the dead shells, light driftwood, and bleached sponges and coral blown up on the inner beach, I noticed some of the familiar rhomboidal fruits of a *Barringtonia*.

There were no land birds. The sea birds were identical with those of Bird Island. Young unfledged gannets were waddling about among the bushes, and as regards the other birds, their nesting season also seemed to be over. I did not notice any petrel burrows, but everywhere near the beach were the burrows of a littoral crab, a species of the genus *Ocypoda*. On the rocks at the northern extremity were multitudes of the widely distributed *Grapsus variegatus*. When chasing them over the rocks of the foreshore, I observed that they were reluctant to take to the water, but preferred to keep clear of me by scampering away over the coral further inshore. The cause of this strange behaviour on their part soon became apparent; for the rockpools about the foreshore were tenanted by savage grey eels, ranging in length from two to three feet, and I saw that the moment an unlucky crab was forced to enter one of these pools, he was immediately snapped up and devoured. I was surprised to see the coolness with which an eel would every now and then raise its head above the water in which it lay, and look about over the adjacent rocks to see if any crabs were near. On starting an eel from its hiding place, it would scuttle with astonishing rapidity over the low rocks which separated it from the water's edge, so that it. was no easy matter to secure one without the aid of a gun Shooting them, as they wriggled off in this way, was rather good sport.

The island is evidently visited by turtle during the breeding season, for we saw several of the excavations in which they were in the habit of depositing their eggs.

We got under way at seven o'clock in the morning, and after running several lines of soundings over the outer edge of the Amirante bank, steamed over to Eagle Island, which lies about thirteen miles to the southward of African Islands, and again dropped anchor.

Eagle Island is somewhat oval in shape, and is a quarter of a mile long by one-eighth in breadth. It is entirely of coral formation, is low and flat, is covered with a thick growth of stunted bushes, and in other physical features is much the same as the African Islands. There was, however, an increase in the fauna in the shape of a small red-legged partridge, which was very abundant, and afforded us some good shooting. Owing to the thickness of the scrub, and weedy undergrowth of grasses, ill-conditioned gourds and calabashes, it was found very difficult to recover the dead birds, so that I fear there were a good many shot which were never bagged. The only other land-birds on the island were domestic fowls gone wild. Of these we saw an old cock and hen, and some three or four chickens, which, on being disturbed, rose and took to flight like pheasants.

In the interior of the island, among a tangled scrub of bushes, we found the remains of an old stone-built hut, which from the solidity of its four walls would seem to have been originally intended as a permanent dwelling for Europeans.

I took several specimens of a small species of lizard, and also some of the tiny spherical eggs of the same. I stowed away the eggs in a matchbox with some sand, and left it open on the table of the deckhouse on board. After a day or two the young lizards began to break out of their eggs, and to wander about among the materials on my work-table. I broke open one egg, and found that the youngster was at once able to run about. After it had wandered about the table, and up and down the sides of some bottles standing near, it returned to the matchbox and remained for a long time hovering about it, as if terrified at the immensity of the world, and loth to venture away from its former narrow dwelling.

In some small holes about the centre of the islet we found a land-crab, apparently similar to that of Bird Island; and from some large burrows issued the peculiar groaning sounds made by the night petrel.

One of the most singular features in the zoology of the islet was the abundance of a hermit crab,—occupying a *Neritina* shell,—which was to be seen and heard creeping over the stems and branches of the bushes in all directions. They seemed for the time to have entirely adopted terrestrial habits.

We got under way again on the morning of the 20th of March, and, after spending the day in sounding from the ship, steamed up to Darros Island, and again anchored.

This island is somewhat circular in shape, and has a maximum diameter of three-quarters of a mile. It is inhabited by a Frenchman and his wife, who are assisted by nine negro labourers from Mahé. Adjoining are nine small islets, bearing a rich crop of cocoa-nuts. Darros Island itself as yet produces next to nothing, but it contains a large plantation of young cocoa-nuts, which in five or six years will doubtless be productive. Immediately behind the Frenchman's house, and affording an agreeable shade, was a handsome grove of *Casuarinas* about eighty feet in height. They were nineteen years old, as we subsequently ascertained. Many introduced plants—such as papaws, cotton, pumpkin, etc.—were growing in a neglected state over the island.

We dredged from the ship as she lay at anchor in twenty-one to twenty-two fathoms, over a bottom which was mainly composed of coral *débris*, and among the living organisms brought up were three species of stony corals. This circumstance is of interest as regards the bathymetrical distribution of corals, inasmuch as Dana, judging from the results of observations made by various authorities, considers that twenty fathoms may be regarded as the limit in depth at which reef-forming corals live. Polyzoa were numerous. I noticed representatives of the genera *Retepora, Crisia, Eschara, Cellepora, Lepralia*, and *Myriozoum*. There were also some examples of *Sertularia* and other flexible hydroids.

Our gropings over the platform of fringing reef, which formed the foreshore at low water, resulted in the acquisition of several species of holothurians. Among these was a large *Synapta*, which was abundant, and a very tough-skinned holothurian—of the genus *Moliria*—provided with organs resembling teeth at its posterior extremity.

On March 23rd we moved over to Poivre Island—a few miles distant—where we anchored, and remained for part of two days.

Poivre Island was colonized for the first time in the year 1820. It is now the property of a Frenchman residing at Paris, and is managed by his agent, a Monsieur Bertaut, who, with his wife and family, and some twenty negroes and their wives, form the population of the island, altogether amounting to twenty-seven. Of course the staple produce is cocoa-nut oil, and the island having been planted with cocoa-nuts at an early period in its history, the trees are in good condition for bearing, and cover every available spot of ground. Among the other trees on the island I noticed a *Casuarina* and a *Ficus*. Two shrubs were common; one, called the "Bois D'aimanthe" (*Suriana maritima*), formed a sort of hedge around the island, and the other was a *Tournefortia*, which seems to be the first plant to establish itself on these islands. The fauna included a black-and-white rabbit—of course introduced—which was very abundant, and some pigeons of a dark-brown plumage. Pigs and domestic poultry seemed to be largely favoured by the colonists, and were indeed in a thriving state.

Like all the Amirantes, Poivre Island is low and flat, and is only exceptional in being the most prosperous island of the group, for which it is indebted to the zeal of the earlier colonists who planted its splendid grove of cocoa-nuts. The island is oval in shape, about two miles in circumference, and it has a broad fringing reef composed of drift coral and sand, but exhibiting no live corals and very few shells.

We cast anchor off the north-west side of Isle des Roches on the evening of the 25th of March, and stayed there for four days. This is the largest island of the Amirante Group, being three and a half miles long, and having an average width of half-a-mile. It is visible for a long distance off, on account of its possessing several large groves of tall *Casuarina* trees, many of which are one hundred and eleven feet in height. On the shore, immediately opposite to our anchorage, was the settlement, which then exhibited a rather desolate appearance, as many of the houses were in an abandoned condition, most of the inhabitants having recently gone back to Seychelles. Only two individuals remained, French creoles, who seemed to have acquired, from their solitary situation, habits of taciturnity, which they found it difficult to break through. At all events, we could not succeed in extracting much information from them. They were well off for supplies, having a large stock of pigs and poultry, besides fruit and vegetables. Cocoa-nuts had been planted extensively, but as yet few of these trees were old enough to bear fruit. At the time of our visit, the natives were engaged in planting vanilla cuttings about the bases of the casuarina trees, which furnished excellent supports for the creeper to attach itself to.

The flora was more extensive than that of the other islands. There was a large-leafed shrub with thick branches like cabbage-stalks, the *Scævola Kænigii*, which over ran the island. There were also herbaceous plants of the families *Malvaceæ*, *Solanaceæ*, *Cinchonaceæ*, and *Convolvulacæ*. Among the trees I noticed a *Ficus*, which, however, may have been introduced; and here I obtained the only fern met with among the Amirantes, the *Nephrolepis exaltata;* it was growing near the sea beach at the eastern end of the island.

There were six land birds : viz., a red-legged partridge, a pigeon, a large brown finch, and a small yellow-breasted finch, a red-capped weaver-bird, and a waxbill (?). Of these I could only obtain specimens of the small finch and the weaver-bird. The yellow-breasted finch is gregarious, and mostly frequents the tops of the cocoa-nut trees and the upper branches of the tall casuarinas, where it keeps up an incessant melody of song, pleasant to the ear in the variety and succession of the notes, and somewhat resembling the song of the canary. In the large casuarina grove, near the western end of the island, I succeeded, but with much difficulty, in procuring some male specimens of the weaver-bird (*Foudia Madagascarensis*). The females were nesting. I observed one of the latter flying away from the tree in which its nest was constructed, and from which I had disturbed it. It differed from the male in having the red-coloured feathers confined to the head, the rest of the plumage being of a dull brown. The nest was an oblong affair, having a lateral opening, and was constructed of a parasitic plant of creeping habit, which the creoles use for making a substitute for tea. The nest hung from the extremity of a casuarina branch which projected horizontally. The male bird was to be seen perched singly on the summits of the large casuarinas, where it made its presence known by a peculiar and characteristic twittering note which it emits about four times in a minute. It was very wary, and difficult to approach within a sixty yards' range, so that it was only by most careful stalking that I could succeed in bringing down a specimen. The brown finch was not abundant, and seemed to confine its range to the plantations of young cocoa-nuts, where it was continually shifting its perch. The waxbill was a very small bird, which was to be seen every now and then flitting in large flocks among the maize plants and low bushes. I was much surprised to find that the four small birds above mentioned were so very wary, as there were no predatory birds on the island, and it was unlikely that they had ever been shot at before. Nevertheless, the motion of raising one's gun at a distance of sixty yards or more was enough to scare away any of them.

The partridge was identical with that already seen at Eagle and Darros Islands. The pigeon, which I have included among the list of the birds, I saw only once. But one of the creoles living on the island told me that it was an indigenous species, and was quite distinct from the domestic pigeons which roost about and restrict their range to the houses and trees about the settlement.

Although this island has been classed as one of the Amirante Group, it would be more correct to look upon it as distinct and apart from the main group, inasmuch as the bank on which it rests is separated from the Amirante bank by a deep water channel eleven miles wide. We sounded across this channel, and obtained no bottom with one hundred fathoms of line. Isle des Roches is, moreover, peculiar in forming part of an atoll, most of which is submerged, and is covered with from two to five fathoms of water. The circumscribed patch of deep water in the interior has a depth of about fifteen fathoms.

During the week subsequent to our departure from Isle des Roches, we anchored successively off the four remaining islets of the group; viz., Etoile, Marie-Louise, Des Neufs, and Boudeuse. They are mere cays, formed of coral and drift sand, and are uninhabited. Owing to the heavy surf which broke all round their shores, we found it unsafe to land.

With our brief visit to the islets just mentioned our survey of the Amirante Group came to an end. I will, therefore, before quitting the subject, make a few general remarks on the group as a whole. The Amirante Group consists altogether of twenty-one low coral islets, resting (with the exception of Isle des Roches, which is on a separate bank) on an extensive coral bank, whose long axis lies in a north-north-east and south-south-west direction, and is eighty-nine miles in length, with an average breadth of nineteen miles. It is included between the limits of $4°\ 50\frac{1}{2}'$ and

6° 12½' south latitude, and 53° 45' and 52° 50½' east longitude, and is about seven hundred miles distant from the nearest part of the East African coast. Some of the islets and cays of which it is composed, and which are included in the above enumeration, are so grouped into clusters, that for all practical purposes the group may be considered as consisting of nine islets, which have been named African Island, Eagle Island, Darros Island, Poivre Island, Des Roches Island, Etoile Island, Marie-Louise Island, Des Neufs Island, and Boudeuse Island. Of these only three are inhabited; viz., Darros (including the adjoining islet " St. Joseph," which is occupied by part of the same establishment of creoles), Poivre Island, and Isle des Roches; the population consisting of French creoles and negroes imported from Seychelles, who make a livelihood by cultivating cocoa-nuts, and altogether do not exceed forty in number. The islets are all low and flat, are formed entirely of coral and coral-sandstone, and their general surface has an altitude above high water mark not exceeding fifteen feet, while in the case of African Island, the lowest, it is not more than seven feet. Most of them, however, are conspicuous from a long distance at sea, on account of their possessing clumps and groves of casuarina trees, which tower to heights ranging from eighty to one hundred and eleven feet above the soil, as ascertained by trigonometrical measurement. The casuarinas at Darros Island, which were eighty feet in height, had been planted nineteen years prior to the time of our visit by a Frenchman named Hoyaeux, whom we subsequently met at Providence Island.

All the islets above-mentioned possess " fringing reefs," but are distinguished from the coral islets of the South Pacific, and of the other parts of the Indian Ocean, by the entire absence of " barrier reefs." The soundings which we made over the Amirante bank showed a general uniformity in the contour of its surface; whilst at the same time there was abundant evidence that the central portions were more depressed than the margins. Soundings in the latter situation gave a depth ranging from ten to fourteen

Nature of the Coral Bank.

fathoms, and as each line of soundings reached the central depressed area of the bank, a depth of about thirty fathoms. The islands were for the most part situated near the margin of the bank, and were in every case surrounded by a zone of shallow water. Hence it is obvious that if the entire structure were suddenly to undergo an elevation of about fourteen fathoms, or eighty-four feet, it would present the appearance of an atoll studded with comparatively lofty islets, and enclosing a lagoon of still water sixteen fathoms in depth.

The outer edge of the bank was exceedingly abrupt, for within a ship's length the soundings changed from ten or fourteen fathoms on the margin, to no bottom with one hundred fathoms of line immediately outside the edge. This precipitous character of the reef-edge was found to be the same throughout its entire extent. At various points over this area growing corals were obtained at depths ranging from twelve to twenty-two fathoms, the latter being somewhat greater than the limit in depth at which it is generally agreed that reef-forming corals can live. It therefore follows, that if the entire bank were now to subside bodily at a faster rate than the corals can by their growth raise the surface upwards, these organisms would soon be immersed below their natural limit, and would consequently die. But we have no evidence of a subsidence having occurred, beyond the fact that the bank, as a whole, bears a resemblance to a submerged atoll, while on the other hand there are some positive evidences of elevation to be seen in the overlying islands. At Eagle Island, the general surface—that is to say, all the land within the inner, or coral-drift beach—is level, and consists of dead coral *in situ;* so that if denuded of its present covering of low vegetable growth, it would present much the same appearance that a broad platform of fringing reef might, if elevated above high-water mark and allowed to remain exposed to the weather for a few years. The same is the case as regards the greater part of one of the African Islands which we visited; while its northern extremity was composed of upraised coral sandstone, standing *in situ*, and exhibiting excavated grottoes and jagged pinnacles, resulting from old marine degradation. It may therefore be inferred that these two islands have been subjected to a movement of elevation to the extent of at least a few feet at some period subsequent to the formation of their present reef-coral surfaces. Again, at Isle des Roches, which, however, it should be remembered lies on a separate, although adjacent bank, there were along its southeastern margin stratified beds of hard coral sandstone occupying a position above high-water mark, and presenting to seaward an abrupt eroded face of hard rock which was undergoing degradation, and was being undermined by the action of the waves on a soft subjacent stratum. As regards the other islands of the group, I have seen no evidence of elevation beyond the fact that they are higher than either African or Eagle Island; one of the most southerly being as much as fifteen feet above high-water mark. I may add that the absence of "barrier reefs" throughout the group militates against the probability of subsidence having taken place. There is, therefore, reason to believe that the entire group have undergone elevation rather than subsidence; and if the forces which produced this condition be still in operation, and continue so until a further elevation of fourteen fathoms has been effected, there will result an atoll over eighty miles long by twenty in width, and studded with lofty coral islands, somewhat resembling the high islands of the south-eastern Paumotus, such as Elizabeth Island, which Dana describes as being eighty feet in height.

The Amirante Group furnishes an illustration of the generally accepted position that corals grow more luxuriantly on the weather than on the lee side of banks and reefs. In this region, a wind, varying in direction between east and south-east, prevails throughout ten months of the year, and consequently gives rise to a proportionately constant surface current; and, on looking at the grouping of the islets, we find that of the eight which rest upon the same bank, six are situated on or about its eastern margin, while the remaining two, which are placed on its southwestern side, are comparatively insignificant sand-cays. Again, Isle des Roches, which rests on a bank to the eastward of the Amirantes, from which it is separated by a deep-water channel eleven miles wide, is situated on the eastern, or weather margin of its own bank—also a partially-submerged atoll.

CHAPTER XII.

CONCLUSION.

ON completing our surveying work at the Amirante Group we steamed back to Port Mahé, Seychelles, in order to replenish our stock of coals. After a stay of a few days we again got under way (17th of April), and shaped a course for Alphonse Island, which occupies an isolated position sixty miles south-west-by-south of the southern extremity of the Amirante bank.

We reached Alphonse Island on the 19th of April, about midday, and saw that in shape, and general appearance, it much resembled one of the Amirantes—for instance, Poivre ; but, however, in one important characteristic was different. It possessed a sort of barrier reef little less than a wash, and sufficiently indicated by a long line of heavy breakers. We steamed round the island, holding a course parallel to the line of breakers, and within a few ships' lengths of it, but we got no soundings with fifty fathoms of line. On attaining a position opposite to the southern extremity of the island, we saw a canoe approaching, the occupants of which, an elderly white man and some negroes, soon afterwards boarded us. The information which they gave us confirmed our impression as to there being no anchorage suitable for a large ship anywhere near the island. We learned that it was the property of a Frenchman named Baudon, who resides in Europe, and that the population consisted of twenty-eight, six being whites—viz.,

John Hickey, the manager, with his wife and children—and the remainder, mulattoes and negroes. The island seemed to us to be covered with cocoa-nut trees, but we were told that only a small number were old enough to bear nuts. The produce consisted of copra, green turtle, hawk's-bill turtle, and pearl-shell. Of the latter, two thousand shells had been exported within the previous two years; and we also learned from Hickey that he then had nine hundred in store awaiting shipment. The shells, which are much smaller than those of Torres Straits, and have a black internal margin like those of Ceylon, are obtained by negro swimming-divers. They are found in the still-water pools, inside the barrier reef, where they lie in four or five fathoms of water; and on account of the danger from sharks they are only sought for in these enclosed pools. Although a good many pearls of small size are met with, the commercial value of the fishery depends on the mother-of-pearl of the shells.

Fish are caught in great abundance, and as poultry thrive well, a large stock of them are kept and allowed to run wild. Fresh water being also plentiful, the inhabitants are not on the whole badly off for the necessaries of life.

After a long interview with old Hickey, who most generously presented us with some turkeys and ducks, we bade him a long good-bye, and steamed away towards Providence Island.

We anchored off the west side of this island on the forenoon of the 21st of April, and lay about a mile from the land, and a quarter of a mile outside a long fringing reef, over the raised outer edge of which the sea broke heavily, forming an almost continuous line of rollers.

Providence Island lies two hundred and forty miles from the Amirante Islands, in a south-west-by-south direction, and is two hundred miles north-east-by-north from the northern extremity of Madagascar. It is entirely of coral formation, is low and flat, and measures two miles in length by one-third of a mile in width. It is surrounded with broad submerged fringing reefs, which at the southern extremity of the island are continuous with a long reef, extending in a southerly direction for a distance of sixteen miles, and partially dry at low tide. At its southern termination are three small islets, or rather sand-cays, which are termed collectively Cerf Islands.

Providence Island belongs to two Seychelle gentlemen; viz., Mr. Dupuys and Dr. Brookes, for whom it is managed by an elderly Frenchman named Hoyaeux. The population consists of Hoyaeux, with his wife and nephew, and a gang of negroes, male and female, amounting in all to thirty-four. The houses of the settlement are situated on either side of a broad avenue which traverses the middle of the island from east to west. The only landing-place is at the western end of this avenue, opposite to which we were anchored; and even here it was always somewhat dangerous, and in bad weather quite impracticable to effect a landing, on account of the rollers which broke over the outer edge of the fringing reef. The latter forms the nearest approach to a "barrier reef" which I have yet seen in these waters; excepting that at Alphonse Island, which we had not time to examine carefully. The depth of water over its general surface is not more than a fathom at low tide; while at its outer edge, which is marked by the line of breakers, the depth is only a foot or so less.

The produce of the island consists of cocoa-nut oil and green turtle. The greater part of the island is covered with cocoa-nut plantations, young and old, for which the soil seems admirably suited. I noticed that here the cocoa-nuts had been planted in the surface soil, and not in pits as at Poivre and Des Roches; and on my making a remark to that effect, Monsieur Hoyaeux, the manager, explained to me the reason. It has been found by experience that cocoa-nuts will not thrive on any of these islands unless they are so planted that the roots may be enabled to reach the bed of coral into which the sea-water penetrates. Hence it follows that when nuts are planted on any but very low coral islands it has been found advisable to put them at the bottom of basin-shaped excavations some three or four feet in depth, so that the roots may have a chance of reaching the moist coral beneath. Providence Island being sufficiently low by nature, it was not necessary to make these excavations.

Green turtle are captured in great numbers during the month of April, when the females come up on the beaches to deposit their eggs. A turtle pond near the settlement contained, at the time of our visit, no less than eighty, all of large size. In connection with this pond a portion of the sandy inner beach was wattled in, so as to serve as a hatching-ground for the captured turtle. As soon as the young ones have become sufficiently strong to take care of themselves, they are turned adrift into the open sea. In this way the young turtle escape the danger, which they are otherwise exposed to when of a tender age, of being destroyed by predatory sea-birds; and thus the maintenance of the stock is favoured. It is a curious thing that young turtle seem to have a difficulty about, or a strong disinclination to, diving beneath the surface of the water. One almost always sees them floating in the ponds, instead of groping about the bottom as the adults do.

The indigenous fauna and flora were almost identical with those of the Amirantes, except that there were no land-birds as at Isle des Roches. Monsieur Hoyaeux very kindly supplied me with the creole names of the trees, shrubs, and one or two herbaceous plants. Among these were the "Bois Blanc" (*Hernandia peltata*), "Sauve Souris" (a low tree with long dark green leaves), "Bois Cu Cu" (a tree with drupaceous fruit, having a curved hook at the apex), "Veloutier Tabac" (*Tournefortia argentea*, a seaside bush of the family *Apocynaceæ*, the leaves of which are sometimes smoked instead of tobacco), and the "Veloutier Blanc" (*Scævola Kœnigii*, a very common seaside bush of the family *Goodeniaceæ*). Some of the bushes and *Casuarina* trees (called "Cedre" by the creoles) were overrun with a parasitic creeping plant, *Cassytha filiformis*, which they use for making a sort of tea, and to which they give the name " Liane sans feuilles."

The huge land-tortoises of Aldabra have been imported, and seem to find a congenial home in the island. There was a herd of seven roaming about among the bushes, one of which was said to be able to carry two men on its back.

Among the introduced plants and vegetables we saw the papaw, custard-apple, pepper, sweet potato, onions, lettuce, capsicum, etc.

Pearl-shell is collected on the reefs, but not as yet in sufficient quantities to establish a lucrative industry. In this respect the island is not so fortunate as Alphonse, for there are no sheltered rock-pools in which the shell can be collected by swimming-divers without danger from the sharks; the sea everywhere flowing in over the outer edge of the broad fringing reef, and the great reef to the southward only drying in patches at low tide.

Small water-worn fragments of precious coral (*C. rubrum*) are from time to time picked up on the reef, but we could not glean any information as to its precise *habitat*. We met with none in our dredgings, which ranged up to a depth of twenty-two fathoms. It probably inhabits the deeper water on the outer slope of the bank. Madame Hoyaeux, who was most kind and hospitable, presented me with some fragments which had been picked up on the reef, and which resembled the *Corallium rubrum* of the Mediterranean.

There are many wells on the island, but in all the water has a saline taste. It is serviceable enough for washing and cooking purposes; but for drinking, the inhabitants rely upon the rain-water which they collect.

On the forenoon of the 28th of April we anchored about a mile and a half to the westward of three small islets, which rest on the southern extremity of the Providence Reef. I then accompanied the captain on a boat-trip to the islets, visiting the two which lay nearest. The most northerly of these we found to be a low and almost barren sand-cay, crescentic in outline, about two hundred yards in greatest length, and thirty yards in width. Near the eastern extremity were two rude fishing-huts which seemed to have been recently inhabited. They contained a turtle-spear and some other fishing appliances, a hatchet, a bag of salt, a tinder-box, and some other small bags which were closed up, and which a delicate regard for the sacred rights of private property deterred us from examining. A few pearl-shells of the species peculiar to these islands lay in a heap near one of the huts. I appropriated, without any scruple, some specimens of these, leaving, however, in exchange, a big lump of tobacco, which I deposited in one of the bags hanging from the rafters of the hut.

Close to the concave margin of the islet was a small turtle-pond, composed of stakes driven vertically into the soft sand, and lashed together so as to form a circular enclosure through which the shallow water flowed freely at all times of the tide. It contained six large turtle.

The only plants growing on the islet were a very young cocoa-nut, scarcely six inches high, and a weed, without flowers, somewhat resembling a *Mesembryanthemum*, and evidently growing wild. The latter may, I think, be considered to be the only indigenous plant on the islet. In strolling over the piled-up sand and broken coral, of which the surface of the islet was composed, I came across three fruits of the widely-distributed *Barringtonia speciosa*, which had evidently drifted on to the beach, and had then been blown up above tide mark.

We subsequently visited a second islet which lay about a mile to the westward of the above, with which it was connected by a shallow reef, probably laid bare at low tide. This second islet proved to be utterly devoid of vegetation, and showed no signs of having ever been inhabited. Strewn over its surface were great quantities of dead shells, among which I saw examples of the genera *Harpa*, *Dolium*, *Bulla*, *Cypræa*, *Littorina*, *Voluta*, *Conus*, etc. From here we obtained a good view of the third islet, and could see on it two large huts and several clumps of bushes, but nothing in the shape of a human being. (One of our boats visited this islet on the following day and reported that the huts were uninhabited, although showing signs of having recently been in use.) There were three plants; viz., the Veloutier Tabac (*Tournefortia argentea*), the Bois D'aimanthe (*Suriana maritima*), a bush with lanceolate woody leaves, and a small herbaceous plant. After a good deal of groping and wading about the shores of the islet, we returned at about 5 p.m. to the place where we had left our boat, but found, to our dismay, that the tide had fallen so low since we had landed, that the boat was now hard and fast on the bare reef, and after repeated efforts to drag it over to the reef-edge, a distance of nearly half a mile, we were obliged to make up our minds to wait for the rising tide. As we were unfortunately without any provisions, our position was not the most agreeable, especially as the boat was not floated off till near midnight.

On the morning of the 1st of May we weighed anchor and steamed over to the island of St. Pierre, which lies about ten miles to the south-west of our last position. We spent some hours sounding off the island in deep water, and as it was reported that there was no safe anchorage, the captain did not attempt to land. Seen from a distance of about half a mile—the nearest we approached to it—St. Pierre appeared to be of a very different character from the islands recently visited. It was somewhat circular in outline, and was covered by a dense growth of scrubby bushes, above which appeared the crowns of three or four isolated palm trees. The mean level of its surface was about thirty feet above the water, so that it was three or four times as high as Providence, or the Amirante Islands. It presented all round a precipitous rock-bound coast worn into jagged pinnacles above, and undermined below by the wear and tear of the heavy ocean swell, which thundered against it and testified to its eroding power by the jets of spray which we saw shot upwards from blowholes through the upper surface of the rock.

Du Lise Island—Flora.

On the 3rd of May we anchored off Du Lise Island, the most northern of the three islets which compose the Glorioso Group. These islets lie about two hundred and seventy miles to the south-west of Providence Island, and one hundred and twenty miles in a west-by-north direction from the northern extremity of Madagascar.

Du Lise Island is of a very irregular shape, both as to its surface and outline, and measures about a quarter of a mile across in various directions. It seems to be formed entirely of coral sandstone, conglomerate, and breccia, and presents to the sea on its north-west side low jagged cliffs of consolidated coral breccia, and on the opposite side a sloping beach composed of hard coral sandstone arranged in gently inclined slabs; while its surface is in one place raised into a large mound about thirty feet in height, covered with trees and rank grass, and probably composed of blown coral sand. Among the tufts of grass on the sloping sides of this mound were great numbers of *Spirula*-shells in a tolerably perfect condition. Many of them lay in sheltered places where they could hardly have been deposited by the agency of the wind alone, and yet if they had been dropped by birds after the latter had devoured the soft body of the mollusc, one would expect to have found the fragile shells in a more or less mutilated state, which was not the case. The circumstance is, therefore, a rather puzzling one to account for satisfactorily.

The flora was more abundant in species than at any of the coral islands to the northward. There were, moreover, no signs of the island having been inhabited; and consequently we saw no palms, for the cocoa-nut does not seem to be *indigenous* at any of the islands recently visited. The prevailing tree was a good-sized banyan, of which many examples appeared to be very old. There were also several Hibiscus trees. As to bushes, there were a few isolated examples of the "Veloutier blanc," while the low central part of the island, into which the seawater penetrated so as to form a filthy salt-marsh, was covered with a dense impenetrable thicket of "Bois d'Aimanthe." Herbaceous plants were numerous, and comprised species of the families *Solanaceæ*, *Malvaceæ*, *Eupharbiaceæ*, and *Granuiceæ*.

The fauna, which was not extensive, included a brown rat, which was to be seen climbing along the upper branches of the trees, apparently in search of small birds or their eggs; a lizard; a large brown dove, pronounced by Mr. Bowdler Sharpe to be a new species of Turtur; a *Zosterops*, and a sun-bird, a large crab of the genus *Birgus*; terrestrial hermit-crabs, and many spiders.

We did not find any fresh water. The soil on the upper parts of the island was a dark loam; and although sea-birds in the shape of gannets and frigate-birds were abundant and bred on the island, I saw very little guano.

I spent the forenoon of the following day in examining the broad fringing reef, a great extent of which was laid bare by the low-water spring-tide. It was composed of coral sandstone and coral breccia, and presented a rather sterile appearance, being entirely devoid of living corals, and containing very few zoophytes in its rock pools. I was, however, interested at finding on the surface of this reef a few isolated rounded stones which were quite foreign to the surrounding formation, and whose source remains a mystery difficult of solution. One was an oblong block of hard black basalt, about a foot long, by four inches in width, while the other was a lump of clear quartz the size of an orange, and much worn by attrition. Darwin, in his "Journal of a Naturalist," mentions a similar occurrence at the Keeling Islands; and in endeavouring to account for it, inclines to the belief that such stones have been transported by floating trees, in whose roots they were originally entangled, and from whence they have become detached after the stranding of the dead tree.

From the rock-pools we picked up some large Cone-shells, as well as a few Murices, Littorinas, and Turbos. We also saw some Ophiurids, and one Holothurian.

We got under way again on the 5th of May, and, after spending several hours in taking soundings, came to an anchor in eleven fathoms, about two miles to the northward of Glorioso Island. This is the largest island of the three which constitute the Glorioso Group (Vert Island is very small indeed), and is somewhat squarish in shape, measuring a mile and a half each way. It consists of a central depressed plateau, in which the wells yield only brackish water, enclosed by two lines of circumvallation, which are composed of sand hills forming continuous ridges, and ranging from thirty to forty feet in height above the level of the sea. The outer of these two ridges is about forty yards from highwater mark on the beach, and is separated from the inner ridge by a broad and deep furrow, which sustains a luxuriant growth of "Veloutier" and "Bois d'Aimanthe" bushes. Near the centre of the island we saw the muddy bed of a marsh, now dry, which one of the negroes informed me was at certain times of the year full of salt water.

Glorioso Island is the property of a Frenchman named Carltot, who, at the time of our visit, was away somewhere in Madagascar. The population consisted of the manager—an old Frenchman—one other white man, and fifteen negro labourers; who, with their wives and families, amounted in all to twenty-seven. They were endeavouring to cultivate cocoa-nuts, but so far as we could judge, without much success; for the number of these trees bearing fruit scarcely amounted to twenty. The poor people were in great distress for want of clothes and provisions, not having seen any vessel for ten months before our arrival. They had latterly been subsisting wholly on turtle and fish, without vegetables, meal, or bread of any kind. The island was so infested with rats that it was found almost impossible to raise any vegetables. In fact, commercially, it has proved a failure, so that the wretched inhabitants were only awaiting the first opportunity for quitting it and returning to Mahé.

The flora resembled that of Du Lise. The banyan tree, called "Fouce" by the creoles, was conspicuous, and in many instances seemed to be of great antiquity. I noticed the same land-birds as at Du Lise, but there was an addition in the occurrence of the Madagascar crow. Frigate-birds were numerous all over the island, and, strange to say, were frequently to be seen perching on the branches of tall forest trees. In using the word "forest" for the first time whilst speaking of these islands, I should add that a great portion of Glorioso was covered with a dense growth of virgin forest, upon which the clearing operations of the colonists had made comparatively feeble inroads. I need scarcely add that our proximity to the great island of Madagascar was rendered apparent by the above-mentioned novelties as to fauna and flora which we encountered on our voyage southward.

The greater portion of the circumference of the island is fringed by a broad reef of dead coral and coral sandstone, on which rests in many places a thin coating of mud or sand. This platform of reef, and also the sandy beach proper, together exhibited examples of a good many shells, most of which, however, were dead specimens. We saw representatives of the genera *Conus, Turbinella, Fusus, Cypræa, Trivia, Nassa, Natica, Neritina, Haliotis, Dolium,* and *Oliva.* Besides these shells there was little else to be seen, except fragments of organpipe coral (*Tubipora musica*), and the bleached tests of an *Echinus*, a species of *Hemiaster* (?).

On the morning of the 8th of May we were again under way and sailing for Mozambique Island, which is about five hundred miles from Glorioso. On the evening of the 10th we passed within a few miles of Mayotta, one of the Comoro Islands, and had a fine view of its high volcanic hills,—a sight peculiarly grateful to eyes now for some time accustomed to seeing land only in the shape of low coral islands. As we passed to the eastward, the shadow cast by the western declining sun on the face of the island brought out the outline of its hills in the form of a bold silhouette.

May 12th, about midday, looking to the westward we saw a great flat-topped hill appearing above the horizon. This was our first view of the east coast of Africa, and proved to be Table Mountain, a hill two thousand feet high, and situated some twelve or fifteen miles inland. Being of such a height it was visible to us from a distance of fifty miles, when nothing was to be seen of the coast itself or of the intervening lowlands. Shortly before dusk we steamed up to the north side of Mozambique Island, and anchored for the night in an open roadstead, whence, on the following morning, we moved into the inner anchorage.

Mozambique Island has been in the possession of the Portuguese since the middle of the fifteenth century. About the year 1505 they commenced to build a large fort on the northern extremity of the island. It was designed on a scale of great magnitude, and although constructed entirely of stone, and entailing an immense amount of labour, was completed within a period of about seven years. Having then by means of this stronghold established themselves securely and made this island a base of operations for further conquests, they began to annex nominally a great extent of territory along the neighbouring coast of Eastern Africa. For the next two hundred years, or thereabouts, most of the trade of the coast passed through Mozambique, and the position was therefore of great importance, both in a commercial and political point of view. The produce consisted of ivory, cocoa-nut oil, india-rubber, gold, amber, and calumba root. Of late years Zanzibar has monopolized most of the East African trade, and, consequently, Mozambique has been losing its importance, and has now almost ceased to be a centre of commercial industry. Indeed, the only African export of any moment which now passes through Mozambique is india-rubber, which is said to be of good quality, and of which large supplies are forthcoming.

The coast tribes have never properly fraternized with the Portuguese, and although a large force of troops is maintained at the fort, the few colonists who now reside on the mainland are practically at the mercy of the natives. At present, a large tribe, the Macolos, hostile to the Portuguese, and numbering about fifteen thousand, were encamped in the neighbourhood of Pau Mountain, a hill which we could see from the ship, and which is only twenty miles distant. The Macolo dialect is the same as that used by the black natives of the island.

Mozambique Island is a mile and a half long by a quarter of a mile in width, and is separated from the mainland by a shallow channel one mile broad, through which the ebb and flood tides run with great velocity. Considering the small area of the place the population is dense, amounting altogether to seven thousand. It is composed of African blacks, Banyans from Kutch and Gudjerat in Hindostan, Portuguese, Arabs, and English. There are only five of the latter nationality; viz., the British Consul, Mr. O'Niel (late Lieut. R.N.); Mr. Cassidy, superintendent of the telegraph cables; Mr. Parlett, agent for the British India Steamers; and two telegraph operators. The number of Portuguese forming the garrison of the island amounts to two hundred and fifty; and, besides these, there is a detachment of sixty soldiers stationed on the adjoining shore of the mainland.

There is a local trade in an intoxicating liquor called " Caju," which is made from the fermented juice of the soft part of the cashew fruit, by distillation. It is said that a tablespoonful of this liquor is sufficient to intoxicate an ordinary man, and to give him a fearful headache as well.

I spent several hours, while the tide served, in exploring the neighbouring reefs for shells and other marine specimens. Among the former were three species of cowries, *C. Tigris*, *C. Mauritiana*, and *C. Moneta*; a large *Fusus*, a *Haliotis*, a *Volute*; an *Ostræa*, a *Conus*, a *Tridacna*, and a *Pinna*; while on the beach we found *Naticas*, *Neritinas*, and *Pinnas*. Several *Echinoderms* were also seen, comprising four *Ophiurids*, and three or four *Asterias*. Of the latter, there was one huge species of a blood-red colour on the upper surface, and gaudily variegated with round blotches of yellow. Among *Crustaceans*, the most common form was a *Calappa*. *Grapsus* was also represented, and a few *Maioid* species were also captured. On opening a couple of clam-shells some curious commensal crabs were found inside, two in each shell; they seemed to be very reluctant to leave their old quarters.

Fringing the adjoining shore of the mainland was a large extent of reef covered with fine sand, and bearing a luxuriant crop of short green sea-wracks (*Zostera*). Under shelter of this weed we found a great number and variety of Holothurians. A long *Synapta*, unpleasant to handle on account of the pricking sensation which its spicules imparted to the skin, was here obtained, and a small conger eel dwelt in burrows projecting downwards from the bottom of small pits in the sand, where it might be seen protruding its head on the look-out for its prey.

The most frequent shell on this part of the reef was a species of *Pinna* about eight inches long, which, in numbers of three or four together, was generally to be seen anchored vertically in the sand by means of its long byssus. The lips of the shell were so very fragile, and the byssal attachment was so firm, that it was no easy matter to root up an uninjured specimen. About the roots of the green sea-wrack nestled in great numbers a tiny cowrie, the collection, of which gives occupation to great numbers of women and children, who may be seen scattered over the reefs every day at low tide. Great quantities of these shells are exported to the west coast of Africa for the benefit of the negro tribes there, who still make use of them as the current coin of the country.

With our arrival at Mozambique terminated the surveying operations of the *Alert*, so that it only remained for us now, on receiving our mails, to make the best of our way to England. We accordingly sailed on the 22nd of May, and proceeded on our voyage towards the Cape of Good Hope, which we expected to reach in about a fortnight's time. However, the weather proved to be most unfavourable, for on passing to the southward of Madagascar, where we had calculated on meeting with the south-easterly trade wind, we encountered instead a westerly breeze, accompanied by a rather heavy sea, so that our progress for the time was far from satisfactory. On reaching the latitude of Algoa Bay, on the east coast of Africa, it was decided on running in there for coal, which we accordingly did, anchoring off the town of Port Elizabeth on the 9th of June, and remaining there until the morning of the 11th, when we resumed our voyage to the Cape.

We arrived at Simon's Bay, Cape of Good Hope, on the 14th of June, and made a stay of fourteen days, which was necessary in order to enable us to refit and revictual the ship, and otherwise prepare for the homeward voyage through the Atlantic.

On one of the few days which I here spent on shore, I made the acquaintance of a Mr. Black, a fine hale old man, a shipwright by trade, who supplemented his regular work by collecting and preparing for sale various curiosities of natural history, especially the skins and horns of many South African animals of the antelope family. His latest trophy was a very large specimen of the egg of the *Epiornis* of Madagascar, a gigantic bird which would seem to have become extinct almost within the historic period. He had purchased this egg, as a commercial speculation, from the supercargo of a trading schooner, and hoped to realize a considerable profit by disposing of it to one of the European museums. It was indeed of enormous proportions—although not actually the largest on record—for it measured eleven and three-quarter inches in length and eight and a half inches in breadth, while it had a capacity of about eight quarts. The shell was one-eighth of an inch in thickness, as I ascertained by measuring it at the smaller end, where there was an aperture large enough to admit the thumb. He could not give me any information as to the conditions under which it was found, and although he had paid a large sum for it seemed to be unaware of the fact that somewhat similar specimens existed. It appeared to be in a sub-fossil condition, and was dotted over externally with fine pits, so that its surface somewhat resembled that of an old half-decayed human skull. About one-third of its surface was stained uniformly of an earthy colour, suggesting the idea that it must have remained for a long time partially imbedded in the ground.

On the direct homeward voyage we stopped for a few days at St. Helena, and also at Fayal in the Azores, finally reaching Plymouth Sound on the 3rd of September, 1882, after an absence from England of nearly four years.

GENERAL INDEX.

Aborigines, Australian, 185, 188, 204, 205.
Abrolhos Bank, 18.
Aconcagua, 82.
Adelaide, 201.
Admiralty, 1.
"Adventure," H.M.S., 1.
Adzes, stone, 163.
Africa, 2; coast of, in sight, 241.
African Islands, 218, 226.
Albany Island, 193.
Albatrosses, 22; flight of, 89, 141.
Aldabra Island, 215.
"Alert," H.M.S., 2.
Algoa Bay, 244.
Alikhoolips, 55.
Allen, Captain, 183.
Almirante Cochrane, 41.
Alphonse Island, 230, 232.
Altamirano Bay, 134.
Amadtha, 164.
America, South, 1.
Amirante Islands, 2, 218, 225.
Andalien River, 97.
Angol, 99, 100.
Angona, 163.
Annita, attacked by Fuegians, 55.
Anson, Commodore, 54.
Ant-Thrush, habits of, 142.
Anuario Hydrografico, 130.
Apparatus Boats, 197.
Arabs, 242.
Araucania, 95.
Araucanians, 29.
Arctic Expedition, 2.
Arnaud, Mons., 131, 135.
Atoll, 227, 229.
Australia, 1, 180.
Axes, Fuegian, 52.
Azores, 245.

Bahia de la gente, old colony at, 35.
Bailie's Sounding Apparatus, 18.
Baker, Mr., of Tonga, 170.
Bakola, 162.
Ball at Tahiti, 151.

Balsam Bog, 31.
Bandurria, 36.
Banka Island, 210.
Banks' Group, 179.
Banyans, 242.
Butcher Bird, 85.
Baron Collinson, 13.
Barrier Reef, Great, 184.
Barrier reefs, 226, 228, 232.
Basil Hall, Captain, 83.
Batteries, crushing, 203.
Bau, 160, 162.
Baudon, Mons., 230.
Bea, town of, 170, 173.
Beagle Channel, 56.
"Beagle," H.M.S., 1, 130.
Beche-de-mer, 190.
Beech-trees, deciduous and evergreen, 36, 80.
Bell, Mr. F. J., 71.
Bellavista, 24.
Bethell, Lieut. G. R., 3.
Berberry plants, 35, 38, 41, 104.
Beresford, Sub-Lieut. C., 4, 69.
Bertaut, Mons., 222.
Biobio River, 95, 98, 99.
Bird Island, Australia, 192.
Bird Island, Seychelles, 211—219.
Birds of Amirantes, 223, 224.
,, Peckett Harbour, 38.
,, Port Darwin, 207.
,, Seychelles, 212, 213.
,, St. Ambrose, 86.
,, Tahiti, 150.
,, Torres Straits, 200, 201.
Black, Mr., 244.
Black police, 185.
Bligh, Lieutenant, 168.
Bois Blanc, 233.
,, Cu Cu, 233.
,, D'aimanthe, 222, 236.
Bolsa, 31.
Bomberos, 81.
Bonitoes, 13.
Booby Island, 199.

General Index. 247

Boomerangs, 186, 189, 206.
Borja Bay, 40.
Boudeuse, frigate, 145.
" Island, 225, 226.
Bougainville, Mons. de, 145.
Bounty, H.M.S., 168.
Bowen, town of, 188.
Boyd, Mr., 178.
Brazen Head, 10.
Brazo del Norte, 111.
Brazo Point, 59.
Brenchley, 173.
Bridges, Mr., 113.
Brillador, mines of, 93, 94.
British Museum, 54.
Brodie, Mr., 214, 215.
Brooks, Dr., 216, 232.
Buckets, bark, 53.
Buckley, the sealer, 113, 116.
Buenos Ayres, 13, 28, 29.
Bullock, collision with, 101.
Bure Kalou, 162, 166.
Buréta, village of, 166.
Burial of Fuegians, 56.
Burmeister, Dr., 29.
Burney's voyages, 54, 68.
Bushes, wind-swept, 109.
Butcher bird, 183.
Byron, Commodore, 51.
Byron Island, 103.

Cache Diablo, 68.
Cacobau, King of Fiji, 159, 160, 165.
Caju, 242.
Calamary, 139.
Calandria, 26.
Callaghan, Governor, 31.
Canal of Fitzroy, 128, 136.
Canary Islands, 12.
Canoe, Fijian, 163.
" Fuegian, 43, 51, 64.
Cape Bowling Green, 190.
" de Verdes, 15.
" Gamboa, 66, 71.
" Gregory, 34.
" of Good Hope, 2, 244.
" Santa Maria, 21.
" Tres Montes, 103.
" Virgins, 34.
" Pigeon, 18, 105, 141.
Carouru, 38.
Carpincho, 26.
Casimiro, 29.
Cassidy, Mr., 242.
Catholic mission, 169.
Cave at Port Rosario, 69.
" Tongatabu, 176.
Cedar, 42.
Cedre, 233.

Cerf Islets, 232.
Cetaceans, 72.
Ceylon, 210.
Chacabuco, 41.
Challenger, voyage of, 77.
Channel Fuegians, 42, 48, 56, 103, 123.
Chasm Reach, 79.
Chickens, gone wild, 220.
Chili at war, 81.
Chillan, 99.
Chinamen, 203.
Chrysalis at sea, 21.
Clack Island, 191.
Clairemont Islands, 192.
Clark, Mr., 98—101.
Climate of West Patagonia, 45.
Coal apparatus at St. Vincent, 15.
Coalmines, Skyring, 131.
Cockatoos, white, 185.
Cockle Cove, 104.
Coco-de-mer, 214, 215.
Cocoa-nuts, method of planting, 232.
" at Seychelles, 215.
" " 170.
Colombo, 210.
Colon, trip to, 22.
Comoro Islands, 240.
Compañia smelting works, 93, 94.
Concepcion Channel, 59, 103, 112.
" town of, 95, 96, 141.
Conferva, oceanic, 13, 177.
Cook, Captain, 145, 168, 173.
" Mr. William, 4.
Cooktown, 190.
Copigue, 46.
Copper trade at Coquimbo, 83.
Coppinger, Dr. R. W., 4.
Copra, 147.
Copra-mill, 216—217.
Coquimbo, 82, 93, 142.
Coral on ship's bottom, 151.
Corals, distribution of, 221.
Coral, red, 234.
Cordillera, 64, 75, 89, 99, 128, 135.
Corea, steamship, 194, 198.
Cormorants, 42, 106, 107, 110, 111.
Covadonga Islands, 137, 139.
Corona Island, 127.
Cox, Mr., of Talcahuano, 62.
Coypo of Magellan, 48.
Crabs at African Island, 219.
Crania, 179.
Croker, Captain, 170.
Crooked Reach, 117, 124.
Crosshatchings, 75.
Culebras bank, 177.
Cunningham, Mr., of Beagle, 191.
Cunningham, Dr., of Nassau, 61.
Curaçoa, voyage of, 173.

Currant-bush, 134.

Danger Islands, 154.
Darros Island, 221, 225, 226.
Darwin, Mr., 27, 31, 83, 97, 106.
Davita, our guide, 171.
Dayot sloop, 146, 151, 152.
Dean Island, 185, 186.
Deedes, Lieutenant James, 3.
Deer, in West Patagonia, 64.
Delgado Bay, 59.
D'Entrecasteaux, 168.
Des Neufs Island, 225, 226.
Diadem Peak, 146.
Diddle-dee, 31, 41.
Dido, H.M.S., 159.
Dinwoodie, Mr. John, 4.
Dolphin, 144.
Drawings by aborigines, 191.
Dredging at St. Vincent, 16.
,, Madeira, 10—11.
,, Hotspur Bank, 18.
,, Victoria Bank, 19.
,, Port Molle, 187.
,, other, 193, 207, 217, 221.
Drongo, 207.
Duck, crested, 38, 68.
Du Lise Island, 237.
Dungeness Point, 34.
Dunsmuir, Mr., 37.
Dupuys, Mr., 232.
Durazno, trip to, 24.

Eagle Island, 220, 225, 226, 227.
Earthquake at Coquimbo, 83.
East, Sub-Lieut. W., 4.
Eastern Archipelago, 209.
Eastlake, Mr., 181.
Eden Harbour, 104.
Edwards, Captain, 168.
Edye, Mr., of Durazno, 27.
Eels, voracious, 219.
Egg of *Epiornis*, 244.
Eighth-Degree Channel, 210.
Elevation of land, 83, 128, 134, 138, 171, 175, 201, 227, 228.
Elizabeth Island, Paumotus, 228.
,, ,, Magellan, 38.
Ellis, the missionary, 145.
Elton, Mr., 141.
England, return to, 243.
English Narrows, 79, 104, 123, 139.
Etoile Island, 225, 226.
Equatorial current, 7.
Evans, Sir Frederick, 3.
Eyre Sound, glacier at, 79, 137.

Fakaata or Bowditch Island, 154, 158.
Falkland Islands, 77, 31.

Fallos Channel, 111.
Favorite, H.M.S., 170.
Fayal, 245.
Felis, sealing vessel, 113.
Fenton, Dr., of Sandy Point, 36, 117.
Ferns, 200
,, of Amirantes, 223.
,, Patagonian Channels, 46.
Fiji, 2, 159, 167.
Finisterre, Cape, 5.
Fire, Fuegian, 44, 53.
Firestone, Fuegian, 119, 120, 121.
Finow, Tonga chief, 168.
Fish, 63, 218.
Fish-weirs, Fuegian, 125.
Fitzroy, Admiral, 48, 54, 55, 65, 130.
,, Island, 190, 198.
Flinders Island, 192.
Flint-flaking, 119.
Flora of Amirantes, 222, 223.
,, Du Lise Island, 237.
,, Providence Island, 233.
Flowering plants, Patagonian Channels 46, 80.
Flycatchers, 183.
Flying fish, 12.
Flytrap plant, 93.
Fox of Falklands, 33.
Foxbats, 173.
Francisco Bay, 71, 72.
Freia, German vessel, 123.
Friendly Islanders, 175.
Fringing reefs, 226.
Fuegians, Channel, 49.
Funchal, Madeira, 8, 9, 10, 11.
Fur-seal of Magellan, 114.

Garajas, Point, 10.
Gatcombe Head, 180.
Gates at Tongatabu, 169.
Gaucho, 23.
George, King of Tonga, 172.
Giant's Causeway, 15.
Glacier, marks of old, 66, 74.
Glacier at Glacier Bay, 124, 125.
Gladstone, town of, 182.
Glasgow Bank, failure of, 13
Globigerina ooze, 18.
Glorioso Group, 237.
Godeffroy & Co., 169.
Goldfields of North Australia, 203.
Goldmines at Sandy Point, 36.
Goode Island, 198.
Goose, Brent, 57.
,, Kelp, 56, 57, 104.
,, Upland, 38, 39.
Gordon, Sir Arthur, 164.
Gott, Mr., 208.
Grabham, Dr., 11.

General Index.

Grallina, 183.
Grasstrees, 181.
Graves of Fuegians, 54.
Gray Harbour, 139.
Grebe, 38.
Greenstone, 74, 77.
Grenfell, Lieutenant, 4.
Guanacoes, 34.
Guia Narrows, 73.
Gulf Stream, 7.
Gulf-weed, 7.
Gulls, habits of, 60.
„ „ of Talcahuano, 97.
Gunn, Lieutenant Gordon, 4, 27.
Günther, Dr., 137, 139.

Haase, Mr., 131.
Hailstone rock, 75.
Hale Cove, 140.
Halicott, Mr., 153.
Hammond Island, 198.
Hanslip, Mr., 175.
Hapai Islands, 168, 169.
Haswell, Mr., 180, 183, 185, 191, 200.
Hawk, 15.
Hawksworth's voyages, 144.
Henderson & Co., 157.
Hermit crabs, 221.
Hickey, John, 231.
Hifo, village of, 173, 175.
Hinchinbrock Island, 190.
Hindostan, 242.
Holloway, Mr., 11.
Honey-eater, 183.
Horn Island, 198.
Horses of Sandy Point, 37.
Hoskyn Cove, 79.
Hotel Universal, at Buenos Ayres, 28.
„ Oddo, at Santiago, 90.
Hoyaeux, Mons., 232, 235.
Huemul, 55, 91.
Huillin, 98.
Huts of Fuegians, 53.
Hydroid coral, 71.

Iceberg Sound, 104.
Icebergs in Messier Channel, 104.
Icy Inlet, 137.
„ Reach, 79.
Independencia, rock at, 24.
Indian Reach, 137.
India-rubber trade, 241.
Inocentes Channel, 112.
Isabella, labour versel, 181.
Isla de los Reyes, 96.
Island harbour, 80, 104.
Isle des Roches, 223, 225, 226, 229.
Isthmus Bay, 41.
Ivi tree, 172.

Jerome Channel, 117, 127, 136.
Joashim Suarez, 26.
Joe, Ratu, 159, 160, 163.

Kaicolos, 165, 166.
Kanakas, 196.
Kava, 174.
King Charles South Land, 56.
Kingfisher, 107.
King George's Island, 144.
Kitchen-middens at Tom Bay, 57.
Kite, Australian, 207.
Komba Island, 209.
Kosmos Line, 35, 64.

La Compania, 91.
„ Rance Bank, 177.
„ Sagittaria, 144.
„ Venus, frigate, 145.
Labour vessels, 155, 181.
Lagoon at Tom Bay, 58.
Lalis, 161.
Lalla Rookh Bank, 158.
Lambert, Mr., 84, 93.
Lamiré, sealer, 55, 74.
Land-crab, 200.
Landshells, 62, 200.
Larikias, 204.
Latitude Cove, 112.
Las Cardas, trip to, 84.
„ Piedras, 25.
„ Tablas, Bay of, 101.
Lasikaus, 162.
Latorre, Captain, 130, 131.
Laughing jackass, 183.
Lawrence, Mr., of Concepcion, 98.
Leadbetter, Captain, 123.
Letore, Senor, of Uruguay, 23.
Levuka, Fiji, 159, 160, 165, 178.
Lifonga, 168.
Limestone, "ripple-marked," 68.
Limpets, 48, 67.
Lisbon, 6.
Livoni, 165.
„ River, 166.
Lizards, 199, 220.
Lizard Island, 190.
Llallai, 90, 92.
Lobos Island, 21.
London Missionary Society, 158.
Long Island, 184.
Loo Rock, 9.
Low, Mr., 54.
Lucas sounding machine, 7.

Maafu, 172.
Machico, 9.
Maclear, Captain John, 3, 82, 98, 173, 174, 191.

Macolos, 241.
Madagascar, 231, 237, 243.
Madeira, 5, 7, 8, 9, 12.
Madre de Dios Island, 47.
Madura Island, 209.
Magellan, Straits of, 1, 34, 112, 117, 127.
Magellanes, Chilian vessel, gunboat or corvette, 40, 130.
Mahé, 211, 213, 214, 218.
Malacca, Straits of, 2, 210.
Malay Archipelago, 2.
Maldive Islands, 210.
Maldonado Point, 21.
Mallicollo, New Hebrides, 179.
Manga Reva Island, 152.
Mariner of Tonga, 168, 169.
Martin, Dr. John, 169.
Maranhense, s.s., 123, 124.
Marie Louise Island, 225, 226.
Matavai Bay, 144.
Maté drinking, 28.
Maurelle, 168.
Mauritius, 214.
Mayne, Adam, 157.
„ Harbour, 42.
Mayotte Island, 240.
Mc Corkill, Mr., 165.
Megalithic structure, 173.
Mendaña, 144.
Merilava, 179.
Mequin Pass, 90.
Messier Channel, 103, 104, 111, 123.
Miers, Mr. E. J., 11.
Moa, town of, 173.
Monsoons, 206.
Montague Bank, 20.
Monte, 27.
Montenegro, 90, 92.
Monte Video, 22, 124.
Moraine profonde, 76.
Moreno, Senor, 30.
Morice, Dr., 204.
Morne, Captain, 166.
Moseley, Mr., 166.
Moss, curious growth of, 108.
Moths on the ocean, 20.
Mound bird, 201.
Mozambique, 2.
„ Island, 240, 241, 242.
Mulhall, Mr., 30.
Museums at Buenos Ayres, 28, 29.
Mussels, 48, 67.
Nares, Sir George, 2, 3, 11, 63, 82, 106.

Narrows, English, 62.
„ First, 34.
„ Guia.
Nassau, H.M.S., 1, 54.
„ Island, 152.

Natives of West Patagonia, 48.
New Hebrides, 179.
North, Mr. Frederick, 4, 43.
Nouvelle Cythére, 145.
Nukualofa, 169, 170, 175.
Nukunono Island, 154, 158.
Nutria, 58, 97, 126.

Oatáfu Island, 154, 155.
Obstruction Sound, 55, 65.
O'Neil, Mr., 242.
Oranges, 148.
Orchids, 199.
Ores of copper, 94.
Organ-pipe Range, 67.
Ostriches of Uruguay, 26.
Otaheite, 145.
Otter of Magellan, 48, 58.
Otway Water, 117, 127, 128.
Ovalau, 159, 160, 165, 166.
Oyster-catcher, 39, 55, 68.

Pachuros, 142.
Palmas, 12.
Palmerston, town of, 201, 202.
Pampas, 97.
Pandora, 168.
Paofai, 151.
Papiéte, 146.
Paraquay tea or "yerba," 29.
Parlett, Mr., 242.
Paroquets, 183.
Parr, Mr., of Fiji, 165, 166.
Parrayon, Mons., 151.
Partridge, red-legged, 220.
Patagonia, 128, 136.
Patent Log injured by sharks, 82.
Pau Mountain, 242.
Paumotus, 228.
Payne, Mr. Alfred, 4.
Pearls, 198.
Pearl-shell of Alphonse Island, 231.
Pearl-shelling, 194, 196, 197.
Peat avalanche, 31.
Pecherays, 55, 123.
Peckett Harbour, 38.
"Peeter," 156.
Pelagic animals, 17, 168, 179.
Peñas, gulf of, 48, 51, 73, 80, 103.
Penco, 95, 96, 99.
Percy Islands, 183.
Petrels, 13, 17, 87, 88, 89, 105.
Petley, Lieutenant W. H., 4, 185.
Philippi, Dr., 90.
Phosphorescence, 8.
Picton Channel, 73, 74.
„ town, 51.
Pigafetta, 140.
Pilot fish, 13.

General Index.

Pinery at Madeira, 11.
Plate River, 21, 112.
Playa Farda Cove, 41, 124.
Plaza de Armas, 90.
,, Vittoria, 30.
Plymouth, sail from, 5.
,, return to, 245.
Point Venus, 149.
Poivre Island, 222, 226.
Pomare, King, 146.
,, Queen, 145.
Porpoises, 14.
Port Albany, 193.
,, au-Prince, 168.
,, Charua, 75.
,, Curtis, 180.
,, Darwin, 201, 202, 204, 206.
,, Denison, 188, 189.
,, Elizabeth, 244.
,, Famine, 35.
,, Gallant, 122.
,, Grappler, 79.
,, Henry, 59, 62, 66, 67, 68.
,, Molle, 184, 185, 186.
,, Riofrio, 137.
,, Rosario, 47, 69.
,, Tamar, 1.
Portage for canoes, 42, 59.
Portland Bay, 63.
Porto Santo, 7, 15.
Portuguese, 241, 242.
Possession Island, 198.
Praslin Island, 214.
Prince of Wales Channel, 194.
,, ,, Island, 198.
Protectorate, French, 146.
Providence Island, 231, 232, 237.
P.S.N.C. (Pacific Steam Navigation Company), 35.
Puerto Bueno, 137.
Punta Wallichii, 29.

Queensland, 180.
Quillapan, 98, 99, 100, 101.
Quiriquina Island, 101.
Quiros, Pedro de, 144.

Rada de las Minas, 130.
Railway at Coquimbo, 83.
Rainfall in W. Patagonia, 45.
Raised beach, 138.
Rat, white-tailed, 184.
Ratu, 159.
Rescue, sealing vessel, 112.
Rewa River, 165.
Richards, Mr., 94.
Ridley, Mr. S. O., 18, 71.
Rio Grande, 84.
Rio Negro, 26.

Robleria, bridge at, 99, 101.
Roca Partida, 54.
Roches moutonnées, 76.
,, perchées, 76.
Rock of W. Patagonia, 47.
Rock-drill at work, 94, 95.
Rookery, seal, 49, 136.
Rooper, Lieut. G., 3, 139.
Root-of-war, 160.

San Antonio, 15.
,, Rosendo, 99.
Sandy Point, 35, 36, 37, 112, 113.
Santa Cruz River, 29.
,, Fé, 99.
,, Ines Island, 117.
,, Lucia de Santiago, 91.
,, ,, de Uruguay, 25.
Santiago de Chilé, 89, 90, 91, 99.
Sapodie Island, 209.
Sargasso Sea, 8.
Sarmiento, 35, 68.
,, Channel, 41.
Sauve Souris, 233.
Sea lion, 44.
Seals, breeding time of, 48.
Seal-hunting, hardships of, 115.
Sealskins, value of, 114.
Seal trade in Magellan Waters, 114.
Sea-water, discoloured, 13, 141, 177
Seychelle Islands, 2, 210, 214, 230.
Shark, 13, 15.
Shell Terraces of Coquimbo, 83.
Shrikes, 183.
Silvertop Mountain, 69.
Simon's Bay, 244.
Singapore, 2, 209, 210.
Skua, Antarctic, 110, 141.
Skull of Fuegian, 70.
Skyring Water, 55, 127, 128, 130.
Small-pox, 141, 206.
Smith, Mr. Edgar, 62, 139.
Smyth's Channel, 130, 137.
Snipe, Magellan, 137.
Soil-Motion, 75.
Soilcap, structure of, 47.
Solomon Islands, 181.
Sombrero Island, 103.
Somerset, settlement of, 193.
Southport, 203, 204.
Sparrowhawk, 5.
Spears of Channel Fuegians, 52.
Sphynx Moths, 20.
Spider, Trapdoor, 118.
St. Ambrose Island, 85, 86, 87.
,, Felix Island, 85.
,, Helena, 245.
,, Pierre, 236.
,, Vincent, 15.

General Index.

Staffa Columns, 15.
Stanley Harbour, 31.
Starling, soldier, 38.
Steamer ducks, 39, 55, 61, 62, 104.
Stole, John, 112.
Stone Runs of Falklands, 32, 77, 78.
Straits of Magellan, 1.
Strangers' Club, 29.
Structure of Amirantes, 226, 227.
„ „ Oceanic Islands, 218.
Submarine cable, 202.
Sumatra, 210.
Sumbawa, 209.
Suva, 167, 179.
Swallow at sea, 7.
Swallow Bay, 125, 136.
Swan, black-necked, 112, 129, 136.
Swift at sea, 209.
Swifts in cave, 176.
Sydney, 166, 167, 180.
Syenite, 74, 76.
Symonds, Mr., 175.

Table Mountain, 241.
Tahiti, 144.
Talca, 99.
Talcahuano, 95, 96, 101, 141.
Tamitao, 150.
Tanjon Paggar, 210.
Tapa, 162.
Tapacola, 85.
Tasman, 168.
Tea-plant, 31.
Tchuelches, 30.
Tekeenicas, 55.
Tema Reef, 153.
Terotero, 97.
Thompson, Sir William, 7.
„ „ Wyville, 21, 32, 77.
Thouars, Admiral du Petit, 145.
Thrush of Magellan, 37.
Thursday Island, 194, 196.
Tierra del Fuego, 34, 112.
Tilly Bay, 118, 125, 127, 136, 117.
Timor Island, 209.
Tom Bay, 42, 43, 56, 57, 60, 61, 111, 112.
Tonga Islands, 168, 169.
Tonga, Mr. David, 173.
Tongatabu, 167, 169.
Torres Straits, 194, 195, 180, 201.
Tortoise of Aldabra, 215.
Totoonga Valley, 165.
Topar Island, 78.
Tower at Funchal, 9.
Trammel net, 60.
Treachery of Fuegians, 112.

Tree silicified, 102.
Trees of W. Patagonia, 46.
Trepangs, 190.
Tribes of Fuegians, 55.
Trinidad Channel, 54, 68, 71, 73, 75, 103, 104, 111.
Trumpet-shells, 67.
Tucker, Captain, 198.
Tucutuco, 26, 27, 35, 38.
Turtle, 21, 219, 231, 233.

Uea, 175.
Union Group, 154.
Uruguay, 22.
Ushuwia, mission station, 56, 112.

Valparaiso, 3, 78, 80, 82, 89, 90, 93.
Vanilla, 148, 216, 223.
Vavau, 169.
Veloutier Blanc, 233, 237.
„ „ Tabac, 233, 236.
Venus, transit of, 145.
Vereker, Lieut. the Hon., 3, 10.
Veronica, 67.
Victoria Bank, 20.
Victorieuse, ironclad, 146.
Vines at Madeira, 12.
Viti Levu, 162, 165, 160, 167.
Vocabulary of Fuegian words, 122.
Vunivalu, 160.

Wager Island, 103.
„ Loss of, 51.
Waidou, 179.
Wallis, Captain, 144.
War canoes, 148.
Ware, Mr., of Durazno, 27.
Water-kite, 6, 7.
Watts, Dr., 32.
Weir, Mr., of Compañia, 84, 93, 94, 95.
Wellington Island, 73, 78, 111, 138.
„ Gnu, 172, 173.
Wesleyan Missionaries, 169.
West Island, 198.
Wetter Island, 209.
Whales and shrimps, 72.
Wide Channel, 78, 137.
Wilkes, Captain, 149.
Wilson, Mr., 29.
Winter's Bark Tree, 36.
Wolsey Sound, 68.
Woomerahs, 205.

Yacanas, 55.
Yi, River, 27.
Yoronha, 147.

INDEX OF NATURAL HISTORY TERMS.

ZOOLOGICAL.

MAMMALS, *genera and species of* :—
Arctocephalus Falklandicus, 114.
Cervus Chilensis, 64, 91.
Chlamydophorus retusus, 30.
Ctenomys, 27, 35, 38, 129, 142, 143.
Epiodon, 30.
Glyptodon, 29.
Hydromys, 184.
Lutra felina, 58, 115, 137.
,, Huidobrio, 98.
Machairodon, 29.
Mylodon, 29.
Myopotamus coypu, 58, 97, 126, 137.
Otaria jubata, 44, 114.
Physeter macrocephalus, 20.
Pteropus Keraudrenii, 173.
Toxodon, 29.

BIRDS, *genera and species of* :—
Ægialitis, 201.
Anas cristata, 38, 39, 68, 136.
Anous, 186,
Anseranas melanoleuca, 208.
Artamus, 200.
Bernicla antarctica, 56.
Bruchigavia, 201.
Buteo erythronotus, 129.
Campephaga, 200.
Centrites niger, 37, 38.
Centropus, 201.
Ceryle stellata, 107.
Chætura, 209.
Chalcophaps, 201.
Chibia, 201.
,, bracteata, 207.
Chloephaga magellanica, 38, 57.
,, poliocephala, 57.
Cinclodes, 39, 129, 133.
Climacteris, 201.
Collocalia spodiopygia, 176.
Cygnus nigricollis, 112, 136.
,, coscoroba, 136.
Dacelo, 201.
,, gigas, 183.
Daption Capensis, 18, 87, 141.
Dicœum, 200.

BIRDS, *genera, etc., of (continued)* :—
Diomedea exulans, 22.
,, fuliginosa, 22, 141.
,, melanophrys, 89, 141.
Donacola, 201.
,, castaneothorax, 207.
Epiornis, 244.
Erythrauchena, 201.
Foudia Madagascarensis, 224.
Gallinago Stricklandi, 137.
Gallinula, 209.
Geopelia, 201.
,, placida, 207.
Grallina, 201, 207.
,, picata, 183.
Graucalus, 183, 201.
Hæmatopus, 201.
,, ater, 56.
,, leucopus, 56.
Halcyon, 201.
,, sanctus, 201.
Haliaster, 207.
Haliœtus leucogaster, 181.
Larus Dominicanus, 60, 97.
,, glaucodes, 97.
,, maculipennis, 97.
Lestris antarctica, 141.
Megapodius, 201.
,, tumulus, 201.
Merops, 201.
Mimeta, 201, 208.
Myiagra, 201.
,, plumbea, 201.
Myzantha garrula, 183.
Myzomela, 200.
Nectarinia, 200.
,, Australis, 201.
Nycticorax, 201.
,, Caledonicus, 201.
Oceanites grallaria=T. gracilis, 141.
Œdicnemus, 201.
Œstrelata defilippiani, 86, 101.
Ossifraga gigantea, 87.
Pachycephala, 200.
Pelecanoides urinatrix, 106.
Pelicanus, 201.

BIRDS, *genera, etc., of* (*continued*):—
Phalacrocorax magellanicus, 106.
,, imperialis, 106.
Piezorhynchus nitidus, 207.
Plictolophus, 201.
Porphyrio melanotus, 201.
Pteroptochus, 85, 129,
,, albicollis, 85.
Ptilinopus, 201.
,, superbus, 201.
,, Swainsoni, 201.
Ptilotis, 184, 200.
Sauloprocta, 201.
Stercorarius chilensis=L. antarctica, 110.
Sterna, 201.
Sphecotheres, 201.
Sula, 86.
Tachyeres cinereus, 56, 61.
Thalassidroma leucogaster, 87.
,, Leachii, 5.
,, pelagica, 5, 13, 18.
,, Wilsoni, 87.
Trichoglossus, 200.
,, chrysocolla, 183.
,, Novæ Hollandiæ, 183, 208.
,, rubitorquis, 183, 208.
Troglodytes, 129.
Tropidorhynchus, 201.
Tropidorhynchus, corniculatus, 183.
Turtur, 238.
Upucerthia, 142.
,, dumetoria, 142.
Zosterops, 201, 207, 238.

REPTILES, *genus and species of*:—
Monitor, 199.
Sphargis, coriacea, 30.

BATRACHIANS, *genus of*:—
Cacotus, 139.

FISHES, *genera and species of*:—
Callorhynchus antarcticus, 71.
Exocetus volitans, 12.
Galaxias, 63.
Haplochiton zebra, 63.
Myxine, 35.
Naucrates ductor, 13.
Neophrynicthys latus, 137.
Periophthalmus, 166, 218.
Platycephalus, 193.
Squalus glaucus, 13.
Thinnus pelamis, 13..

MOLLUSCS, *genera, etc., of*:—
Arca, 16, 22, 39, 187, 217.
Atlanta, 179.
Baculites, 102.

MOLLUSCS, *genera, etc., of* (*continued*):—
Bulimus Beddomei, 200.
Bulla, 235.
Calyptrœa, 70.
Cardium, 10, 16, 102.
Chilinia, 62, 63, 139.
Chiton, 70.
Cleodora pyramidata, 19.
Concholepas, 67, 68.
Conus, 235, 240.
Criseis aciculata, 6, 18, 19.
Cuvieria, 18.
Cyprœa, 10, 187, 255, 240.
,, mauritiana, 242.
,, moneta, 240.
,, tigris, 242.
Dentalium, 10, 22.
Dolium, 235, 240.
Eurybia Gaudichaudi, 168, 179.
Fissurella, 70.
Fusus, 240, 242.
Haliotis, 240, 242.
Harpa, 16, 235.
Helicina reticulata, 200.
Helix, 62.
,, Buxtoni, 200.
,, Delessertiana, 200.
,, Krefïti, 200.
,, Spaldingi, 200.
Hippopus, 187.
Hyalea, 17, 19, 22.
Ianthina, 17, 18.
Lima, 187.
Littorina, 16, 235.
Mactra, 105.
Melo, 192.
Mytilus, 39.
Nassa, 240.
Natica, 240, 242.
Nerita, 185.
Neritina, 221, 240, 242.
Oliva, 10, 240.
Onychoteuthis inogens, 139.
Ostræa, 132, 185, 242.
Patella, 16, 39, 70.
Pecten, 10.
Pinna, 187, 242.
Pneumodermon, 19.
Ranella, 207.
Rossia, 71.
Siliquaria, 185.
Spirula, 16, 237.
Stilifer, 188.
Strombus, 16.
Succinea, 62.
Terebra, 235.
Teredo, 202.
Tridacna, 187, 242.
Trivia, 240.

Special Index—Zoological.

MOLLUSCS, *genera, etc., of* (*continued*) :—
Trochus, 39.
Trophon, 39.
Turbinella, 240.
Unio, 62.
Voluta, 39, 235, 242.

POLYZOA, *genera of* :—
Amathea, 187.
Biflustra, 187.
Canda, 20.
Cellepora, 20, 207, 187, 222.
Cribrillina, 20.
Crisia, 182, 187, 207, 222.
Eschara, 18, 187, 207, 222.
Giguntopora, 20.
Lepralia, 207, 222.
Idmonea, 207.
Membranipora, 8, 20.
Myriozoum, 187, 222.
Retepora, 187, 207, 222.
Rhyncoporn, 20.
Salicornaria, 187.
Scrupocellaria, 187.
Smittia, 20.

TUNICATA, *genera of* :—
Pyrosoma, 168.
Salpa, 18.

INSECTS, *genera, etc., of* :—
Halobates, 17.
Phylloxera vastatrix, 12.

CRUSTACEA, *genera, etc., of* :—
Actæa, 19.
Alpheus, 182, 187, 193, 218.
Arcturus, 71.
Atergitus, 218.
Birgus, 238.
Corallana, 19.
Calappa, 242.
Egeria, 193.
Galathea, 173, 217.
Gelasimus, 172, 182, 218.
Geograpsus, 200.
Glaucothöe, 9.
Goniograpsus, 187.
Grapsus, 191, 218, 242.
„ variegatus, 86, 187, 219.
Iliastemis, 187, 207.
Huenia, 187.
Lambris, 187, 207.
Leucosia, 191.
Lithodes antarctica, 58.
Macrophthalmus, 189, 218.
Matuta, 189.
Mycteris, 189.
Myra, 187, 207.
Ocypoda, 218, 219.

CRUSTACEA, *genera, etc., of* (*continued*) :—
Ozius, 182.
Parampelia saxicola, 191.
Phlyxin, 191, 207.
Phyllosoma, 18, 179.
Pinnotheres, 187.
Porcellana, 171, 218.
Remites scutellatus, 16.
Scilla, 218.
Serolis, 71.
Squilla, 187.
Thalamites, 217.
Thalassina, 182.

ANNELIDA, *family, etc., of* :—,
Amphinomidæ, 187.
Nereis, 10.
Polynöe, 187.
Sagitta, 179.
Spirorbis, 8, 13, 14, 19.
Tomopteris, 142.

ECHINODERMATA, *genera, etc., of* —
Asteracanthus, 189.
Asterias, 242.
Astrophyton, 182, 187, 188.
„ Lymani, 71.
Cidaris, 11.
Comatula, 187, 193.
Echinus, 10, 70.
Gephyrea, 40, 105.
Goniocidaris, 187, 193.
Hemiaster, 240.
Holothuria, 187.
Moliria, 222.
Ophiuridea, 187.
Pentaceros, 193.
Peronella, 189.
Salmacis, 187.
Spatangus, 191.
Synapta, 193, 222.

CÆLENTERATA :—
Actinia, 17, 71.
Astræa, 187.
Caryophyllia, 187.
Corallium rubrum, 234.
Fungia, 152.
Gorgonia, 182, 187, 193.
Labiopora, 71.
Meandrina, 187.
Medusa, 17.
Orbicella, 187.
Physalia, 17.
Plumularia, 187.
Porites, 187.
Sertularia, 187, 222.
Tubipora, 187.
„ musica, 240.
Virgularia, 207.

PROTOZOA :—
Aphrocera, 20.
Aspergillum, 118.
Chalina, 20.
Cladochalina, 19.
Globigerina, 14, 17.
Grantia, 20.

PROTOZOA (continued) :—
Nardoa, 20.
Orbitolites, 6, 218.
Pyrocystis, 8, 19, 22, 179.
Thalassicolla, 179.
Vioa, 20.

BOTANICAL.

Aleurites, 172.
Alsophila, 140.
Apocynaceæ, 233.
Aristolochia, 93.
Barringtonia, 219.
   „   speciosa, 235.
Berberis, 134.
   „   empetrifolia, 46.
   „   ilicifolia, 42, 46, 104.
Bougainvillea, 12.
Calceolaria, 35.
Campsidium chilense, 44, 51, 80, 104.
Cassytha filiformis, 233.
Casuarina, 212, 221, 222, 233.
Cheilobothrium, 129, 134.
Cinchonaceæ, 223.
Conferva, 13, 14, 18.
Convolvulaceæ, 223.
Dendrobium, 199.
Desfontainea Hookeri, 46.
Drimys Winteri, 44, 46, 53.
Echium, 24.
Embothrium, 46, 129, 134.
Escallonia, 134.
Fagus antarctica, 46, 80.
   „   betuloides, 46, 80.
Ficus, 222, 223.
Fuchsia magellanica, 42.
Gaultheria antarctica, 42.
Goodeniaceæ, 233.
Gramineæ, 238.
Hepaticæ, 46.
Hernandia peltata, 233.
Hibiscus, 237.
Hymenophyllum, 46, 62.

Hymenophyllum cruentum, 80, 138.
Ilex Paraguayensis, 27.
Jungermanniæ, 104.
Lapageria rosea, 46.
Libocedrus tetragonus, 42, 44, 46, 52.
Lindsaya ensifolia, 200.
Lychnis, 129.
Lygodium scandens, 200.
Macrocystis, 40.
Malvaceæ, 223, 238.
Mesembryanthemum, 235.
Mitraria coccinea, 138.
Myrtus nummularia, 35.
Nephrolepis acuta, 200.
   „   exaltata, 223.
Panax, 134.
Pandanus, 199.
Philesia buxifolia, 41, 42, 46.
Polypodium quercifolium, 200.
Pulcea nitida, 200.
Ribes magellanica, 134.
Sargassum bacciferum, 7.
Scævola Kœnigii, 223, 233.
Solanaceæ, 223, 238
Spondias dulcis, 173
Suriana maritima, 222, 236.
Tetraplodon mnioides, 108, 138.
Tournefortia, 212, 222, 236.
   „   argentea, 233.
Vacciniaceæ, 140.
Veronica decussata, 67.
Weinmannia trichosperma, 138.
Xanthorrea, 181.
Zostera, 243.

www.ingramcontent.com/pod-product-compliance
Lightning Source LLC
Chambersburg PA
CBHW031329230426
43670CB00006B/283